# Model Ships

RAU IX
BREMEN

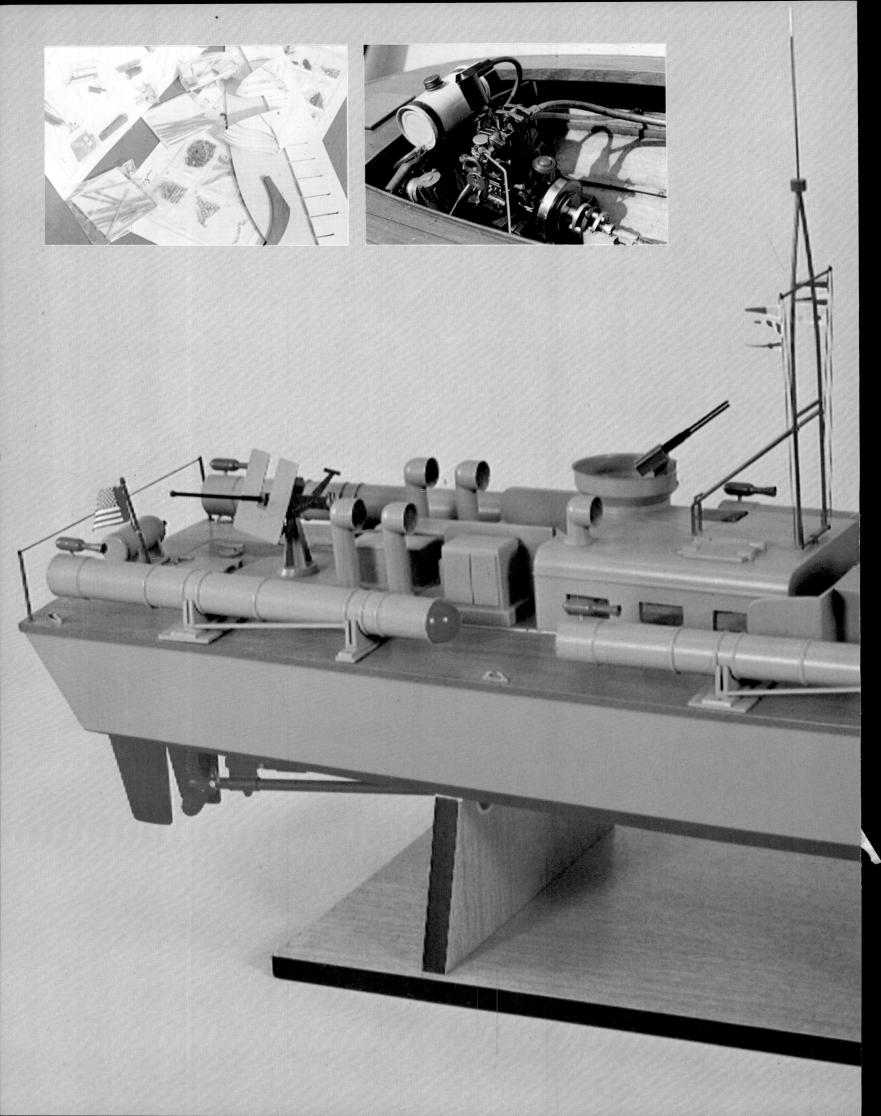

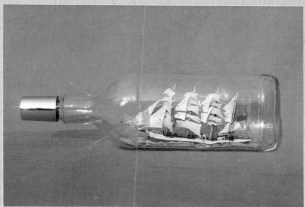

# Model Ships

## Vic Smeed

PT109

# HAMLYN

LONDON · NEW YORK · SYDNEY · TORONTO

 A BISON BOOK

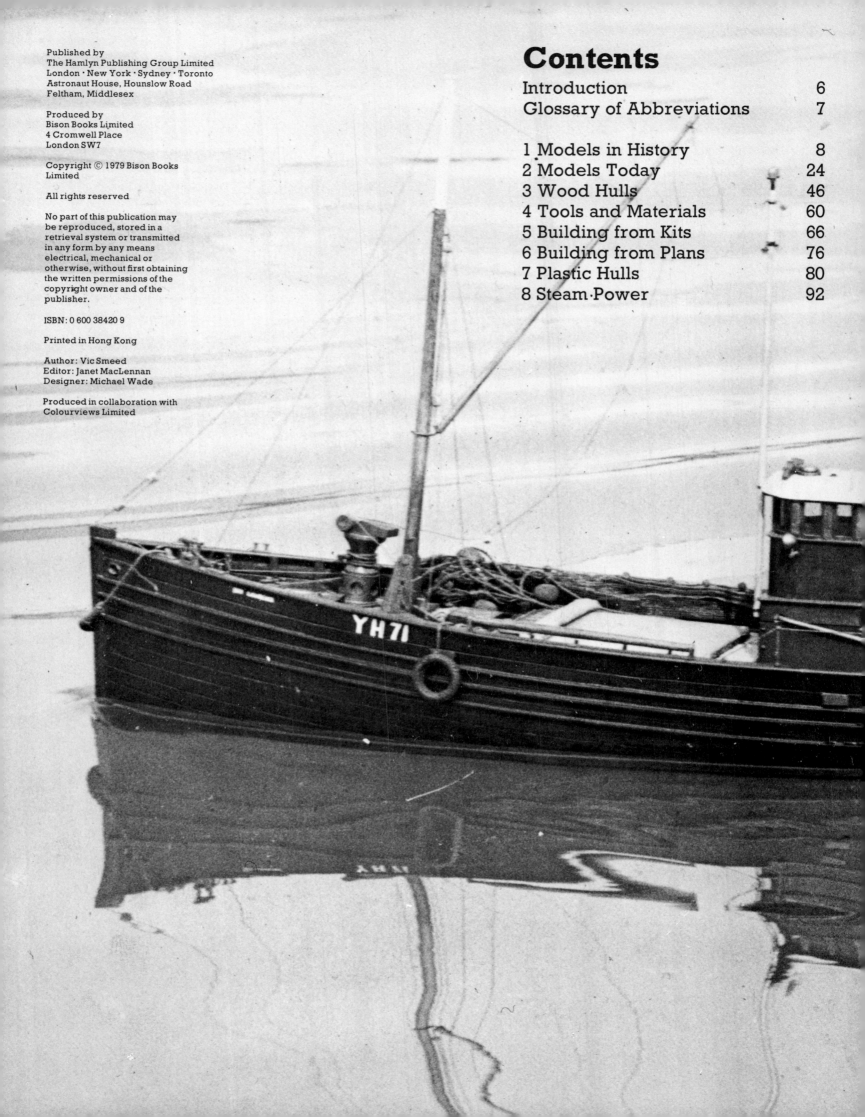

Published by
The Hamlyn Publishing Group Limited
London · New York · Sydney · Toronto
Astronaut House, Hounslow Road
Feltham, Middlesex

Produced by
Bison Books Limited
4 Cromwell Place
London SW7

ISBN: 0 600 38420 9

Printed in Hong Kong

Author: Vic Smeed
Editor: Janet MacLennan
Designer: Michael Wade

Produced in collaboration with
Colourviews Limited

# Contents

*Unless otherwise indicated, photographs come from the author's collection.

YH 71

# Introduction

The history of ships can be traced back over some five thousand years, and no other of man's inventions–not even the wheel–has had so great an effect on the development of the human race. Evidence of model-making recurs from time to time throughout those five thousand years, but as a pastime, less than two hundred years covers the traceable history, and only in the last thirty years has model ship or boat construction and operation become a hobby or sport attracting really significant numbers of enthusiasts, backed by its own trade. In that time marine modelling has expanded into a many-faceted leisure pursuit with a capability for educating as well as entertaining which is now taken seriously by governments and national sports organizations in many countries.

This book sets out to describe every aspect of what so many people are finding an absorbing and rewarding hobby in the hope that it will not only interest and attract those who have always felt that they would like to make a model, but also that it will help to avoid the compartmentalizing of those who already engage in one or other of its various sides. Specialization seems a characteristic of modern-day life, and while it may be necessary to reach the top in a particular field, a great deal of pleasure and interest can be missed by not understanding what other modellers are doing.

Building a model teaches one to read a plan, to concentrate, to develop skills with tools, to think and plan ahead, to discover the uses and limitations of many materials, to increase powers of mental arithmetic, to cultivate patience, and to begin to understand something of the natural laws that govern our existence. A modeller has to be a little of a cabinet-maker, engineer, electrician and mechanic, to list only the basic skills. He becomes more observant, ingenious, dextrous, resourceful and knowledgeable as his experience grows, and finds challenge but also relaxation and contentment in the exercise of craftsmanship. All this and more from a leisure occupation which needs no great investment of time or money, and which can be followed by anyone who has the urge to use his hands. Model-builders are a happy, friendly and enthusiastic section of the human race–come and share our pleasure!

# Glossary of Abbreviations

| | |
|---|---|
| a | amp |
| ABC | Aluminum-Brass-Chrome |
| a/h | amps per hour |
| a/m | amps per minute |
| BDC | Bottom Dead Center |
| cc | cubic centimeter or centimeters |
| CE | Center of Effort |
| CLR | Center of Lateral Resistance |
| cm | centimeter or centimeters |
| cu | cubic |
| dB | decibel |
| Deacs | nickel cadmium button cells |
| dm | decimeter or decimeters |
| ft | foot or feet |
| gm | gram or grams |
| grp | glass reinforced plastic |
| HMS | Her Majesty's Ship |
| hp | horsepower |
| HP | High Power |
| hr | hour or hours |
| ic | internal combustion |
| in | inch or inches |
| kg | kilogram or kilograms |
| kHz | kiloHertz |
| km | kilometer or kilometers |
| kph | kilometers per hour |
| lb | pound or pounds |
| loa | length overall |
| lwl | load waterline |
| m | meter or meters |
| mA | milliamps |
| mHz | megaHertz |
| mm | millimeter or millimeters |
| mph | miles per hour |
| MV | Motor Vessel |
| nicads | nickel-cadmium cells |
| oz | ounce or ounces |
| PS | Paddle Steamer |
| psi | pounds per square inch |
| R/C | Radio control |
| rpm | revolutions per minute |
| RTP | running round the pole |
| Rx | receiver |
| SG | Specific Gravity |
| sq | square |
| SS | Steamship |
| TSS | Twin Screw Ship |
| Tx | transmitter |
| USS | United States Ship |
| v | volt or volts |
| yd | yard or yards |

# Models in History

Model ship and boat construction as a popular hobby is a relatively recent development, dating back only to the 1950s. There were, of course, practitioners long before that, but it tended to be a minority interest, with only a few hundred devotees in any country. Yet the history of model ships extends back some 5000 years, proving in doing so that models, or miniature reproductions of familiar objects, have always exerted an attraction on mankind.

Water craft were man's first means of transport and very probably the objects of his first attempts at construction, other than perhaps some basic improvements to natural shelter. From simple swimming aids—driftwood, bundles of reeds, inflated animal skins—rafts developed by assembling such naturally buoyant materials. Soon gourds were used and, later, pottery vessels as flotation cells. Where large trees were available, dug-outs evolved, the hollowing being carried out initially by fire, followed by chipping; canoe-

**Right**
Polynesian outrigger canoe, kitted primarily for school use by a West German firm.

**Above far right**
Miniature Roman merchant ship by E P Heriz-Smith photographed through its glass case at an exhibition. Models have to show practical arrangements which can be glossed over in paintings.

**Below far right**
Egyptian ship of the 5th Dynasty researched and built by F F Robb and seen displayed at a Model Engineer Exhibition.

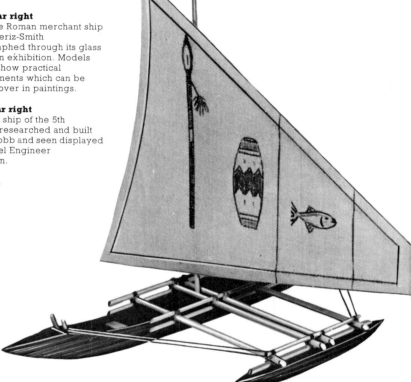

type hulls were made by manipulating areas of bark from suitable trees.

Much of the early evolution of boats must be conjectural, although ethnographers studying marine cultures have, with archaeologists, adequate grounds to make assumptions which can in most cases find reasonable confirmation in primitive craft still in use today. Inflated skins, reed rafts, hollowed log and bark canoes are still fulfilling useful functions in Tibet, the Sudan, Peru, and many Asian countries, as well as in Eastern Europe.

It seems probable that much of the early progress in watercraft evolution took place in tropical areas bounding the Pacific, where conditions were ideal for the development of communities living partly on forest products and partly on sea foods; traces of such groups dating from the middle stone age have been found. However, the earliest firm evidence of shapes and building methods so far available originates from the

Nile, from about 3000 BC onward. Much of our knowledge of the vessels of Ancient Egypt came from decoration on pottery and, from about 2500 BC onward, from models found in tombs of noblemen, until the discovery in 1954 of a ship some 140ft (43m) long in the great pyramid of Cheops.

Clay or pottery models, or drawings and sculptures, have given a fair glimpse of the development of ships in the comparatively sheltered Mediterranean; a Phoenician wreck of circa 1250 BC was found in 1959, and remnants of Ancient Greek and Roman ships have more recently been discovered, but no contemporary models have survived. From bas-reliefs, vase paintings, bronze models of ships' bows and sterns, and measurements of building slips it has been possible for skilled modellers to construct convincing representations of vessels of this period, while finds such as the Kyrenia ship have provided details of constructional methods and confirmation of basic shapes.

Moving forward, one of the most important discoveries was the pair of ships dated (from coins) 170 AD, raised from Lake Nemi near Rome in 1928–30. These ships, 230ft (70m) in length, were housed in 1939

in a specially erected building which was, alas, destroyed completely with the ships in 1944.

The state of preservation of these ships owed much to freedom from attack by the more voracious wood-boring worms encountered in most seas. Here the Baltic has an advantage and many wrecks which are expected to have remained reasonably well preserved have been pinpointed for salvage when funds and time permit. Knowledge of Scandinavian ships of about the 10th century is almost complete thanks to the discovery of entire ships buried by the Vikings. Recovery of even a few of the known wrecks (like the *Vasa*) could in due course lead to a complete picture of ship development in Northern Europe.

It will be clear, even from this very brief survey, that anyone wishing to undertake the construction of a model of a vessel of any period up to Viking times must become involved in some research from fairly limited sources. Museum experts have in many cases gathered evidence and built models of some of the more important craft, but as far as it is known, very little of the evidence has been collated for publication; photographs of the models and brief notes are often available,

**Half title page**
Extensive use of formed and molded plastics make construction of a detailed model like this Graupner *Rau* whale catcher very straightforward. *(Courtesy Ripmax Ltd)*

**Title page**
Another popular model is John F Kennedy's torpedo boat PT109, available from more than one manufacturer. This one is 45³/₄in (1160mm) for electric power and radio. *(Courtesy Micro-Mold Ltd)*

**Page 2 top left**
Part of a Spanish period ship kit. Apart from the basic keel, bulkheads, planking etc, hundreds of tiny fittings in wood and metal are supplied.

**Page 2 top right**
A *Gannet* 15cc ohv engine, the last to be built specifically as a model four-stroke on a commercial basis. A small batch is still made from time to time by the English manufacturer.

**Page 3 top left**
Skippers racing radio yachts; the rules say that they must all stay in a compound near the judges. This can help to prevent one transmitter near the models swamping out the others.

**Page 3 top center**
Four-masted barque in a whisky bottle. This is built as described, except that the shrouds are glued to the outside of the bulwarks rather than threaded through.

**Page 3 top right**
Gasoline-engined (or spark ignition) hydroplane; motor is mounted on its side to reduce height of center of gravity and improve stability. An unusual model from Coventry.

**Contents page**
An early steam drifter nicely built from commercial plans. Note the clutter on the deck and the overall matt finish which helps to make it look realistic.

**Page 6–7**
Competitors' enclosure at a British A Class Championship, which is sailed over a week and normally attracts between forty and fifty entrants. These are the largest models raced.

but information in depth is scattered through catalogs of pottery collections and sculptures, friezes and rock drawings and the like; there are often clues in the work of such writers as Homer, so that research is likely to be a long-term essay in detective work.

There is a gap of some 600 years after 1000 AD in which evidence is very scant, relying almost entirely on suspect pictures and tapestries, city seals, and votive and other religious models. This lack of 'real' evidence is particularly unfortunate since this was a period which saw considerable progress in ship development and navigation.

**Left**
The brig USS *Washington* was built for the US Revenue Service in 1837 but used by the US Navy as a survey vessel for some ten years. Built in wood to 3/16in scale (1:64) by J B Walton, the model is attractive and an excellent record.

**Below**
Mediterranean galley in plastic, including vacuum-drawn plastic sails, quite a popular inclusion in period ship kits at one time.

Artists often included stylized ships in the backgrounds of religious paintings, seeming satisfied that they were recognizably ships and paying little attention to accurate representation. In the same way, tapestries featuring ships were usually produced by workers with little accurate ship-building knowledge – some may not even have seen a ship – although occasional crumbs of information can be found. It is obvious, for example, from the Bayeux tapestry that the Norman ships of the time showed a strong Viking influence.

Seals of towns with nautical associations show developments in ship design in some cases. For instance

seals have shown the emergence of fighting castles and the introduction of a centrally hung rudder rather than a steering oar. What are known as 'votive' models also contribute a small amount of knowledge. These were models of ships, hung in churches, often as a thanksgiving for a successful voyage or escape from shipwreck. They, however, tended to be decorative rather than accurate, and some that have survived show signs of restoration and even modification, in most cases carried out more with enthusiasm than with accuracy. Perhaps the most valuable of these models to the ship historian is the Catalan Nao, believed to be early 15th century and now in the Rotterdam Maritime Museum. This is probably the oldest wood-built model existing, and was obviously constructed by someone with knowledge. (It has that indefinable feel of rightness which a good model will always bring to an enthusiast.) The Spanish Mataro model is another well-known votive ship, though later alterations reduce the trust which can be put in it.

In the late 15th and 16th centuries matters began to improve, with artists beginning to create more accurate representations and, of greater value fragments of drawings of some technical conviction. lists of spars with sizes, and so on. Towards 1600, complete scale drawings have survived. However no specific ship details in the form of builders' technical drawings have ever been identified, and models of classic vessels such as Columbus' *Santa Maria* and Drake's *Golden Hind* are based on typical ships of their time, guided by references in contemporary journals. How accurate such a model may be will depend on the quality of the detective work put in by the researcher, though it is possible now to obtain plans drawn up by experts which are in general agreed to be 'most probable.'

After 1600 much more reliable sources begin to appear. Marine painters became very much more concerned with accuracy, particularly French and Dutch artists, and shipyard technical drawings began to be retained more carefully. The main supply of knowledge is provided, however, by the practice of building detailed models of projected ships which began at this time. A common procedure in shipyards, even until quite recent times, was to carve a half-model incorporating the characteristics known by experience to produce the required results, and, when approved by the future owner, to saw it into sections and scale up the shapes to full-size on a mold-loft floor. This method of design by eye was followed by construction by eye by skilled but illiterate shipwrights; there are still many small boat-builders even in sophisticated countries

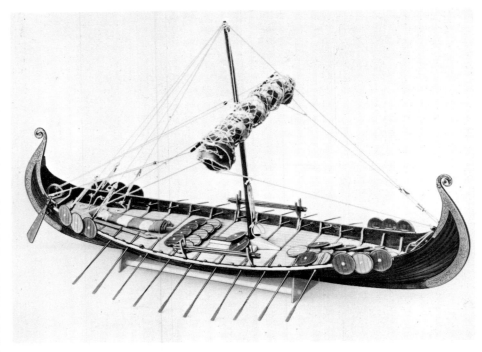

who never draw plans but rely on models or skill and experience to produce boats of traditional types.

The ship models of the 17th, 18th and early 19th centuries were to a large extent a continuation of this idea, but with ships becoming larger and much more complex, the models were primarily built to sell possible ships to customers; in many cases this meant the Board of Admiralty. Frequently the earlier models were made of the hull only, but gradually more and more fully rigged subjects were built. Early models tended to show an unplanked hull, but later it became the practice to plank the hull sides above the waterline. Other ship-building nations adopted the same sales technique, but usually with fully planked models.

An Admiralty order of 1649 was the first of its kind ever issued *requiring models* of projected vessels. It has been suggested that this order originated from Cromwell. Firm evidence is available to show that Phineas Pett of Chatham had used detailed models some forty years before, and there can be little doubt that the members of the Board set great store by them, not only for their value in decision-making but as beautiful artefacts in their own right. Over a period of a hundred years, scores of lovely models were built, largely in the Royal Dockyards, and many have survived, though now they are spread round the world. Several of the most important are now in the Henry Huddleston Rogers Collection in the US Naval Academy at Annapolis, but the National Maritime Museum at Greenwich and the Science Museum in Kensington display a good number, and there are others in the ship sections of many other museums in Britain, America, and in European collections. A considerable number have been lost, alas, especially in Europe during the 1939–45 war.

It was possibly the cost of these models which led to simplification; two bills of 1741 show a total of about £90 for carved work and painting alone, and that sum was a very respectable year's income at that time. Early in the 18th century a swing to carved models occurred, sometimes planked on the outside and, since they were hollowed to a very thin shell, fitted internally. Some more elaborate models, or models of parts of a ship demonstrating innovations, continued to be made, but at the other end of the scale increasing use of half-block models was seen.

War with France (1793–1815) interrupted the flow of Dockyard models, but in their place came, coincidentally, the models built by French prisoners-of-war. Although the bone and ivory models are the most publicized, the wood ones produced by craftsmen

among the prisoners are in general far more accurate and reliable guides to French ships of the period.

After the war, the Dockyards again turned to models, but of simple type in general, and the practice slowly faded with the advent of steam power. Later in the 19th century warship models were to reappear on a more limited scale and for different purposes.

Compared with the wealth of surviving drawings and models of warships, very little of merchant-ship development in the 17th and early 18th centuries remains, though the practice of copying lines of outstanding captured vessels by the Admiralty has meant the preservation of a number of drawings. Published manuals on rigging and so on provide information which has enabled later researchers to produce works of value for ship historians and model makers. The emergence of the clipper era in the 19th century saw much greater use of models, often half-block but occasionally more detailed, and some of these still exist. The availability of more adequate information has enabled present-day enthusiasts to make fine models of these ships; strangely American clippers are better documented than British.

The middle of the 19th century saw iron and later steel construction and the beginnings of mechanical propulsion. As the flow of materials and goods accelerated during the industrial revolution, so competition increased to build the ships needed. Models were used as advertising and sales aids, and in the naval services, following the end of pressing, models could be used to assist recruiting.

While reasonable numbers of accurate contemporary models have survived in European countries, notably Sweden, Holland, and France, comparatively few now exist in the USA, though it is known that models were extensively used, particularly around 1800, when American ships were establishing such an excellent reputation for speed and serviceability. American museums do, however, have a good selection of models, either obtained from other countries or recently built, and of course several examples of full-size ships remain.

As science began to influence art in ship design, models began to be used for research, and in the second half of the 19th century testing tanks began to be built for increasingly sophisticated measurements of performance characteristics. Such tests are very widely used today, and a development has been to build man-carrying models of ships, both for more accurate

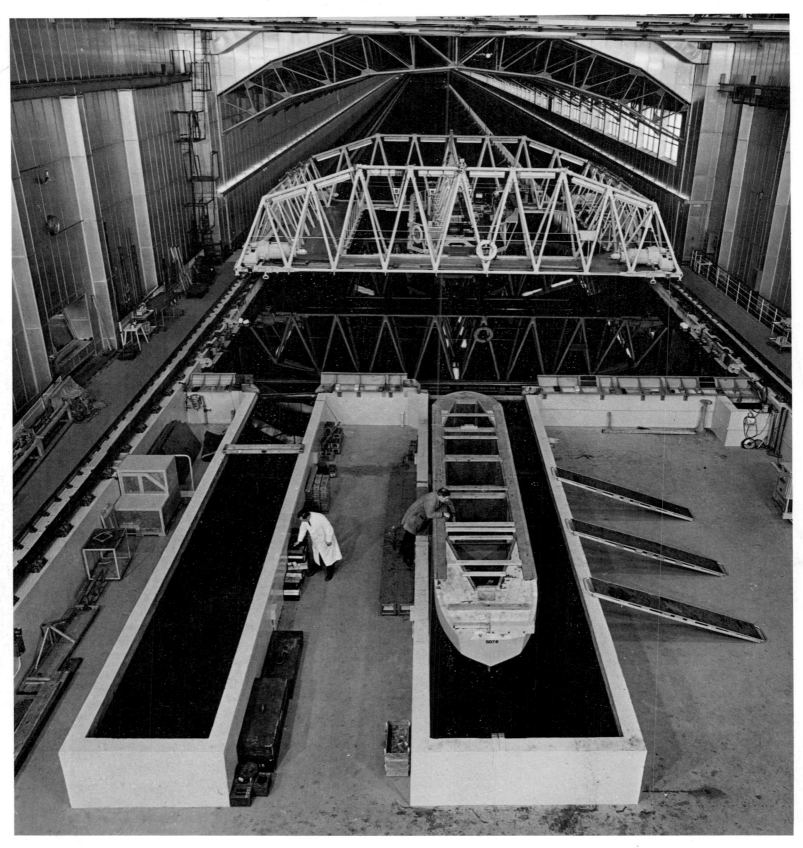

assessment of some aspects of performance and to
provide training in handling such vessels as large
tankers.

The construction of builders' models for advertising
or, in some cases, record purposes has diminished of
late, largely because of the considerable expense of
building such models, which in turn is partly a result of
the increasing size and complexity of ships. It is also a
fact that a much higher proportion of those concerned
with ships are nowadays able to 'read' drawings and
can assess a vessel from written statistics. Models for
advertising and recruitment are still made but usually
in simplified and even mass-produced form. Most of

the modern super-detailed models are built by amateurs undertaking the task from enthusiasm and love of
ships. A very few professional builders continue to
produce fine models for museums or private collectors,
and several of the major international auction houses
conduct regular model sales in which ships figure
prominently and command remarkable prices.

## MODELS FOR PLEASURE

Watch a group of youngsters playing with twigs in a
stream and it seems obvious that there must always
have been delight in dabbling with models, however

rudimentary, and water. There is no hard evidence
that models were popular a couple of thousand years
ago; however, since clay dolls have been found and
clay ship models were buried in Cretan and Egyptian
tombs, it is not an unreasonable step to surmise that
clay ships were made as toys. Quite elaborate and
accurate sailing models of local craft are found today in
fishing communities in Asia, where the men and boys
have raced such models for centuries, and anyone with
experience of the way the talk goes when boating
enthusiasts get together will not find it difficult to
believe that even quite primitive people would have
enjoyed sailing models.

The average model is not made of particularly
durable materials, and it would be no surprise to find
that models used as decoration, or even gathered
together as a collection, would not survive for long
periods in medieval or earlier conditions. Most surviving votive ships, hung in churches and therefore
subject to less handling and better protection, are
little more than faded blocks of wood with a few dowels
in the remnants of the rigging. The obvious apprecia-
tion of model ships, coupled with better living standards and greater security from the 17th century onward, meant the preservation of at least some models
in collections; possibly the availability of glass played

a part, since a glass case provides the best protection for a delicate model and still allows enjoyment of it.

Written mentions of models (or drawings or paintings including obvious models) are rare before 1600, and one of earliest appears to be that quoted by Rudyard Kipling in 'Rewards and Fairies' which refers to experiments made with metal floating models by Simon Cheyneys of Rye, a friend of Sir Francis Drake.

Boating for pleasure was known in Ancient Egypt, but the foundations for today's vast small-boat industry were laid by Charles II, who was presented with a small fast vessel called a *jaght* by the Dutch, in the 1660s. Courtiers commissioned similar craft, and racing developed, although the first 'yacht club' proper was not formed until 1775.

Word-of-mouth stories handed down indicate that racing of models was not uncommon in fishing com-

*Model Engineer* appeared and included information and advice on marine models as well as locomotive and stationary engines; this magazine is still published.

Electric power arrived towards the end of the century, but the cumbersome size and weight of the early batteries and motors in relation to the power available offered no challenge to the steam engine as a propulsion unit for model boats. The first real rival, the internal combustion engine, made its debut in model size in about 1904, but the early examples were hand-built and could be temperamental; it was to be another 25 years before gasoline began to supplant steam as a popular prime mover.

Clubs formed during the last half of the 1800s and the beginning of the 1900s formed loose associations in order to employ common rules; although easier transport by train and tram increased the opportunities for

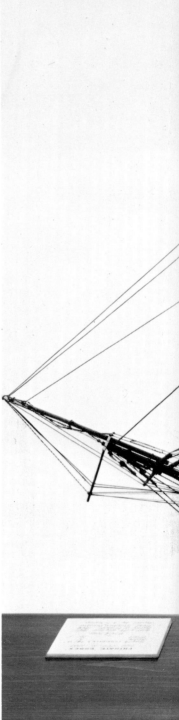

munities in the late 18th century, with annual regattas and intense inter-village rivalry. It seems likely that some models were bought and taken home to inland cities; at least one London model-boat pond dates from the late 18th century. The arrival of railways would possibly have exposed coastal modelling to a larger visiting audience, and Victorian pride in the Navy made people ship-conscious.

The first formal model yacht clubs were formed in the 1850s and 60s, mostly in Britain but also in the USA, and some of these clubs are still in being. The oldest rating rule can be traced back to 1878, and the degree of interest then existing is suggested by the publication, for a brief period in the 1880s, of a magazine shared between model yachtsmen and canoeists.

With the advent of steam power and the spread of mechanical knowledge and technology, model power boats began to appear. One firm advertised parts and accessories for models as early as 1789, and another, to become a well-known source for nearly a century, began advertising steam parts in 1845 and, in 1868, complete ready-to-operate steam models. A number of toy manufacturers, especially German, started to produce simple steam and, later, clockwork powered models, and it is likely that ownership of examples of these imbued innumerable fathers and sons with the desire to make their own models. In 1898 the magazine

inter-club matches, in the case of yachts in particular, clubs were sufficiently scattered for the further ones to compete only perhaps once a year, and it was essential that firm rules were laid down for model classes and methods of sailing so that everyone was on an equal footing. Accordingly, in 1911 the Model Yachting Association was formed. In the same year the first recorded international race was sailed at Enghien-les-Bains in France, between French, Belgian and British teams; as an incidental aside, the top-scoring boat (one of the British) earned for its skipper a Sèvres vase, presented by M Poincaré, the then-President of the French Republic.

Because the greatest concentration of power-boat enthusiasts was in the London area, the need for a national body was perhaps not quite so urgent, and it was not until 1924 that the Model Power Boat Association was formed. International meetings followed from 1925 onward.

Although international sailing races took place between England and the USA (from 1922) and Denmark (1923/24), the concept of an international controlling body was not formalized until 1927 when the International Model Yacht Racing Association was created. For various reasons, the founder countries revised the constitution, and in 1936 the International Model Yacht Racing Union was established; this body still controls the sport in the sixteen member countries which have separate national model yachting organizations and exerts a guiding influence in those European countries whose yachting activities are liable to the combined power/sail authorities, affiliated to Naviga.

Power boating on an organized scale was for many years confined to a very small number of countries, and despite occasional suggestions, the need for a formal international organization did not seem particularly urgent. The 'active' countries had evolved classes and racing methods from experience in racing together, and it was not until the sudden explosion of interest internationally after World War II that the lack of a broad-based controlling body became an obvious handicap. Eventually in the late 1950s, a group of European countries got together to form a European controlling body to be known as Naviga, which rapidly

spread to include most Continental countries. Nearly all these countries had one central national body embracing both power and sail, and Naviga rules therefore catered for both categories.

Britain, regarded as the leader in model boating and certainly with the greatest number of participants and longest experience, disappointed the others by declining an invitation to become a founder nation of Naviga, but despite this, much of the basic legislation was based on British practice. A small group of English enthusiasts supported Naviga meetings, and eventually, in 1967, Britain became the fifteenth member country. In 1976, with a membership of 22 countries, Naviga was persuaded to accept applications from countries outside Europe, and became an acceptable world body.

The tremendous upsurge of interest from about 1948 onward is ascribable to a number of factors, a major

**Below**
The 32-gun frigate *Essex* at $\frac{1}{8}$in (1:96) scale from a US kit. She actually carried 40 32pdr carronades and six long 18s in 1812, and 42 guns after capture by the British. *(Courtesy Model Shipways Co Inc)*

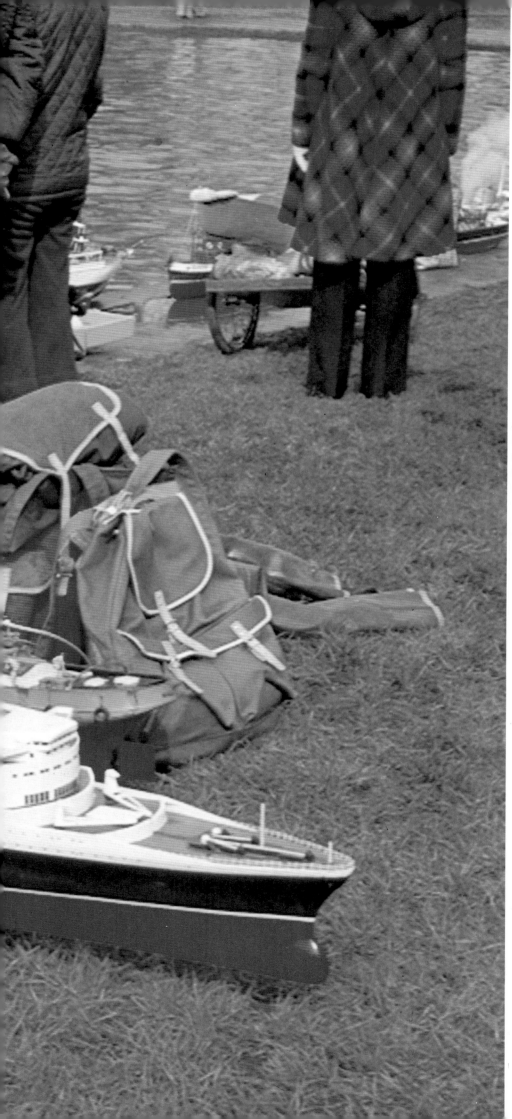

one being the wide availability for the first time of cheap and efficient small engines suitable for marine use. The major one, however, was the advent in about 1950 of commercially available radio control equipment, which was to prove a watershed in the history of working model boats. Club and association officials were usually enthusiasts for, and experts in, the existing types of model, but the new technology attracted large numbers of newcomers with a very different approach to modelling. Clubs found it necessary to adopt new attitudes in order that existing waters could harmoniously be shared among the devotees of differing aspects of the same basic hobby. A transition period of some ten years was required before power boaters were happily settled, and it took even longer before model yachting achieved full equilibrium. Much of this time is accounted for by the need to explore the horizons opened by the innovation of radio, especially in view of the very rapid technical advance of the radio equipment itself.

In America quite a different story has unfolded. Model yachting clubs formed in the 19th century came together to form the Model Yacht Racing Association of America, roughly parallel with the British MYA. The peak of MYRAA activity was undoubtedly in the 1920s and 1930s, with dozens of clubs forming from coast to coast (53 clubs and 553 registered boats in 1938). Gradually, however, after World War II, sailing models lost support until the Association was down to a handful of clubs racing with vane steering gear. Pressure to adopt radio racing and some reluctance to do so without adequate exploration led to the formation at the end of the 1960s of the American Model Yachting Association, sailing radio boats only, and rapidly growing to over a thousand registered boats.

On the power side, very little organized activity appears to have been reported in the first half of this century, though many individuals were building models, and there were several clubs affiliated to the American Model Power Boat Association. From what little information is available standards of construction and performance among the best boats were on a par with the Europeans, where the models could be compared; possibly due to distance, American competitions and model categories have always been quite different from those of the rest of the world. These differences still persist, but with increasing US awareness of, and in one or two instances participation in, international regattas, there is hope that the areas of common ground will widen—world records claimed when all countries are not using the same yardstick must have a hollow ring.

Radio control made an impact on American model boating in the 1950s similar to that experienced in Europe, and there now exist numbers of clubs and a growing manufacturing industry. The proportion of enthusiasts to total population in the USA is, however, very much lower than that in England and West Germany in particular.

One other country which is active in model boating and only now beginning to adopt generally used classifications and rules is Japan. Once again, the boom in activity can be traced to the introduction of radio control, which has had more far-reaching effects in that country than most, since it is probably true to say that half of the model control equipment used in the world originated in Japan. Similarly, perhaps a quarter of all model internal combustion engines and nine out of every ten electric motors are of Japanese manufacture, and it is the one country in which production of goods for modelling purposes must have had a measurable effect on the national economy.

**Left**

Liners are complex subjects and the *Queen Elizabeth 2* offers particular problems in deck and funnel shapes. It makes a handsome model nonetheless. This example was photographed during a regatta at St Albans.

## THE MODEL TRADE

Outside Japan there are probably not more than twenty model manufacturers with a turnover in excess of two million dollars US (one million pounds Sterling) per annum. Many firms with worldwide reputations employ only perhaps half a dozen staff, though there has been a tendency over the last few years to follow world patterns in concentrating production into fewer larger consortiums. The model business, however, is one requiring enthusiasts, and most of the successful businesses can be traced back to a single individual who was, and in many cases still is, a keen and dedicated modeller.

Widespread model trade support for boats is not much more than thirty years old. As already mentioned, one or two small firms were supplying steam engines and castings more than a hundred years ago, but until about 1950 most model yachts and power boats were virtually completely hand-built. There were individuals who had a particular expertise in sailmaking, detail fittings, engine construction, and so on, who would supply fellow club members with occasional items, and it was not uncommon for even quite experienced yachtsmen to pay to have a boat built (though comparatively rare for a power enthusiast to buy a complete boat) but in general, the owner made every part of his model himself. This to some extent inhibited the growth of model boating.

Specialist suppliers slowly grew in number and

**Below**
The transition from sail to steam was a fascinating period. USS *Kearsarge* from a wood kit was a civil war gunboat built in 1861 at Portsmouth, NH. *(Courtesy Scientific Models Inc)*

model shops began to appear, particularly during the 1930s when model aircraft began to become popular, but the range of kits and accessories for boats remained very small. Strangely the first aspect of boats (other than steam plant) to receive much trade attention was period ships, for which several kits and a selection of fittings and materials appeared in the 1930s–1940s. Most of these were decorative rather than accurate scale models, but they enjoyed several years of popularity before interest declined, to leave them a relatively minor part of the model scene until about 1970.

The major model-boat market has undoubtedly centered on working power models, more particularly those fitted with radio control, but there was no sudden arrival of interest. Several small manufacturers in the

being made for aircraft, and then to make a suitable coupling and propeller shaft assembly. Once motive power was easily available, a demand for kits could be expected, and for those modellers who were not enthusiastic about internal combustion, electric power had become a reasonably efficient alternative. Steam power went into eclipse, apart from a hard core of enthusiasts, but a strong revival began in 1975. Most of the early products were from aircraft manufacturers, but slowly specialist boat firms became established. Today a strong and independent boat trade produces an enormous variety of kits, engines, fittings and materials internationally.

One noticeable feature in the model boating world is that 'the trade' follows trends in the hobby to a

1946–1956 period were slightly ahead of their time; ten years later their products would have found a ready market but by then most had abandoned their projects and turned to other things. In those early years of modern model boating, much of the supply of materials and goods relied on the extremely healthy model aircraft trade, and the necessity of adapting engines, radio equipment, and so forth for marine use was an accepted part of boating. It took many years before manufacturers, used to thinking in aircraft terms, realized that a very large boat market remained virtually untapped.

Gradually a trickle of products specifically for boats started, in many cases from adaptations of existing items. It was not difficult, for example, to fit a water cooling jacket and a flywheel to an engine already

greater extent than in other modelling fields. For example in aircraft or railways, manufacturers are frequently ahead by developing and promoting new products which they believe modellers will take up; instances which might illustrate this are the introduction of electric flight and smaller gauge railways. In boating, however, innovation is more often in the hands of modellers themselves, and most of the new directions in which the sport has moved have been the result of individual experiments and developments which have been taken up by manufacturers when a demand for them has been proved. It may be that this is one reason why model boating can still be a relatively inexpensive pursuit, and certainly the possibility of initiating a new trend adds to the fascination of a hobby which has held a powerful attraction for so many years.

# Models Today

One of the attractions of model ships and boats nowadays is the remarkable variety of approaches, which give a modeller an almost limitless choice of what to build. There is something to suit all tastes. Categorizing the types is something of a problem, since there are so many possibilities of overlap, but a normal model must basically be working or non-working, sail or power. It can be scale or functional, and if working, free-running, automatically steered, or radio-controlled. If it is a power model, it must also be classified by the form of power unit. Lastly, it can be built for competition or display purposes, or it can be what is loosely termed a 'sport model,' that is intended for the builder's own pleasure, either for pride of ownership or the fun of operating.

## NON-WORKING MODELS

These are given various names—shelf, exhibition, display, static, waterline, and glass-case models are the most common—and cover everything from huge promotional models, sometimes 20–25ft (6–7m) long, down to ships in bottles and miniatures which are sometimes only an inch (2.5cm) or so long. In Naviga classification non-working models are the C group and competitions are held in Europe every second year. Otherwise, apart from club and society exhibitions, the only competition catering for them is the annual Model Engineer Exhibition.

These models are almost invariably scale, that is representations of full-size vessels, although very occasionally one sees a model of what the builder thinks a certain type of ship should look like. An extension of this approach is a professional model of a projected ship built as a sales aid, or on a different level, an individual's model of a small cabin cruiser or cruising yacht which he will pass to a naval architect as an illustration of his requirements. In any event, a scale factor is involved, and there are recognized scales which are usually used unless particular circumstances require an odd scale. The advantages of a common scale in a collection of models for comparative purposes are obvious; an example is the National Maritime Museum at Greenwich where most of the earlier models were built to $1/4$in scale and the museum is naturally keen to retain this scale for any new models acquired.

Metric scales are simple to understand and are expressed as a fraction—1/5, 1/10, 1/25, 1/50, 1/100, 1/200, 1/500, and 1/1000 are the accepted ones—and even a layman has no difficulty in grasping that in, for example, a one hundredth model (1/100) everything is one hundredth of full-size. Imperial scales are more complex, and are expressed in different ways. For example, 16ft to 1in may be referred to as that, or 1/16in scale, or 1/16in to 1ft, or, as a fraction, 1/192. The usual ones are 2in (1/6), $1\frac{1}{2}$in (1/8), 1in (1/12), $\frac{1}{2}$in (1/24), $\frac{1}{4}$in (1/48), $\frac{1}{8}$in (1/96), 1/16in (1/192), 1/32in (1/384), then 50ft–1in (1/600) and 100ft–1in (1/1200).

Choice of scale will depend on several factors, perhaps the most important of which, to the amateur, is the size of the prototype and the amount of space which the model can be allowed to occupy. A large-scale model of a big ship in a modern small house or apartment can cause problems. Then there is the amount of detail the builder wishes to incorporate. Is the model to give an overall impression or is every last rivet to be shown? If commercial fittings are to be incorporated, this may well determine the scale. The model may be one of a series, all to the same scale, and even the size of the workshop or working space can be an influence.

Non-working models can be of any type of vessel, from a coracle to a nuclear submarine, and choice is limited only by the availability of adequate information

A Besahn-Ewer
North European Barge
Built by B.Edwards
Sails by Mrs.Lacey.

ENGLISH HOY
CIRCA 1760

**Left**
A 24in (610mm) kit model of the whaling brig *Kate Cory* of Westport, Massachusetts, 1856. Note the dories and the hull coppering and the fact that despite her specification she is brigantine rigged. *(Courtesy Model Shipways Co Inc)*

**Top**
A besahn-ewer barge, used in a similar manner to the hoy on northern European waters. Model by B Edwards, photographed at the Model Engineer Exhibition.

**Above**
An attractive non-working model of an English hoy of the 18th century, beautifully planked by T W Dickey. These little cargo vessels were used on inland rivers and broad canals and occasionally ventured along the coast.

or the amount of research the builder is willing to undertake. The types can roughly be grouped as follows:

**Early Period Ships** These have been discussed in the previous chapter. Museums can offer some help. Some drawings have appeared in model journals, but can usually only be obtained in back issues or possibly as photostats. There are no kits available except for one or two wood Viking ships and occasional plastics of Greek and Roman vessels, and only one or two plans published (in England, France, Italy, and possibly Poland).

**Period Ships** This term usually covers vessels from about 1400 to 1900 and tends to be used only for sailing craft. It embraces the 'galleon' era–many people erroneously apply the term to any ship model with square sails–and there have probably been more kits of the *Santa Maria* and *Golden Hind*, of varying degrees of probability, than of any other two vessels. Once again museums are helpful, but for after about 1600 there are numerous commercial sources for plans, books, and kits. The most popular period is perhaps the 18th cen-

possible to track down adequate information on a particular vessel, but a very wide selection of plans can be obtained. Books are not quite so easy, and often the best source is earlier issues of full-size shipping journals, which may involve a journey to a museum or one of the few libraries having such archives. Plastic kits offer a choice of several dozen ships, and there are some wood or wood/plastic kits which can be built as either static or working models.

**Native Craft** This term covers a very considerable number of smaller vessels common to particular regions, built at any time in traditional ways. Random examples are Chinese junks, Eskimo umiaks, Arab dhows, Indian canoes, Irish curraghs, Polynesian catamarans, Maltese dhgaios, and so on. The difficulties of research and the help available from museums and publications vary; frequently modellers of such boats have the opportunity to examine actual examples. There are a very few plastic kits and there have been occasional simple wooden kits (such as the *Kon-Tiki* raft) though current wood ones tend to be of slightly more elaborate Mediterranean vessels such as xebecs.

**Below**
Neat waterline model of the modern freighter *Orchidea* built by R L Packham and displayed at the Model Engineer Exhibition, where it was very highly commended.

tury, and so much information is readily available now that mistakes should be easily avoidable. In the same way, a great deal of information on 19th century clippers and schooners and so on can be obtained without difficulty.

**Warships** Although first rates and frigates and the like were warships, the usual interpretation of this title in this context is for powered vessels from the early steam and ironclad ships to the present day. In general a great deal of information exists and there are plenty of books and plans available; there are many plastic kits, but virtually no wood ones. One of the biggest problems in warship modelling is getting a particular ship correct for a particular period, due to the practice of refitting and, usually altering warships every few years, and this can involve research.

**Merchant Ships** Again, this tends to refer to steam and motor vessels, sailing vessels usually being more closely specified, for example, East Indiaman, merchant brig, etc. With so many thousands of ships having been built in the last hundred years or so, it is not always

**Fishing Craft** Since much of man's experience afloat is in the search for food, fishing vessels can reasonably be expected to have their own category, especially as the variety of craft built for specific activities is considerable. A few examples from the British Isles are zulus, fifies, Leigh bawleys, Hastings luggers, Colchester smacks, cobles, Mounts Bay luggers, Morecambe Bay prawners, scaffies, nobbies, and many more, while some of the better-known American craft are Grand Banks schooners, Friendship sloops, Cape Cod catboats, and Chesapeake bugeyes and skipjacks. A number of these vessels still exist, and the usual sources of museums, books and publications make research not too arduous. Plans for some of the craft are commercially available, but there appear to be no kits, even plastic, for the smaller ones; some American types are kitted.

**Miniatures** What constitutes a miniature depends on the size of the prototype to some extent, since a $\frac{1}{8}$in scale model of say a 32ft cabin cruiser would be 4in (10cm) long and would be classed as miniature, but a destroyer at the same scale would be about 40in (1m)

long and would not; in the latter case the largest scale to qualify would be likely to be 25ft–1in (1/300). A maximum overall length of 16in (41cm) is one criterion sometimes used. Just as much information is needed to build a small model, though the constructional techniques and materials may differ. Very few wood kits are made nowadays, but quite a selection of plastics can be bought.

**Waterline Models** These are simply models which show the subject set in a sea, so that only the above-water part is modelled as opposed to a *full-hull model*. A waterline model may be shown at anchor or under way; several models may be grouped to form a *diorama*. Some modern plastic kits embody a thinned band round the waterline, so that the model may be built as full-hull or easily cut through to be mounted as a waterline subject. As far as is known, no wood kits are now sold.

**Recognition Models** Naval training employs small-scale (1/1000 or 1/1200) simplified waterline models to teach ready identification of ships, usually warships.

**Above**
Ships in bottles have their own fascination. This example demonstrates the need to choose the best possible distortion-free bottle.

**Right**
More models shown at the M E Exhibition. Glimpsed in this picture are two tugs, two E-boats, an RAF crash tender, a lifeboat, a modern frigate, a paddle steamer, and a trawler.

**Below**
Cast metal miniatures at 1:1200 scale have become a collecting vogue in recent years. The longest model in this group is about 3½in (90mm).

Quantities of these models were disposed of after World War II and attracted collectors; some were also used by 'wargamers.' Several manufacturers now produce die-cast metal models in these scales incorporating considerable detail and requiring only careful painting to make an attractive collection. As the models have become more elaborate, so the cost has risen, but they are still much cheaper than commissioning hand-made miniatures. Wargamers have tended towards smaller scales (1/2000 or 1/2500) for convenience and the models are often rudimentary. These too can be bought in cast form.

**Ships in Bottles** Most serious modellers are interested in building an accurate replica of a ship and regard the specialized techniques of building a ship in a bottle or in a light bulb as a hindrance to a faithful model. Nevertheless, the public is always enormously intrigued and it has been demonstrated that a good model can be presented in this way. Some kits including a suitable bottle are produced, but in general this type of model is considered as a separate art from ship modelling itself.

# WORKING MODELS

An immediate and obvious division in working craft is the basic method of propulsion; sail or power.

There are a few modellers who are equally happy with either, but the majority are devotees of one or the other and, while usually interested in the models of their opposite numbers, belong to different clubs or, where a water is shared, operate at different times. This is partly because unless a lake is very large, the different sorts of boats get in each other's way and the risk of collision is not worth taking; scale power boats will not normally run at the same time as yachts or speed models because of their vulnerability to damage, and sailing craft prefer not to be on the water with fast power boats for the same reason. The other inhibition is that only a limited number of radio-controlled boats can operate simultaneously, so that the more models present, the less running time each gets.

# SAILING MODELS

Since sail is the older method of propulsion, perhaps it should be considered first. Most sailing models are functional, even if an attempt is made to give a scale-type appearance, and this is because of a factor known as the cube law. To give a simple illustration, if a quarter-size model is drawn up, the length is obviously one quarter of the full-size. The sails, however, are one quarter as long and one quarter as high, that is, one sixteenth of the area, while the hull is one quarter as long, one quarter as wide and one quarter as deep, or one sixty-fourth of the volume and thus one sixty-fourth of the weight. In other words, the smaller the model in relation to the prototype, the less stable it is likely to be.

This is not to say that scale models cannot be made and sailed successfully, but in nearly all cases a false keel is fitted for sailing, having the function of improving stability but also providing side area to prevent excessive leeway—the tendency of the boat to be blown sideways through the water. Leeway is also related to the scale factor (in the example above the sideways thrust of one sixteenth of the sail area has one sixty-fourth of the water volume resisting it) and to the very easily disturbed top surface of the water which can displace upwards; a model working in the top two or three inches of water will not 'grip' in the same way as one with a draft of a foot or so.

Sailing models of dinghies are not feasible (except in very light wind) without a fin or exaggerated centerboard carrying ballast at the bottom. These boats in full-size rely on movement of the crew for stability, and there have been few really successful models. Model catamarans can be extremely fast and do not necessarily need ballast, though fin area is desirable to prevent excessive leeway. They tend to suffer the drawbacks of full-size versions, particularly reluctance to change direction quickly and tripping over the bow of the lee hull, the more so because anticipation is more difficult when the 'crew' is on the bank.

Convenient sailing categories are as follows:

**Scale Fore-and-Aft Rig** Schooners, Thames barges and other comparatively small prototypes without square sails make the best sailing models bearing in mind the foregoing comments. The rigging is much simpler and sail adjustment easier, with or without radio, and they will sail reasonably close to the wind. A well-chosen prototype, carefully built so that as much internal ballast as possible is carried, can sail without a false keel and can be very fast and handy. Working plans can be obtained for a few models, and there are one or two helpful books as well as occasional articles in model publications which offer guidance. There are one or two kits of ketch or yawl type yachts, and odd examples of grp or plastic hulls. Plans of a number of full-size vessels are available for those who may care to design their

A large Greek caique, another excellent choice for a scale fore-and-aft sailing model, combining good sailing characteristics with a long and interesting history.

own structures. There are not many clubs specializing in scale sailing models, but individuals are often seen on popular lakes.

**Square Rig** People who like a challenge go in for square-riggers; they look very beautiful afloat but require tremendous patience and can be frustrating. It is unusual to achieve successful sailing performance without a false keel, particularly sailing to windward. Most square-rig models will sail across or downwind, but are not too good at sailing towards the wind. It will take a square-rigger perhaps a dozen tacks to work as far to windward as a fore-and-after makes on one leg, unless most of the square sails are furled and the model is sailed only on its fore-and-aft canvas. This is, of course, what happened to a large extent in full size. The time taken to bend on or stow sails can be considerable, and trimming the sails can be time-consuming unless there is out-of-scale simplification of the running rigging Once again, there are only a very few clubs in which square-rig models are regularly sailed, but individual models are not uncommon. There are no kits as far as is

known, and only one or two working plans, but articles and books are available.

**Native Craft** Apart from the odd felucca, xebec, dhow, or junk very few sailing native craft are seen in Western countries although in many cases they could make excellent working models. Little information has been published and no drawings or kits specifically for working models are known, though small-scale sketch plans have appeared once or twice in magazines.

**Fishing Craft** Most sailing fishing craft were fore-and-aft rigged, with gear intended for easy handling and therefore simple. Drawings of some prototypes are available, but only one or two actual working plans. Remarks above on fore-and-aft models apply.

**Sport Models** This can cover either non-scale models having the appearance at a distance of, for example, a barge, through to simple small or non-class functional yachts. There are working plans available for one or two of the former and for quite a number of the latter.

**Left**
An intruder! A large model brig cuts across racing radio yachts. Note that despite the yards being trimmed as far fore and aft as possible, the model is still sailing dead across wind, compared with the yachts at about 40 to the wind.

**Opposite left**
A German model yawl of scale type. Points to note are the full keel rarely seen on racing models, the curled leach of the mainsail which battens would improve, and the absence of roach on any of the sails.

**Opposite right**
A large ketch-rigged radio-controlled yacht photographed at the Nürnberg Toy Fair. Hull is made for a 10-rater, and the extra sail area could only be carried in light wind.

**Left**
A scale sailing model of a Brixham trawler photographed on the famous Round Pond in Kensington Gardens, London. A Thames spritsail barge can just be seen in the background; both make good scale sailing subjects.

Basically, any model which is not to scale and does not fit in any of the recognized racing yacht classes must be classified as a sport model, built for the pleasure of construction and/or sailing rather than formal competition. There are several kits, usually with vacuum-formed styrene hulls, for yachts of scale-type appearance, mostly intended for radio control installation, and much of the information published on class models applies. Toy yachts, little ones bought ready-made, have not always been successful sailers under all conditions, but in recent years some better ones have appeared, though most can be improved by slight modifications here and there. A hand-built model can have more time and care bestowed on it and should be expected to outsail a commercial product, which a manufacturer has to cost and build within a price limit.

**Below**
Natural lakes with shelving banks make waders essential for sailing yachts. These are 36R vane yachts. Note the 'black water' indicating an area of water totally devoid of wind.

# RACING YACHTS

Which boat is fastest, or which skipper has the most skill, must be questions as old as boats themselves. A competitive spirit is part of man's nature, and though it varies in intensity in individuals, the widespread interest in games and sports is an indication of its strength. It is therefore only to be expected that when two or three model boats are together, the questions as to which is fastest or most maneuverable should be of interest. With sailing craft, performance is affected by a number of factors, the most important of which are sailing length and sail area. Comparisons can only be made when limits are placed on these factors. Hence rating rules, which establish maxima or interrelate performance factors so that an advantage gained in one

place is offset by a restriction elsewhere, were created. A rule should produce yachts of virtually equal performance so that winning depends on the skill of the skipper.

Not everyone wishes to build and sail a large model yacht, and not everyone wants a small one, so that more than one rating rule is required to give a choice. Over many years, just about every variant must have been tried, but now there are just three classes which are accepted worldwide; there are several others which are used in some countries only, and the list which follows includes all those currently sailed.

Racing yachts are divided into two basic categories: free-sailing, normally with a vane steering gear, and radio-controlled. Despite a number of experimental classes having been introduced over the years, model yachtsmen have settled for the same rating rules for

**Below**
Getting ready to release a pair of 36R yachts. Near boat is the prototype of the author's *Gosling* design, an extremely popular beginners' model.

either category, distinction being made only by inserting an 'R' before the class letter or number.

In order of size, then:

**36in Restricted Class (36R or, with radio, R36R)** This British class, about 50 years old, is sailed to a limited extent in other countries. The hull must fit inside a box 36 ×11 ×9in (914 ×279 ×229mm) and the total displacement (weight) must not exceed 12lb (5.45kg). Apart from minor restrictions on bow shape and so on that is all. Sail area is unlimited and a bowsprit can be used. There are one or two kits and several working plans available.

**36/600 Class** This is the American equivalent of the 36R and differs in that hull beam and draft are not restricted

33

in any way, but sail area may not exceed 600sq in (38.75sq dm). One or two kits and plans fitting the rule are available.

**10/40 Class** This European equivalent of the above originated in France and was used for a short time by Naviga, but is now only occasionally heard of outside France. Hull length is 1m, sail area 40sq dm. Some plans are available in France, it is believed, otherwise only one is published, in England.

**Naviga X Class (DX, or, with radio, F5X)** A Continental class which receives some support, this is the simplest rule of all, simply limiting sail area to 50sq dm (775sq in). There are no other restrictions. Unfortunately none of the major model yachting countries has taken this class up, but it should clearly be possible to produce very fast models. No plans and certainly no kits are known, but other classes could be adapted by changing sail area.

**Marblehead Class (M, RM with radio, often 50/800 in USA)** By far the most popular and numerous class of yacht in the world, the Marblehead class is sailed in every country having organized racing. The rule dates from about 1930 from the USA, and its popularity is due to its simplicity and the convenience of its size. The basics include an overall length of 50in (1270mm) and a sail area not exceeding 800sq in (51.7sq dm). There are no restrictions on displacement, beam, or draft. Some critics feel that the rule produces a less-than-graceful craft, since by simply limiting overall length and not waterline length, the waterline is normally extended to the extreme bow and stern, giving vertical ends without overhangs. This makes a fast but wet hull. Kits for Marbleheads, usually with grp hulls, are currently made in England, the USA, West Germany, France, South Africa and Japan. In addition a range of grp hulls and plans can be obtained. Average displacements are between 12 and 20lb (5.5–9.0kg).

**International 6m Class** Dating back to the 1920s, this class is officially international but has only ever been used once in an international race and has been out of favor for many years. There were strong fleets in the 1930s particularly in Scotland and the USA, and currently there are the beginnings of what may be a revival

**Above**
A pair of 36R vane yachts setting off to beat up the lake in fresh conditions which have necessitated changing down to third suit sails.

**Left**
Racing 10 raters at Birmingham. This picture gives an excellent idea of the size of these boats which are the fastest of the model classes.

**Above**
Vane Marbleheads racing at
Dovercourt. From the sail and
vane settings it can be seen
that the course is a reach, ie,
the wind is blowing across the
pond.

**Left**
A German and a Belgian A
class yacht about to start on
the famous lake at Fleetwood.
The German mate steadies the
boat with his pole, normally
used to turn the boat out when
it comes to the bank on the
beat.

of interest. The rule is fairly complex, based on a full-size rule giving in effect a scale model; it is rather constricting. Boats are about 54in (1375mm) loa (length overall) and 45in (1140mm) lwl (load waterline), displacing around 25–30lb (11–14kg) and are limited on girth and draft. Sailing performance is attractive, though slower than the similar-size Marblehead class despite being allowed in the region of 1100sq in (70sq dm) of sail area. Only one available plan is known, published in 1955.

**American X Class** Little is heard of this class now, but it attracted a number of builders and some lively debate in the 1930s through to the 1950s. Its basis was merely a sail area limited to 1000sq in (64.6sq dm) and there were certain prohibitions on hulls and fins. Possibly interest dwindled because the rule was not sufficiently specific and too wide a variation in performance could result.

**10-rater Class (10r or 10R, with radio R10R)** The second most internationally popular class for radio control, this is the fastest class of model and uses a simple rule relating sail area and waterline length, an increase in one requiring a decrease in the other. The basic rule dates back to 1878 in England, but occasional alterations have been made. A typical model is long and slim, possibly 80in loa (2000mm) with a 65in lwl (1650mm), a displacement of about 25lb (11.5kg), and a sail area of

**Below**
Competitors lining up under starter's orders at Fleetwood. Colored sails are spinnakers, only used downwind. The boats are A Class and the occasion is an international vane race.

1150sq in (74sq dm). There are kits made in England, the USA and West Germany, and plans can be bought in those countries as well.

**A Class (with radio, RA)** The A class is the largest class of model and the second most popular internationally for vane racing. Originating in England in 1922, the rule was cleverly framed so that a wide variety of models (and thus design freedom) would have similar performance. Successful models have ranged from 35 to 80lb (16–36kg) displacement, but on average 52–56lb (23.5–25.5kg) on a waterline of 55in (1400mm), 80in loa (2000mm), 13–14in beam (330–360mm), and 12in (305mm) draft would be typical, carrying about 1500sq in (96sq dm) of sail. A number of plans and glass-fiber hulls can be obtained, and there are one or two kits produced in England and France. Most early radio yachts belonged to this class, but possibly because of problems of transport they have long been outstripped in numbers by RM and R10R yachts.

**One-design Classes** In the USA a number of one-design classes are recognized for radio racing, the most numerous being the *Santa Barbara*, about 10R size, the *Soling* M, the *East Coast 12m*, a little larger than a 6m, and, surprisingly, one of the author's designs, *Starlet*, which fits the 36/600 rule. No other country recognizes any one-design class.

# RACING

Methods of racing the two basic types of yacht are quite
different. Radio racing is easily understood since it is
effectively the same as full-size yacht racing, using a
triangular course and from six to thirteen yachts sailing
in each heat (Figure 1). A sixty second count-down
before the starting gun sees all the boats jockeying for
a good starting position, and a race is usually over two
laps, lasting five to six minutes. Racing schedules ensure
that every boat races all the others during a regatta,
and the total of points earned in the heats, less any
penalties that might have been accumulated, decides
the finishing position. Rules of right of way, overlap, and
so on are just the same as in full-size racing.

Vane boats sail on a tournament system, racing as a
series of pairs from one end of the lake to the other then
back, every boat meeting every other during a race
meeting. Three points are earned for winning the beat
in one direction, and two points for the run the opposite
way, total points determining final positions. When
beating, the yachts tack from one side of the lake to the
other and are turned with poles by the skipper on one
bank and his mate on the other; the boat must be stopped if an adjustment to its trim is thought necessary.
Downwind, spinnakers are carried, and in a fresh
breeze these give the yachts sufficient speed to make
their crews very active!

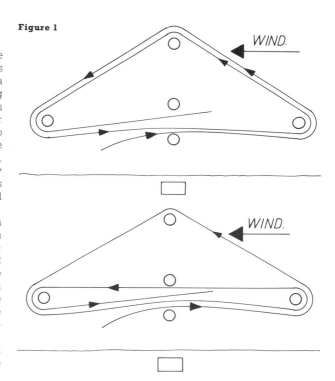

**Figure 1**

WIND.

WIND.

# POWER BOATS

In power models there are various ways of dividing boats into classifications. An obvious one is type of power plant—internal combustion (diesel, glow, or spark ignition), electric, or steam. Then there are tethered, free running, or radio-controlled boats. Or they can be split into functional, scale, and stand-off scale. (These last are models of scale appearance but which are not accurately scaled down to the last detail.) Sport models are frequently of the semi-scale or stand-off scale type, but equally they can be functional. Any boat run for pleasure rather than specifically for competition is in effect a sport model. If, therefore, the recognized classes are listed, it will be understood that a model in any category could be used for fun operation, and there are no boats that would not fit into one class or another.

Internationally the Naviga classifications are most frequently used except, at the time of writing, in multi-racing where world championships are held in different sizes, and in the USA, where a totally different approach to model power boating has developed. Naviga classes are:

**A** Tethered hydroplanes, A1 up to 2.5cc, A2 2.5–5cc, and A3 5–10cc. These models are hooked to a wire giving a radius of 15.923m (1 lap = 100m) and run in a circle, being timed over five laps. Speeds of over 200kph (130mph) can be recorded by top-class boats under ideal conditions. Glowplug engines are used almost exclusively in these sizes, but Britain has additional classes for 15 and 30cc boats in which spark ignition engines can be competitive; steam boats up to a weight of 8 and 16lb are also covered, and a flash steam hydroplane can be capable of more than 100kph (65 or so mph).

Other titles which may be used are 'pole boats,' from running round the pole (RTP) or simply 'hydros.' It is a fairly specialized field, but at Naviga championships about ninety or so boats can be expected. There are no kits but a few plans can be obtained.

**B** This is for tethered hydroplanes which are airscrew driven. There is only one class, B1, up to 2½cc (.15cu in) and speeds of 240kph (150mph) have been approached.

**Above**
A tethered hydroplane in class B, 5cc (.29cu in). Such boats can exceed 100mph (180kph). Fastest internationally are often Russian, Bulgarian or Italian models.

**Above right**
A very typical F1-V5 model, that is, radio controlled speed with up to 5cc (.29cu in) engine. Tool-box carries accumulator for glowplug, meter to check plug, fuel, etc.

**Above far right**
Scale-type three-point hydroplanes for radio running are very popular in the USA but have never really caught on in other countries. This one is kitted, 18in long for .8cc (.049cu in) motors, or 36in long for 6½cc (.40cu in) and radio.
*(Courtesy Dumas Products Inc)*

**Right**
Multi-racing is the most exciting form of power-boat racing. Three models are here turning the end buoy but a fourth has just capsized, center right. Six to thirteen boats, all at 40+mph (64−kph) make for thrills and spills.

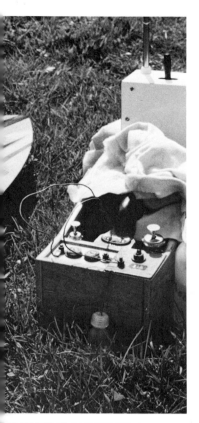
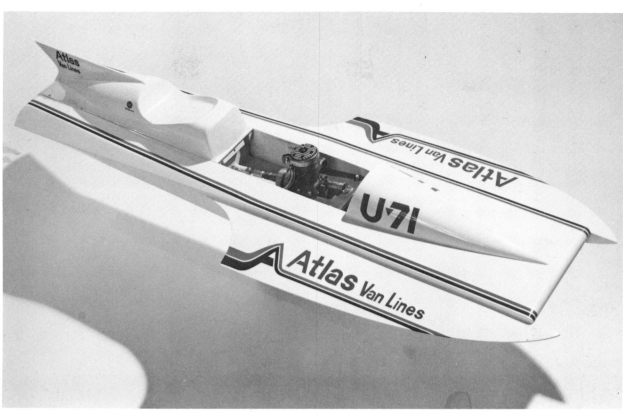

Running occurs on a line as with the preceding models. This is the only form of airscrew-propelled model approved by most national model power boat authorities. One or two plans are available.

**C** As previously mentioned, these are non-working models.

**D** Sailing yachts with vane or other automatic steering.

**E** Frequently known as 'straight runners,' these boats are aimed by the operator at a line of target buoys 60m away, the bull's eye being a pair of buoys 2m apart; passing between scores 100 points. Further buoys at 1m intervals over a 10m line, and buoys along each side of the course, provide reducing scores (see illustration Figure 2). The total for three attempts is recorded.

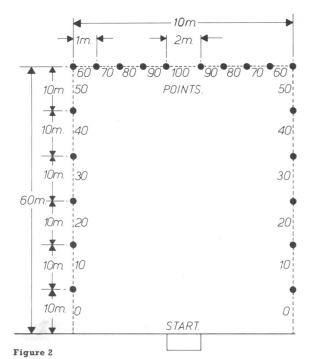

Figure 2

There is no control over the model once it has been released, apart from a timeswitch stopping the motor, and considerable skill and experience is needed to achieve accuracy and consistency, especially in windy conditions or when currents are encountered. The category is sub-divided into: EX models which are functional and may be powered by electric, steam, or internal combustion; EH, scale merchant or pleasure vessels; and EK, scale warships, normally but not necessarily electric powered. These models are judged before running, for scale accuracy, workmanship and so on and are timed when running, their speeds being compared with true scale speeds. Final positions are based on the total of points earned from static judging and running.

In Britain a slightly simpler course is often used with only six target buoys spaced at 1m intervals, scores being five points for a bull, three for an inner, and one for an outer. Other competitions include a nominated time to travel over the course, passing between two buoys about 10m apart; and knock-out, when two buoys are gradually brought closer together and boats which succeed in passing between them continue into the next round, rounds being continued with the buoys

Big class hydroplanes with hand-built 15 and 30cc (.9 and 1.8cu in) motors are raced in Britain, France and Belgium but are not normally as fast as the 10cc (.60cu in) class. Here a competitor prepares a model for a run.

**Left**
An EX class straight runner is released. The absence of superstructure means less effect on the boat from cross-winds. The crowd is obviously absorbed.

**Below**
An East German EK class straight runner. Large models tend to run more consistently and can be faster without losing points for exceeding scale speed.

moved closer together each time until all but one boat are eliminated. Boats must not exceed 12mph (19.2kph).

Almost any boat can compete in such events so that there is a wide choice of kits, plans, and power plants. Regular competitors design and build specific straight-running models, and drawings for one or two can be obtained in England, where this type of model boating is popular.

**F** The F categories are the most numerous, covering all radio-controlled models, speed, steering, scale, racing, and novelties. With the exception of the last, strict and testing standard courses are laid down, as sketched, and this can lead to a certain amount of puzzlement to a newcomer. With speed models, for example, it is the time taken to cover the course which counts, not the actual speed in mph or kph, and reference to 'a fifteen-second model' means nothing to the uninitiated. The explanations accompanying the following descriptions should clarify matters.

*F1*, speed models, are run in three separate classes according to internal combustion engine size, and two electric classes. The course is small, just a triangle with 30m sides, the start line being halfway along the base (Figure 3). Boats make a flying start, followed by one lap in each direction, turning for the second lap halfway along the base line. There are thus six 60° and one 180° turns to be made, so that acceleration and turning ability are essential; top international 10cc boats complete the course in just fourteen seconds or even less, and electric boats can do it in under twenty seconds. The classes are:

F1–V2.5–engines up to 2.5cc (.15cu in)
F1–V5–engines from 2.5 to 5cc (.15–.30cu in)
F1–V15–engines from 5–15cc (.30–.91cu in)
   In practice all top models in this class use 10cc
   (.61cu in) engines
F1E–1Kg–electric models weighing up to 1kg
F1E–500–electric models limited only to 42v input

There are some kits and plans for this type of speed model, but usually a glass-fiber (grp) hull is used and a wide choice of such hulls can be purchased.

In the USA a totally different approach to speed models is evident. Two courses are used, an oval of ½ mile circumference, and a straight 1/16 mile dash. Turning ability and acceleration are thus of far less importance. There are eight classes according to engine size, and each is split into hydroplane or mono-

Friedrich Wiegand
D D R / 66 GREIZ
Ernst-Thälmann-Str. 16

**Figure 3**

**Figure 4**

**Figure 5**

hull classification; a hydroplane normally runs with three points of the boat touching the water, a monohull (that is, a conventional boat) with one. Since turning ability can be largely discounted, flat-out speeds tend to be higher–something like 70mph (112kph) in America against 50mph (80kph) in Europe.

*F2* is for scale models, currently divided into F2a, 75–150cm (29½–59in) and F2b, over 150cm. These models are first judged by experts, from five nations where possible  the highest and lowest points being discarded and the average taken of the other three. They then negotiate a cloverleaf course (Figure 4) through closely spaced buoys, demonstrate control astern, and finish by docking in a rectangular dock, the size of which is adjusted according to the length and beam of each competitor. The total of all points awarded determines their position in the final results.

The standard of models in this category is incredibly high; many would be quite at home in a glass case in a museum. Among items for which points are awarded are originality and amount of work involved, so that a kit model. which would lose points in these areas, has to be superbly made to compete at top level, although in club or inter-club events there are often special awards in the kit category. Plans for detailed scale models are obtainable, but with experience building from shipyard drawings offers unlimited choice.

F3 is for functional steering models, navigating a complicated Christmas-tree course (Figure 5) and earning bonus points for the speed at which the course is completed. Small, highly maneuverable boats are favored, usually using up to 3½cc (.21cu in) engines in F3V and total weight of about 1kg for F3E electric. The course is based on a 30m equilateral triangle and the boat has to pass accurately sixteen times between pairs of buoys spaced 1m apart; a top boat will complete it in around 35 seconds. Plans, some kits, and grp hulls suitable for this type of competition are available.

F4 is now obsolete, but it consisted of bursting a line of ten balloons with a needle mounted on the boat's bow. In the 1950s, with small numbers of entries, this gave light relief, but as proficiency and numbers increased preparation time became out of all proportion to the few seconds needed to pop all the balloons.

F5 covers radio yachts, and has been mentioned.

F6 is most spectacular, involving a team demonstration lasting up to ten minutes. As many as thirty boats have been used in pyrotechnical displays of seaborne invasions, fleet actions, submarine battles with blazing models exploding and sinking, rescue and salvage operations–these shows illustrate the ingenuity of modellers and produce very realistic scenes

F7 is much the same, but limited to a single operator. The general public is, on the whole, aware of radio-controlled boats, but the functions performed by specialist models as used in F6 and F7 can be guaranteed to astonish, and huge crowds are soon drawn by the spectacle afforded by these models in operation.

Also popular with spectators are the two remaining classes, FSR15 and FSR35. These are classes for what are usually termed 'multi-boat racing,' or even 'multi-racing,' where up to thirteen boats race together round an M-shaped course of about 200m for periods of, usually, 20 or 30 minutes, but sometimes one or two hours. Starts are on the Le Mans principle, the drivers dashing for their models and starting up on a signal, and pit stops for refuelling or adjustments or even repairs are all a part of the racing. As may be imagined, it is frenzied and exciting, and demands a high degree of preparation and 'driving' skill.

In the Naviga classes, FSR15 is for engines up to 15cc, although, again, almost all boats use 10cc engines since these are the most highly developed. FSR35 is for spark-ignition engines up to 35cc (2.1cu in), a figure which was originally set because it allowed the use of commercial water-pump and small lawn-mower engines of comparatively low power. Hand-built engines of this capacity are now producing up to 7bhp, and it may therefore be necessary to reduce the size allowed.

**Above**
Paddle vessels are becoming extremely popular. This is the paddle tug *Jean Sallie* which is electric-powered. So far, few have proved as maneuverable as screw vessels.

**Above right**
Novelty model rowing boat, propelled by sculls. This type of fun model is enjoyed by spectators and allows great scope for individual ingenuity.

**Right**
Submarines always attract interest and are very good straight runners. This one is *U47*, 63in (1600mm) in glass fiber by John Darnell. It can be fitted with radio.

There are few kits suitable for FSR classes, but some plans are available and there is a wide selection of grp hulls.

Additional international classes, not officially recognized by Naviga, include a 3.5cc and a 6.6cc class, and one for 2½kg electric boats, with ten minute heats.

\* \* \* \*

It is hoped that the foregoing explanations of classes and competitions substantiate the chapter's opening remarks about 'something to suit all tastes.' Where possible, a newcomer should visit clubs and regattas to see as many varieties of models as possible before making his choice of what to build; model enthusiasts are rarely anything but outgoing, friendly people who are only too pleased to welcome and help anyone who shows interest. Membership in a club is certainly the quickest way to learn. There are club, inter-club, district, national, and international competitions, of course, but even for the non-competitive, the pooled experiences and comradeship of a club are invaluable. The lone hand, with no organization near him, must rely on reading whatever he can find, or what his nearest library can find for him, and should not be put off by something that may seem a little advanced. Read it all— it is amazing what the mind will store, half digested, to prove useful later on.

# Wood Hulls

Ships and boats come in all shapes and sizes, but the first division as far as a hull is concerned is whether it is a planing or a displacement type. A body floating in water displaces an amount of water equal to its own weight (Archimedes) and a vessel which moves through the water remaining on the same mean waterline has a displacement hull. Such a vessel has a maximum critical speed related to its waterline length beyond which its wavemaking becomes excessive and in trying to mount its own bow-wave its trim angle and stability suffer. To exceed a critical speed/length ratio it must be designed to plane, to lift on to its own waves while keeping stability and a reasonable trim angle. This is a planing hull.

The amount of power required to get a hull on the plane is considerable, much more than is needed for maximum displacement speed and more than is needed to keep it planing once the condition is achieved. Planing is therefore confined to relatively small and light boats up to about 120ft (36m) maximum and usually much smaller. The best hull form for planing is flattish-bottomed, fairly broad, light, and with a noticeable change in angle between the hull bottom and the sides, and the simplest way to meet these requirements is to use a 'hard chine' hull. In this the sides and bottom form a definite corner for most of the hull length, and the shape lends itself to construction of a light and relatively inexpensive hull, often using sheet ply or metal.

Without a chine, the area where the hull sides merge into the bottom is called the bilge, and if the turn is sharp, the term 'hard bilged' is used. A hard-bilged hull will also lend itself to planing, though may well demand more power, but it will also be more weatherly or sea-

kindly in rough conditions, in which a hard chine design would be uncomfortable. A hull intended for displacement running only, will normally have a 'soft' or 'easy' round bilge; there can be exceptions, such as when maximum cargo space is more important than performance, or when speed or cheapness of building are major factors.

## HARD CHINE HULLS

Although a hard chine hull, or a sharpie as it is sometimes termed in the sailing world, can be carved from a laminated block, such construction is only likely to be used for a scale model where complex transverse curves exist, or for a 'plug,' which is a form from which a mold is made for glass-fiber hulls or the master pattern over which vacuum-formed hulls are drawn.

The vast majority of chine hulls are built by applying

a skin to a basic framework, and most frequently the skin simply consists of large panels of thin ply. Ply is a fairly easy material to bend in one direction, if necessary by damping, warming, or even steaming, but it is reluctant to bend in two directions. This places some constraints on the design of a hull; any two-way curves which are not basically generated by the geometry of conic projection are likely to be very difficult.

At its simplest a chine hull can be of the dory type, just a flat bottom and the sides, but a V-bottom is much more common. The frame for such a hull will consist of a central keel member, two chine stringers, and two inwale stringers, to which are applied four panels of ply. The two bottom panels can butt to each other over the keel member, or sit in rebates formed along the keel, the rebates either being cut into the keel or produced by attaching a light doubler strip each side. Since the chine stringers provide only a fillet between the

side and bottom panels, they need only be of adequate section to be shaped to the appropriate angle and provide a reasonable gluing area, and they do not normally contribute, except as fillets, to the overall strength of the hull.

In a similar way the inwale strips provide a fillet between the hull side panels and the deck, but in many cases these strips also have to provide an anchorage for deck-edge fittings, and they are therefore normally of slightly heavier section. It is common practice to laminate both chine and inwale stringers from two or even three lighter strips, which makes it easier to negotiate curves and produces a stiffer member when the glue has dried. The strips are applied a pair at a time, that is, one each side, thus avoiding any tendency to distort the framework by uneven loads.

The true method of building the framework is to cut each bulkhead or shadow with an upward extension to a common height, and then to mount them securely inverted on a true and flat building board or jig. A bulkhead is a transverse frame which remains part of the finished hull, and a shadow is a similar frame which is used to position chines and inwales accurately, but is removed completely before decking the hull shell. It is, however, quite possible to construct a hull by using the central keel member as a built-in jig, or to use two parallel fore-and-aft members which may remain in the hull as cabin sides, 'egg-boxing' the bulkheads to these with matching slots and making sure that no twist or asymmetry is allowed to creep in as work proceeds.

Stress in the basic framework can be avoided by using sawn-to-shape members in lieu of bent strips where heavy curves are involved. As an example, many hulls curve rapidly in towards the bows at deck level at such a rate that even laminated inwales would require steaming. This sharp curve can be sawn from ply or timber and the inwale strips rebated into its after end where the curve begins to ease off, thus reducing stress and making construction a good deal easier and quicker.

A curve as sharp as suggested will also prove difficult to skin, the ply needing a lot of coaxing even if left overnight in a tray of damp sawdust. Alternatives are to change to narrow vertical strips of ply or timber forward of the first bulkhead, or to use a bow carved from a solid or laminated block of light timber. In either case the ply skins will be terminated on the first bulkhead and the treatment of the hull forward of this point must be such that a smoothly faired joint will result.

The most frequent difficulty encountered by an inexperienced builder is what to do when the angle between the side and bottom skins is very shallow. Normally the bottom panels are applied first, and it is a good idea to lay an uncreased sheet of brown paper over the framework and lightly rub along the keel and chine to mark the shape required. This shape can then be cut out, checked on the hull, and used as a template to mark out the ply. This should be cut with a little spare material along the chine edge and pinned to the frame. The forward part of the chine is now carefully marked along the corner, until the angle between side and bottom closes to 140° or thereabouts, and after unpinning the panel, an accurate cut is made along this line. The panel is then glued and pinned in place—use hardened steel dressmakers' pins pushed in with pliers, and withdraw them when the glue is dry. Trim the balance of the chine overhang back flush.

Repeat the brown paper template procedure for the side skins, which can have a little spare material left along the deck edge and most of the chine. The bow edge must be accurate, as well as the forward part of the chine edge, which must butt neatly to the edge of the bottom panel. Overhang on the rest of the chine and the deck edge can be trimmed and sanded when the glue is dry and pins withdrawn (Figure 6).

Hard chine hulls almost without exception finish in a flat transom stern. Just occasionally a V or curved transom is encountered, but these offer no problems as

**Figure 6**

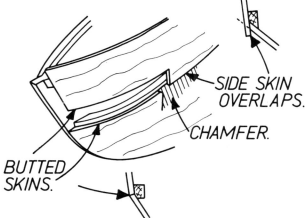

SIDE SKIN OVERLAPS.

CHAMFER.

BUTTED SKINS.

**Left**
The simplest possible bread-and-butter hull is solid, as in this little yacht designed for a television series and since built in thousands. Four vertical balsa laminations and a central spruce sheet keel are all that is required.

**Below**
Stages in the construction of a hard chine hull made in two halves, port and starboard, with the side skins attached before lifting the halves from the building board. The slots for the fin and skeg can be clearly seen. An unorthodox approach, but one which simplifies construction and has proved very successful.

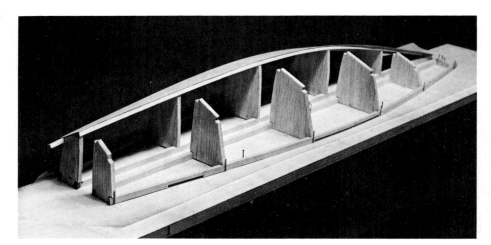

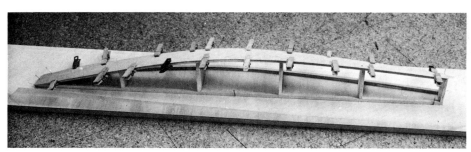

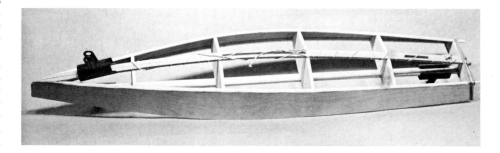

long as there is adequate material left on the bottom skins. In the rare instances where a rounded stern may occur, the panels should be ended on a flat bulkhead and the extremity of the stern carved from block; this is called a fashion piece.

Where transverse or vertical curves exist, it may be necessary to plank the hull with narrow fore-and-aft strips rather than try to induce ply panels to assume complex curves. An alternative is to plank diagonally at about 45° with narrow strips of ply or veneer, preferably fitting a second layer of planks over the first at right-angles to them. Many air-sea rescue launches, with double S-curves in the bottom skins and marked concavity in the sides especially towards the bow, were built in this way, the first planks being covered in canvas before the second layer was applied. Additional stringers are required between keel and chine and chine and inwale at high and low points of the curves,

so that the planks adopt the right shape.

Functional models usually have one-way curves so that ply panels can be used for ease and speed of building, and most stand-off scale chine models use simplified hull shapes for the same reason. If balsa is used instead of ply, it is best to plank in short lengths with the grain running vertically on the sides and across the bottom skins; apart from being easier and more economical on material, the skins are much stiffer and damage which may result from a collision is localized. Ply can be painted in any normal way, but with balsa it is recommended that model aircraft tissue is applied to the outside surfaces by brushing on clear cellulose dope, after which any normal painting procedure can be followed. Applying the tissue reduces the amount of grainfilling needed and produces a much tougher and abrasion-resistant surface.

It is difficult to generalize on the number of bulkhead

**Below**
The result of the top two pictures opposite is *Genie*, a beginner's Marblehead design by the author which has been built all over the world for both vane and radio sailing.

50

and/or shadows needed in a chine hull since much depends on the size and shape of the vessel. Permanent bulkheads are useful in a power boat, dividing the hull into compartments or bays so that the motor, radio, batteries and so on are separated. This can be particularly helpful with an internal combustion or steam engine, tending to restrict oil and fumes to one part of the hull; starting a diesel or glow engine also imposes strain on the hull which fixed bulkheads distribute. On the other hand it is normal to have no bulkheads at all in a yacht hull, but to use deck beams and, if necessary, light internal bracing at particular stress points. Very generally bulkheads or shadows are needed on most models at intervals of 5–7in (125–180mm) but obviously they will be lighter and closer on small models. Large areas of unsupported ply should be avoided by gluing stiffening strips internally from keel to chine and chine to inwale. These and the bottom edges of bulkheads

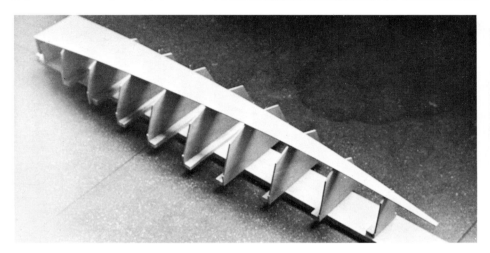

**Top**
Shadows set up for a double-chine Marblehead yacht. Edge-glued ⅛in (3mm) skins are used, so that no chine stringers are needed. Note change of fillet positions at the largest section.

**Center left**
The bottom plank pinned in place on the shadows. Glass tape is later glued along the joint lines of the chines, when the hull shell is lifted off.

**Center right**
Increased stiffness and strength and easier work results from using balsa with the grain 'the short way,' ie, vertically on the sides of this simple model.

**Above**
Using the superstructure as a basic box jig makes it hard to misalign the hull of this all-balsa cabin cruiser. Prop-shaft and engine are lined up during assembly and only chine stringers and skins are now required.

can with advantage be provided with limber holes, small notches between the edges and the skin, so that any water finding its way into the hull will drain to the lowest point, making it easy to sponge or syringe out.

Examples of hard chine hulls include many fast service launches (MTBs, air/sea rescue craft etc) and a majority of ski boats, most wood-built small cabin cruisers and many grp ones, a high proportion of sailing dinghies (Enterprise, Mirror, Cadet, etc), quite a number of larger cruising yachts, barges, lighters, and many other types of small craft. Double chines are found in some coasters and smaller fleet auxiliaries, workboats, tugs such as the wartime *Tid* class, and cruising yachts and dinghies. A look round a harbor or a marina, or through boating magazines, will indicate just how many hulls are made today of hard chine form.

planking on frames. Which is chosen depends to some extent on personal preference and availability of materials but also on the shape of the hull. Some hulls can have quite tricky reverse curves or rapid changes of section which can prove difficult to plank and thus lend themselves to carving, while others, particularly where weight and space may be crucial, are better planked. A present-day consideration may be cost, since good quality timber for a carved hull can be expensive, and most of it finishes up on the workshop floor as shavings and chips; it is usually cheaper to plank a hull. Often a compromise is sensible, using carved areas where the shape is difficult but planking elsewhere. The bow and stern may be laminated with a planked midsection, or the hull bottom may be carved from solid and then the planking started.

**Above**
Cramping up the laminations for a bread and butter hull. Note station lines well marked all round. Cramps use lengths of studding, but long bolts may do.

## ROUND BILGE HULLS

For displacement craft, or even smaller semi-planing boats which spend time on the open sea, the round bilge hull form is safer, more efficient, and more economical in running costs. Increased efficiency means that this type of hull is preferred for model racing yachts, and a scale model of any ship is almost certain to require a round bilge hull. Period vessels of any size from rowing boats upward are traditionally rounded, originally perhaps because of materials and methods of construction available, but certainly later because of strength/weight ratio and seaworthiness. Exceptions are some native craft, such as some Chinese junks, and special purpose craft such as whaling dories. Cargo vessels like canal barges were flat-bottomed and angular for much of their length, but fined off at bow and stern; much the same applies to present-day supertankers and bulk carriers.

There are two time-honored methods of construction for round bilge hulls; carving from a laminated block or

Either method, or any combination of them, works from the body plan of the hull, which is simply a drawing of cross-sections of the hull superimposed one over the other on common axes; the center line and the load waterline. Because a hull usually tapers towards each end, the body plan shows on one half the maximum cross-section and the decreasing sections towards the bow, and on the other half the same main section (or sometimes the next one aft) and the decreasing sections towards the stern. Provided one has a body plan and knows the spacing of the sections along the hull, any method of construction can be used.

## BREAD-AND-BUTTER CONSTRUCTION

At one time it was possible to obtain a large block of, say, yellow pine, well seasoned and free of faults, and carve a complete hull in one piece. Nowadays the cost would be astronomic, but even if it were not, it is far better to laminate planks together to make what is universally termed a bread-and-butter hull, the planks being the bread and the glue the butter. This is much more economical on timber, allows doubtful areas of wood to be avoided, and by laying out the planks beforehand, considerably reduces the amount of hollowing out needed.

The planks may be laminated horizontally (bread and butter on the waterlines) or vertically (bread and butter on the buttock lines), but for a complete hull, horizontal is usual. Vertical laminations are frequently used when only the bow and/or stern are carved; the method of marking out is similar.

In a line drawing, water and buttock lines are shown, the spacing being indicated by the straight lines on the drawing (Figure 7). The hull profile (the sheer plan) will show parallel straight lines running from bow to stern, and these lines are also shown across the body plan. Looking down on the hull, these lines are curved and give the shapes of the waterlines on the third part of the drawing, called the half-breadth plan or simply the waterline plan. This bit also has straight parallel fore and aft lines, shown as vertical straight lines on the body plan and curves–the buttock lines–on the sheer plan. Finally the vertical straight lines on the sheer plan and across the half-breadth plan are the station lines which show the positions of the sections which form the body plan.

If timber of exactly the same thickness as the waterline spacing can be obtained, it is possible to trace off the waterlines from the half-breadth plan. Otherwise the laminations have to be plotted, which is not difficult. Across the body plan draw lines representing the actual

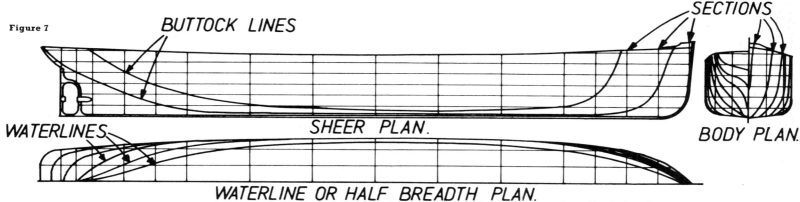

Figure 7

BUTTOCK LINES

SECTIONS

SHEER PLAN.

BODY PLAN.

WATERLINES

WATERLINE OR HALF BREADTH PLAN.

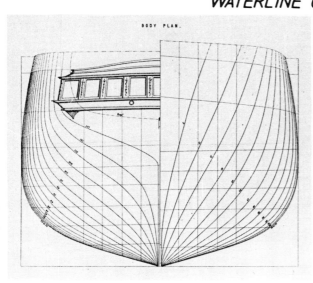

BODY PLAN.

thickness of the timber available, starting from the bottom of the hull or, if preferred, upwards and downwards from the load waterline. Draw lines at the same spacing from the same starting level on the sheer plan; this is necessary to give the position of the ends of each plank. The timber must be at least half the width of the hull, and the object is to make each lamination in two halves, which is much more economical and simplifies removal of most of the center before gluing up.

Make sure the edge is straight and square, then mark along it and across the face, the station (section) positions and the plank ends for the particular plank chosen to start. Identify the top line of this plank on the body plan, then with a pair of dividers or compasses measure the required width of the plank from the appropriate section and transfer it to the station line on the timber. Mark each station with the required width at the corresponding section (Figure 8) to give a series of dots which, when connected with a line drawn with the aid of a spline, will give the shape of the plank. A thin strip of wood or springy wire can be used as a spline. The

**Top**
A bread-and-buttered hull ready for carving; most of the inside has already been removed as seen by the way in which the planks were marked out and sawn.

**Left**
A typical body plan such as is found on museum drawings. Provided the section spacing is known, this is all that is needed to build an accurate hull.

sketch shows a tag which should be cut on each end to provide a parallel grip for a small clamp, used when gluing the halves together and sawn away when the glue has set.

A lot of work can now be saved by cutting out the center of the plank. This is done by marking out a cutting line from the body plan, or to avoid confusion, from a tracing of each section. The desired thickness of the hull shell is drawn on to each section (Figure 9) and the bottom inside point gives the position of the cutting line at that section. It is necessary to draw the hull thickness on the sheer plan in order to establish the ends of the cutting line. When all points have been transferred to the wood and connected, the complete plank has been drawn out, and the center 'waste' may well be large enough to accommodate a smaller half plank from lower down the hull. Alternatively, a half plank can be made in two pieces butt-jointed amidships for minimum waste (Figure 10). There are many cases of smaller models built from the cut-out centers of larger ones!

At all stages the station lines should be kept clearly marked and, after sawing out, squared round all faces, as they will be necessary to align the laminations correctly when they are finally glued up. Each pair of half-planks should, however, first be glued accurately together to make a set of full planks.

It is possible to lay out all the planks on paper rather than directly on to the timber, but they must then be traced. Long, narrow and curved strips of paper stretch and distort if cut out, especially with scissors, and builders who have cut templates in this way and then pasted them to the timber, which again distorts them, have found that they have wasted a lot of wood.

**Figure 8**

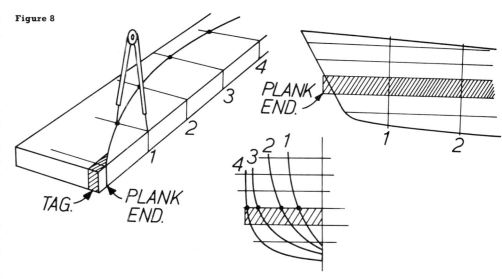

**Below**
Shadows in place on building board and first lamination of backbone pinned in place. These shadows were experimentally lightly tack-cemented, but fillets are recommended.

The number of planks glued into a block at one time will depend on the shuffling time of the glue used, and it is usual to limit it to three or four planks. A series of cramps should be prepared beforehand by cutting lengths of timber long enough to be drilled through outside the maximum hull width. Lengths of studding (screwed rod) are passed through the holes and nutted; with one piece of timber below and one above the hull, connected each end by studding, considerable pressure can be applied. Enough cramps should be made to allow one about every 6in (15cm). Before tightening, a check is made that all the joints at bow

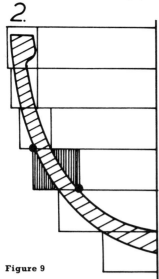

**2.**

**Figure 9**

and stern and all the station lines are accurately aligned.

An alternative method is to place the glued block on a flat surface and lay a stout plank on top, adding heavy weights such as several house bricks. It is more difficult to ensure alignment, but with care and modern adhesives, a satisfactory result can be achieved.

When all planks are glued up, carving is the next step, and holding the hull can be a problem. It is best to drill the bottom plank for two long bolts, passing through the bench, to carve the exterior with the hull inverted, and to use two shorter bolts with the hull right way up to work on the inside. The holes can subsequently be plugged with dowels, unless needed for keel bolts or something similar. Long experience has shown that this is far superior to other methods and well worth accepting the two holes.

Starting with the outside, the corners are planed off the planks and the hull spokeshaved to a smooth shape. A set of templates should be prepared by tracing the sections from the body plan on to thin card or ply and

cutting them out accurately. These templates are then offered to the hull at the appropriate stations (the marks should still be continually renewed as the hull is carved) and further shaving, or crossways rasping or coarse sanding should be carried out until a near fit is obtained. Leave final sanding until the interior is finished.

Turn the hull over and gouge away the internal corners, unless any are needed for equipment mounting. The functionally important points about interior hollowing are hull weight and strength, adequate space, and a reasonable surface for painting or varnishing. Within these criteria how much work is done is a matter of personal taste.

Any internal bulkheads may be fitted from a cut-and-try card template, but usually a bread-and-butter hull is left without bulkheads, having deck beams instead. These are jointed into the thickened area round the top edge (Figure 9) or an inwale strip can be glued round inside the edge to receive the deck beam ends and any deck-edge fittings.

Completion of the model follows normal practice except for fitting the propeller shaft tube(s) for a power model. The hole for this has to be drilled at a shallow angle and may extend for some distance. Long drills can be obtained from engineers' suppliers, or a normal drill can be brazed or silver soldered to a length of rod. The entry and exit points of the required hole should be marked, and a ply or thick card template made to the required angle of the shaft tube to the outside of the hull, the template being taped to the hull close to the center line. With an assistant to sight from the side, an accurate hole can be drilled.

Alternatives are to burn a pilot hole through with a

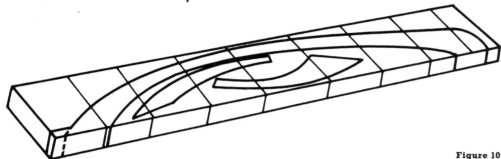

**Figure 10**

red-hot rod, opening up the hole with a rat-tail file, or to chisel out a slot accommodating the tube and shape two wedges to be glued into the slot to secure the tube and restore the hull surfaces.

When working on the hull after carving, padding in the form of an old but clean blanket is desirable to protect the surface from scars and indentations; minor ones will often swell out if the immediate area is damped, but it is better to avoid them. A padded stand should also be made as early as possible, since not only does this protect the hull, but it holds it firmly and greatly simplifies later stages of work.

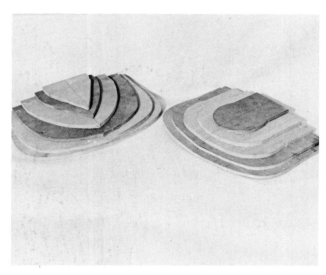

# PLANKED HULLS

There are subtle distinctions in the nomenclature of these hulls. Initially there are carvel and clinker (or clincher) builds, the former referring to flush planking with butted edges and the latter overlapping planks, much used in small boats from Viking times and requiring slightly different treatment. Then there is plank-on-frame, which implies permanent bulkheads or frames, and rib-and-plank, which means the use of shadows (sometimes called molds) which do not remain part of the completed hull.

In either case the starting point is once again the body plan. Normal practice is to draw up the lines with equally spaced station lines, but desired bulkheads may not necessarily coincide with these stations, in which case new sections must be plotted on the body plan by taking the appropriate points off the sheer and waterlines. Simply draw a line across the half-breadth plan at the required point, and a corresponding line on the sheer plan. Take the gunwale height and keel depth from the sheer plan working from the load waterline, and the width of each waterline from the half-breadth, and sketch in the section, which will follow the general shape of the existing sections adjacent to it.

For permanent bulkheads or frames (a bulkhead is a solid partition, a frame will have part or all of its center removed) trace the appropriate sections separately, then draw a line around inside each one representing the finished thickness of the planking, which will be the line to cut to. Mark also notches for inwales and keel member etc, and an extension upward to a common line. For rib and plank the same procedure is followed

except that the cutting line must allow for the finished plank thickness plus the thickness of the rib.

Each bulkhead or shadow when cut out requires a fillet strip screwed to its top edge, and these fillets are screwed, from beneath, to a building board which must be flat and true. The board needs to be good, solid timber, well seasoned, and need only be four or five inches (100–125mm) wide. Some builders screw it to a second piece to make a T shape, which helps keep it flat and also provides a convenient means of holding it in a vice. The board surface should be marked with a dead straight center line and the station positions marked accurately on it.

Because most hulls taper from a midsection, the section drawn will only be correct on its station line, and the thickness of the bulwark or shadow must lie between the station line and the larger section, or the station will effectively be moved forward or back by this thickness. This must be borne in mind when screwing the fillet strips, and the screws must also be driven from underneath, so that they can be unscrewed when the hull is completed.

The keel member and inwales are now added and can be glued into permanent frames but only pinned to

**Bottom**
Yacht hull ribbed ready for planking. Waxed paper prevents unwanted adhesion to shadows. Ribs are pinned with ply 'washers' under pinheads which are removed as planking proceeds.

**Below**
Kit model of Dragon class yacht ready to plank. Shadows here remain in finished hull and are thus bulkheads or, in cabin area, frames.

**Above**
Nicely planked Marblehead yacht. Variation of color in cedar planking indicates the run of the planks well and looks attractive in bright varnish finish.

shadows. Ribs, usually narrow strips of thin ply, are rebated into the keel and inwales, though if solid (that is, non-laminated) inwales are used, cutting rebates may affect the smoothness of their curves. In this case the ribs are secured over the inwales, and packing pieces between ribs later inserted to fill the gaps between inwales and top planks.

A planking plan is now drawn over the body plan by first dividing off the largest section according to the plank width to be used. It is possible to vary the planks, wide on straight or gentle curves, to narrow where curves are sharp. The same number of planks must now be marked on a section towards each end, proportionately reduced in width. Which section is used will depend on the basic shape of the hull and its degree of taper; with a typical yacht hull, perhaps half the planks will terminate on the keel member (backbone), while with a cargo vessel all but the bottom one or two will run forward to the stem and perhaps half will end on the sternpost aft. Connecting the points on the mid-section through those on the chosen sections with straight lines continued through to the center line will show the pattern of planking and give the width of each plank where it crosses each section. Visualizing the application of each plank to the hull will indicate whether a practical plan has been achieved, or whether it should be rubbed out and an altered version tried.

Planking is best started with the top (gunwale) plank. Mark off the planking material with the station lines and spot the appropriate plank width on each. Connect the spots with a smooth line with the aid of a spline and cut out. In every plank, the top edge will be straight and all the curve will be cut into the bottom edge. If equal plank width was decided on at the mid-section, every plank should be the same shape, and it is therefore possible to use the first one as a template to mark the rest. This means that six or eight planks can be planed to shape together. However, cautious builders may prefer to spot the plank widths on the ribs or bulkheads and keep a check as planks are added, cutting a plank with a little extra width as necessary to keep up to the marks.

The top plank each side is applied to follow the line of the inwale and has all its edges left square. In all subsequent planks the straight top edge must be bevelled to a greater or lesser extent, depending on the rate of curve of the sections. The ends will either fit in rebates in a stempiece or terminate on a bulkhead; as in chine hulls, it may be desirable to use a block for the extreme bow and stern, rather than attempt severe curvature of the planks.

Where resistance to adopting complex curves is encountered–for example at the tuck of the stern of a tug–planks may be steamed by sliding them into a length of metal pipe, putting a cork in one end and slipping the other end over a boiling kettle's spout. Ten minutes of this will render them supple, but they should then only be pinned and clamped in place and allowed to dry, or shrinkage may ruin what initially appeared a good fit. When dry they are glued in the normal way.

Tapering hulls such as yachts' require specialized treatment when the planks start to lap on to the backbone. This member will have been shaped to follow the sections, usually sharpening towards the bow but fairly flat towards the stern. As pairs of planks reach the bow, they are alternately overlapped, *viz* the starboard plank is cut to match the backbone surface and the port plank is glued over it. For the next pair, the port plank is cut flush and the starboard one glued over it, and so on. When planking is completed, the pointed line formed by the plank ends is planed away and a strip of timber glued along the flat so formed, to be planed to fair neatly later. Aft of the fin, a narrow strip of planking material is glued centrally along the backbone, leaving a step or rebate each side into which the plank ends are fitted.

When planking is completed, the corners are planed off and a rasp or coarse glasspaper applied across the

grain until all flats have disappeared. Finer glasspaper is now used, rubbing fore and aft until the surface is smooth all over. The hull can now be removed from the building board by unscrewing the fillets. Deck beams should be prepared for fitting as the shadows are knocked or twisted out, to prevent the hull sides springing in or out. Where fixed bulkheads remain, it will be necessary to cut away the top extensions, a job simplified if part of the sawcut was made when the bulkheads were initially cut out.

The inside of the hull needs to be thoroughly painted or varnished and any interior work completed before decking. This includes any additional deck beams and carlings (fore and aft deck support strips). Decking depends on the shape of the hull; the standard camber (thwartship curve of deck) is 1:30 and if the ship has a lot of sheer, a dual curvature exists which may mean that planking is necessary. Usually it is possible to use a sheet of ply with, if required, veneer planks laid on top, or simulated planking drawn or scored on the surface. Where weight is not too critical, melamine-faced laminates have been used.

It is common practice to make up a central keel member incorporating the propeller shaft tube for a powered vessel before the main assembly is started. The tube is likely to be slightly larger in diameter than the thickness of the keel (often ply) and the procedure is to cut a slot to accept it, which separates the keel into two parts, and rejoin them over a doubler piece already grooved as necessary, laying the tube in place and assembling the whole unit over the plan to ensure accuracy. A second doubler is then added and, when dry, the complete assembly is ready to be dropped in the notches in the bulkheads or shadows.

In the case of a yacht, the main backbone may be laminated over a drawing beforehand, or laminated in place on the shadows, or it may be sawn to profile from a solid plank. Modern fin keels tend to be quite thin, and are slid through a slot in the backbone and fitted to a center plank immediately beneath the deck. If necessary local doublers can be glued to the backbone in the region of the slot, extending a short distance ahead and aft of the slot. It is crucially important that the backbone is absolutely true.

Clinker built hulls follow much the same technique of mounting shadows on a jig and spotting off plank widths on every shadow. A photograph shows an easy way to mark each shadow, using a strip of paper and the standard geometric method of dividing an 'unknown length' by parallel lines from divisions on a line of convenient length. Clinker planks tend to vary slightly in curvature. The technique is to cut the planking material to the shape required for the lower edge of a plank, then spot off the width at each station, connect the points, and cut out. Planking starts, fairly obviously, with the garboard plank, that is, the one next to the keel.

In full-size, the overlap of the planks and the timbers, which are bent into place later, is nailed with copper nails; a rove (a dished copper washer) is slipped over the nail protruding inside the hull, the surplus nail snipped off, and the end riveted or clinched over. It is not possible to buy scale copper pins and roves, and in model work it is customary to glue the planks. Short lengths of copper wire can then be used, if desired, to simulate the hundreds of nails in a hull.

Diagonal planking is quite feasible for a round bilge hull, requiring only that several stringers are let into the shadows to ensure that the planks adopt the correct curvature. If double diagonal planking is intended, no ribs are needed and a very light, stiff, and strong monocoque shell can be produced.

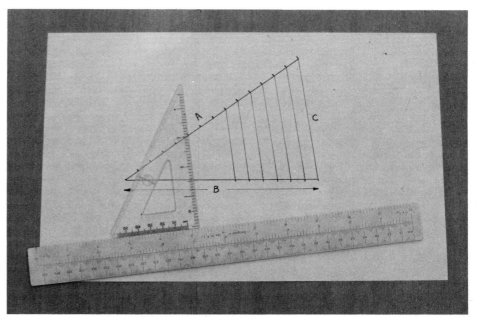

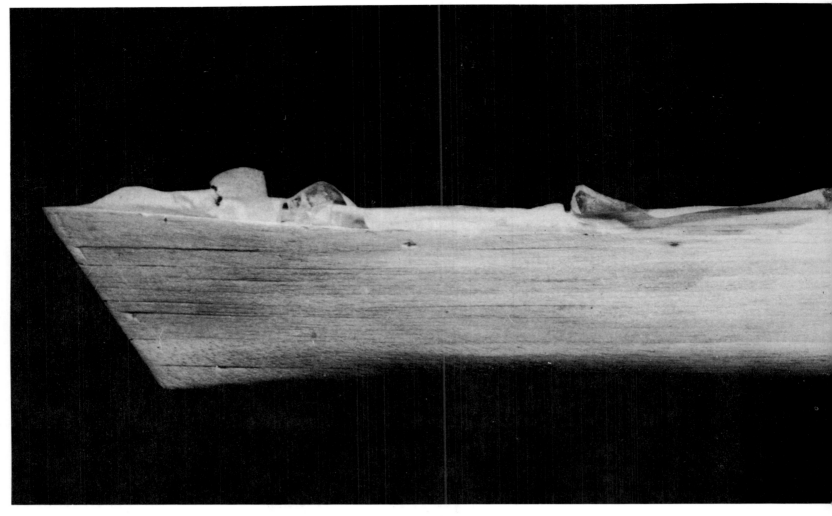

# Tools and Materials

Some people can make a prize-winning model with nothing more than a razor blade, a saw, a drill, and a pair of pliers, while others need a complete power workshop to make even the simplest of things. Similarly, where one man can cut his requirements from one sheet of material, others need two or three. Much depends on the individual and the following suggestions must therefore be considered in relation to one's own preferences and method of working.

The type of person undertaking a model is likely to be something of a handyman and probably already has most of the tools required. Choice of model will be influenced by personal inclination and facilities available, especially working space, although the determination to build can outweigh most disadvantages. Some remarkable work has been done literally on the kitchen table, but there are stages in the production of a model which can be messy or smelly, and a bench in the garage or garden shed is desirable if possible. If not, then a large building board, at least four feet by two feet (120 ×60cm) is a help, as everything can be placed on it and the whole thing lifted out of the way.

## TOOLS

Tools will vary with the type of model under construction, but if for the moment ship miniatures and plastics are set aside, there are a certain basics likely to be used in the building of almost any model. Although listing the basic tools makes quite a formidable total, in many cases the absence of one or two of them would be of little significance as there are always alternative ways of tackling most jobs.

**A desirable tool-kit would include:**

1 An ordinary cross-cut handsaw. 2 A small backed or tenon saw. 3 A fretsaw. 4 A junior hacksaw. 5 A modelling knife, or, better, a heavy duty knife and a light one. 6 A small iron plane. 7 A ½in (12mm) chisel. 8 A wheelbrace and a selection of drills–say a dozen from 1/16in (1½mm) to ⅜in (9mm). 9 Pliers, preferably a sturdy conventional pair and a lighter taper or snipe-nosed pair. 10 An 8in (200mm) file. 11 Three or four needle files. 12 A 6 or 8in (150–200mm) rat-tail file. 13 A steel rule, 12in (300mm) or better, 24in (600mm). 14 A small bench vice, say 3in (75mm) jaws. 15 A soldering iron, about 15 watts. 16 A light hammer. 17 Two or three medium to small screwdrivers. 18 A fine bradawl. 19 One or two small clamps. 20 An oilstone for keeping cutting tools sharp. 21 Most important–glasspaper of several grades and a suitable rubber or cork block.

There will also be a need for paint brushes, oil, rags, and so on and, for a bread-and-butter hull, a padsaw or bowsaw, or if available a bandsaw or jigsaw. Working inside a hull is eased with one or more gouges, particularly a wood-carver's spoon gouge, available from specialist suppliers. Such tools as spokeshave, rasp, marking gauge, and various planes are to some extent extras, but a countersink and small wrenches (spanners) may well be needed. It is best to wait for a need to arise rather than buy a number of tools which may rarely be used.

In the specialist fields the miniaturist requires more than anything two or three pairs of tweezers and a supply of new single-edged razor blades; the period ship modeller needs the tools of the miniaturist plus forceps, tiny pliers and drills, needles and a pin chuck.

**Above**
Tissue has been doped in place on the inside of the balsa planking of this model; the surplus will be trimmed away when dry. The outside will also be tissue-covered for maximum strength and minimum weight.

**Right**
The right tool for the job is essential. For hard balsa, spruce, or thin ply a heavy-duty knife is required, but for lighter work a scalpel-type blade and handle is preferable.

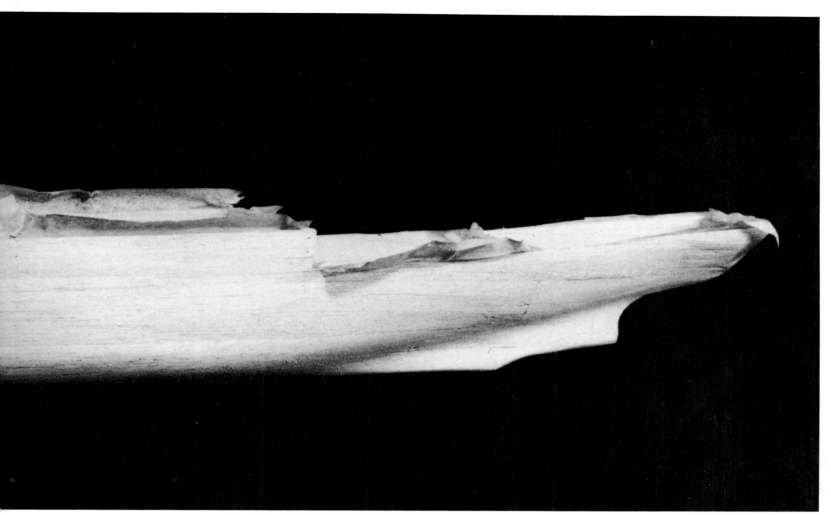

A steam enthusiast making his own plant will use a lathe and one or more blowlamps or gas torches, plus all the engineering tools such as scribes and center pops, reamers, a micrometer and so on. Much depends on the particular side of the hobby which attracts, but in general the tools required are self-evident.

Among 'tools' might be classed books, for certainly they will help the modeller to tackle many jobs. Reading as much as possible is important, not only for better understanding of one's own particular interest, but because methods of solving apparently quite different problems will surprisingly often have relevance to a job in hand.

# MATERIALS

### Woods

At one time it was possible simply to say 'Take a piece of yellow pine . . .' but, apart from the shortage of (or at least difficulty in obtaining) better class timbers, there are now so many recently introduced alternative materials that deciding which is best for a particular purpose can be quite an exercise. While most people with a little common sense can see whether a piece of wood is warped or knotty, or reasonably seasoned, the final result of using, say, polyester resin to make a grp hull will not be evident for some days or even weeks after it is finished. The only answer is to buy from a reliable source and accept the advice of the supplier.

Approaches vary—these enthusiasts are members of St Albans Model Engineering Society where steam boats are popular and model engineering is a primary interest. Tools used are therefore much more sophisticated.

Working in wood still attracts the majority of modellers whose pleasure comes from building, but good quality timber is expensive and can be hard to find. For 'solid' work, such as bread-and-butter, or laminated bow and/or stern blocks, yellow pine is outstanding, but others of the pine family (sugar pine, King William pine, Douglas fir, kauri etc) can also be excellent. Mahogany, cedar, obeche, lime and jelutong are other good timbers; the last two in particular are often used by pattern-makers and some timber yards near large engineering firms carry regular stocks. Two timbers often sold in Do It Yourself stores are parana pine and ramin but these should be last choices, even behind deal or hemlock.

The essential thing is thorough dryness which is only really satisfactorily obtained by seasoning although slow kiln-drying is not unacceptable. Often an aged, dirty-looking plank at the bottom of a stack is a far better choice than a nice, freshly sawn length at the top.

An alternative is used timber–old floorboards or solid doors, old shop countertops or sideboards, and the like. The usual difficulty is persuading a sawyer to cut them to usable sizes, but it can be done. The cost will be a tenth of new wood and the quality is likely to be infinitely superior.

A similar approach can be made to planking, and it can be even easier, since only comparatively small sections are needed. If the local yard has a thicknesser and can be persuaded that no nails, grit, or other foreign bodies should be present, your problems are virtually solved. Timbers suitable for planking are yellow pine, mahogany, cedar, poplar (well dried) and spruce, among the more commonly known woods.

For smaller work where closer grain, sharp corners, and resistance to splitting are desirable, fruit woods such as apple or cherry are good, and a range of more exotic timbers in small sections–walnut, box, lancewood etc–can be obtained from one or two specialist suppliers. Of veneers available, holly is one of the most useful, though any of the close-grained split-resistant ones are valuable in small work and differences in color can often be used to emphasize features. If a large veneered hull is to be built (double or treble diagonalled) a very cheap or free source is the scrap material woven into protection for crates of ply. Although much of it is salvageable it is usually burned as waste in timber yards.

Balsa needs no introduction and; while some serious ship modellers will not use it, it has many advantageous applications provided that its limitations are remembered. Its open grain, readiness to absorb water, and comparatively soft surface can be dealt with by applying a 'skin' of paper tissue, silk, nylon, or glass tissue which seals and toughens the surface. Sanding sealer on bare wood seals the grain but scratch damage and subsequent water absorption occur more readily. Use of balsa means lighter work and usually fewer tools required, while its light weight and general availability in a range of sizes make it a very useful material. On the debit side, it is probably true to say that an all-balsa model will have a shorter life than one built in ply or harder timbers, though some are known to be in good condition after twenty years of regular use, especially where small amounts of ply were used in high-wear areas.

Ply is one of the most useful materials for working models, since it has high strength and stiffness for its weight and is much more consistent than natural untouched timbers. The method of manufacture allows for rejection or correction of natural faults, but like most things, you get what you pay for–top-grade ply is not cheap. It is not always appreciated that it is made in nominal metric thicknesses only, and that there is a high tolerance allowed, so that thickness may be 10% or more different from the nominal size, thinner or thicker. While this allows the use of approximate Imperial measure sizes ($\frac{1}{4}$in ply may be anything from 5 to 8mm) it means that a builder following a plan must check the ply he has obtained and compensate for any difference in thickness. In kits too, slots cut by jig or die may not match exactly from one batch of kits to the next if the ply supplied to the manufacturer varies slightly.

Any ply under 2mm thick is virtually certain to be resin-bonded and waterproof. From 2mm upward, grades and prices vary from aircraft, marine, exterior, and normal, down to cheap grades. The last should be avoided, but normal, good sound ply is quite suitable for model ships and boats provided the joints are nicely fitted, painting inside and out is thorough, and the model is not left with any water trapped inside it. Exterior grade is a better choice, and normally not difficult to obtain. Marine ply is only really needed for specialized purposes, such as the fin of a racing yacht, though of course it can be used throughout a model if easily available. Modern adhesives mean that chances of delamination are very slight with models which do not remain afloat for weeks on end, but if there is any doubt, a small square of ply can be left floating in a jar of water for a day or two and checked now and then as to whether it can be pulled apart.

Most of the ply used in modelling is likely to be birch, which is quite close-grained and hard and varies from off-white to honey, or a close relation of birch. There are, however, various types of mahogany plies to be found; marine ply is frequently one of the mahogany family. Exterior grade is often gaboon mahogany (luanda), which is also used for panelled doors; this is lighter and softer than average and, apart from a slightly open grain, excellent for model work. Faced plies such as afrormosia, sapele, oak and so on are of no particular significance for modelling except when the face is useful for scale effect.

## Fastenings

Metal fastenings such as screws or bolts should always be of brass or, if available, stainless steel. The only exceptions may be steel bolts to hold an engine in place, and these should be checked periodically for rusting; cadmium-plated bolts will often last the life of the model before serious corrosion occurs. Permanent pins are rarely required with modern glues, which is perhaps as well, since they are extraordinarily difficult to obtain in model sizes. Brass, plated brass, copper, or phosphor bronze are all suitable, if available. For planking, bamboo trennals are recommended. These are made by pulling thin strips off a length of bamboo through a drawplate [a hole 1/16in (1½mm) or less in a piece of ⅛in (3mm) mild steel plate] to make them roughly circular in section. Holes are drilled through the planks and into the frames, the bamboo dipped in glue and pushed or tapped into the holes, and the surplus snipped off when dry.

## Adhesives

Adhesives fall into several categories, but it can be mentioned that at the time of writing there is no single-component fully waterproof adhesive suitable for normal construction. There are some which will not soften or yield for several hours, and with adequate painting will be satisfactory, but to be absolutely sure, mixing is the only way. The groups normally used in modelling are as follows:

**Cellulose Cements** Often referred to as balsa cements, these rely for a bond on reasonably deep penetration of the surfaces and are thus suitable for balsa and other porous or open-grain material. As a rule the slower-drying they are the stronger the result. They are not fully waterproof and after a period may become slightly brittle. For best results a thin coat should be applied to each surface and allowed to dry. A second coat can then be applied and the joint held by light pressure for, preferably, several hours. It has some gap-filling qualities, but close joints are preferred.

**PVA** Polyvinyl alcohol, often called 'white' glues are not totally waterproof but clean and convenient to use on wood joints. They usually turn transparent on drying. They are non-gap-filling, and best used with moderate pressure for at least six hours. If water should soak into the wood, the joint may be expected to fail.

**Contact Adhesives** These are non-waterproof and non-gap-filling, but have been used for laminating hull skins of the double diagonal type. They lose strength if soaked but may regain some adhesion when dried out.

**Urea Formaldehydes** These are the best and most economic choice for normal construction in ply and hard woods. They may be either a dry chemical powder *only* requiring mixing with an accurate amount of

water, or a powder to be mixed with water to be applied to one face and a liquid hardener to be brushed on the other face. Neither type should be used in a cold atmosphere (below 10°C). Both are slightly gap-filling and can be made more so with fine wood dust; they need moderate pressure on the joint to achieve maximum adhesion. Setting time shortens with increased temperature and the water-only type takes about three times as long as the other. They are classed as moisture-resistant but for model purposes may be regarded as waterproof. They are colorless.

**Resorcinol Resins** These are a two-part mix, usually a powder and a viscous liquid, and are totally waterproof. They are gap-filling and usually brown. The complete durability is attractive, but they should not be used below about 15°C and it is advisable to leave joints clamped or under pressure for 24 hours.

Always follow the maker's instructions with adhesives. Equal parts means just that—too much of one or the other leads to an inferior joint. *(Courtesy Ripmax Ltd)*

**Polyester Resins** In glass-fiber construction these adhere to many surfaces but without fibrous support may be brittle (not recommended as simple adhesives).

**Epoxy Resins** Epoxy resins are usually mixed in equal quantities from two tubes of very viscous liquids and mix easier when warm. They are invaluable for strong bonds between non-porous surfaces provided they are totally free of grease. Where possible surfaces should be scratched or keyed for maximum strength. The resin can be heated to decrease viscosity and reduce curing time. Two types are usually available, one setting in five to ten minutes (complete cure one to three hours in normal temperatures) and the other nominally twelve hours (cure up to three days) giving a noticeably stronger bond. They are fairly expensive and offer no advantages over urea formaldehydes for normal wood joints, so use should be confined to situations where their special qualities are employed. Incidentally, joint strength is increased by pressure.

**Polystyrene Cements** These are used for vacuum-formed hulls, plastic card and plastic kits and so on. Available as a fairly runny liquid in tubes or as a clear thin liquid in a bottle for application by brush, polystyrene cement is only suitable for styrene (of which it is a solvent) and has little adhesive power for other materials. Always check whether it softens a particular plastic if it is not known positively that it is styrene. For styrene to wood joints, cement as used in plastic plumbing is recommended (see Chapter 7).

**Anaerobic Adhesives** These are engineering-type adhesives used for locking nuts, sealing pipe unions, even making gaskets, and as such have relatively limited applications in model boat construction, but

With all adhesives, cleanliness and absence of oil or grease is vital to strong bonds, and the manufacturer's instructions should be followed implicitly, particularly with regard to accuracy of quantities to be mixed. Avoid trying to stick wet wood–pin it in place and allow it to dry first. In many cases clothes pegs or pins make excellent clamps, or temporary pins will provide enough pressure while the adhesive sets. Weights can be books, bricks, cans of soup etc, and a simple means of exerting pressure is a Spanish windlass, which is simply a loop of stout string into which a short stick is inserted and twisted to produce the required tension.

### Buoyancy Foam

Most other materials–paints and finishes, glass-fiber fuels, styrene sheet and so on–are dealt with in appropriate chapters, but one which might be mentioned

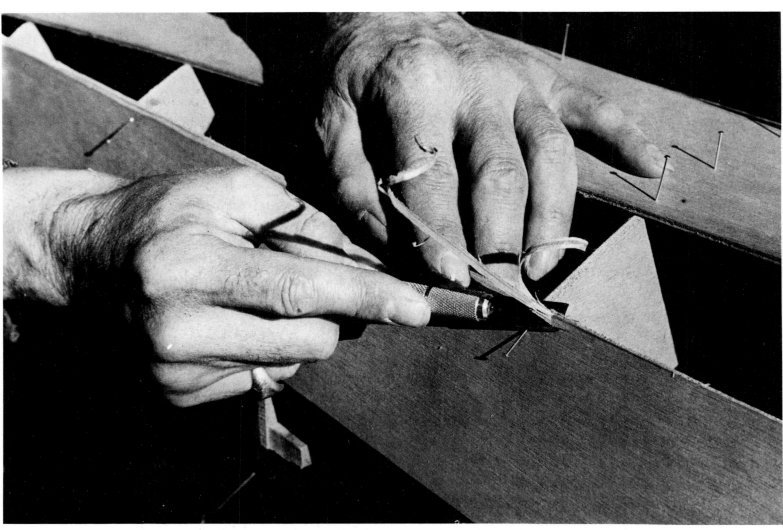

many uses in, particularly, steam plant installation. They are usually thin, watery looking fluids; only a tiny quantity is required, and setting is activated by air humidity. They are expensive but much underrated at present. There are several types for different purposes and they are well worth investigation by modellers with an engineering bent.

**Cyanoacrylates** These are the magic fluids which stick most things in seconds once air is excluded. They are not really necessary to build a model but there can be occasions when they are useful. Usually a thin, water-like liquid in a tiny bottle, only the very minimum amount should be used for the greatest strength. Cyanoacrylates are helpful when assembling tiny detail items. Although they seem expensive, so small an amount is needed that the cost per joint is quite comparable.

here is buoyancy foam. Accidents can happen, and spare space in a hull can be used to house buoyant material. Table tennis balls have been superseded by blocks of expanded polystyrene (try the packing around record players, televisions etc) or that polythene packaging which consists of heat-sealed air bubbles in sheet form, but it is also possible to buy specially made pre-shaped buoyancy bags or made-on-the-spot expanded polyurethane foam. This consists of a two-part mix of syrupy liquids which, when mixed (usually fifty-fifty) will, after thirty seconds or so, foam up to about 25 times volume and after a few minutes harden into a block of quite light weight. By pouring it immediately on mixing into a small hole left in a bulkhead, empty space can thus be filled with foam. Accurate amounts and rapid, thorough mixing are essential, and too little is better than too much. A trial mix can ensure the insertion of exactly the right amount.

# Building from Kits

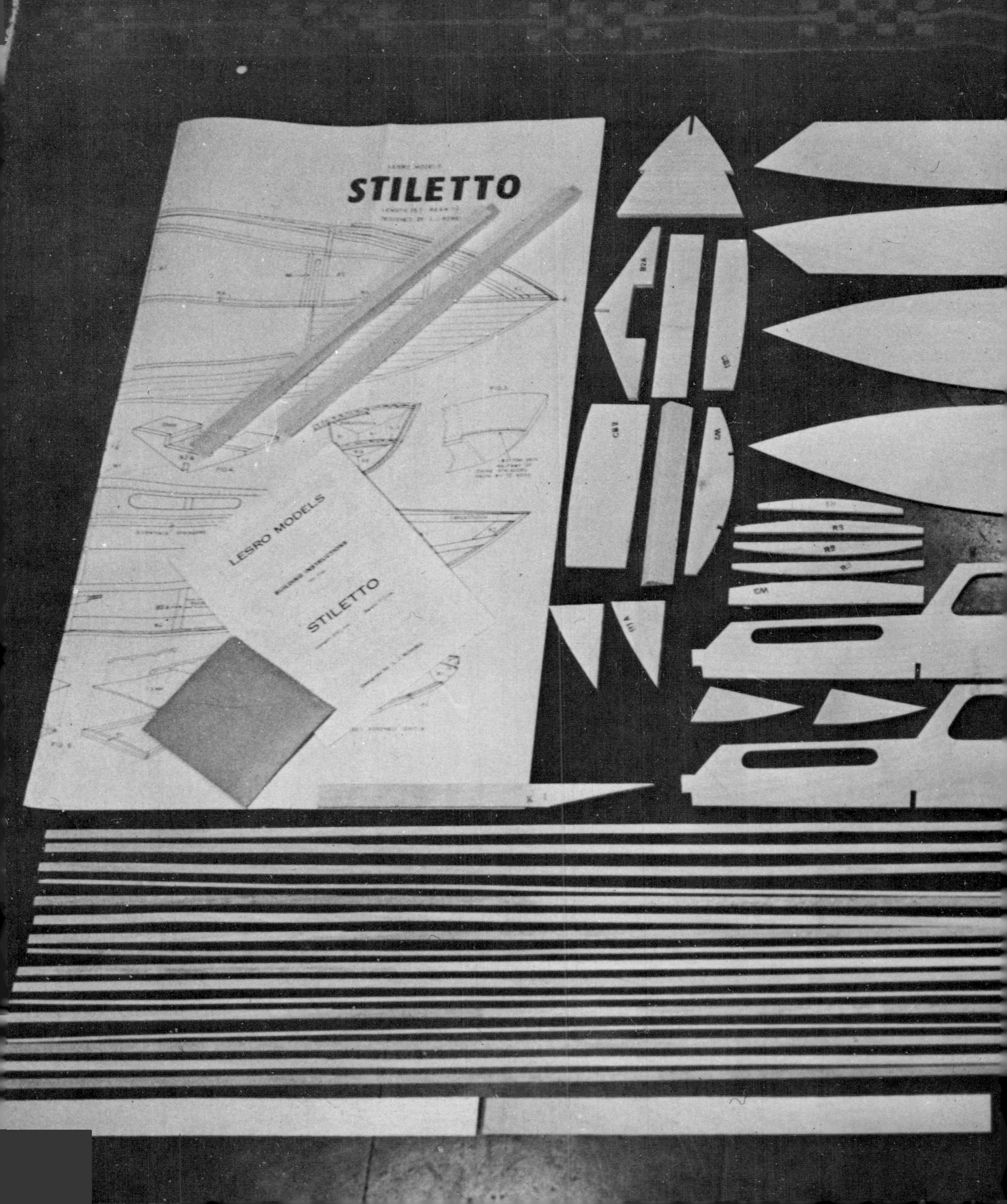

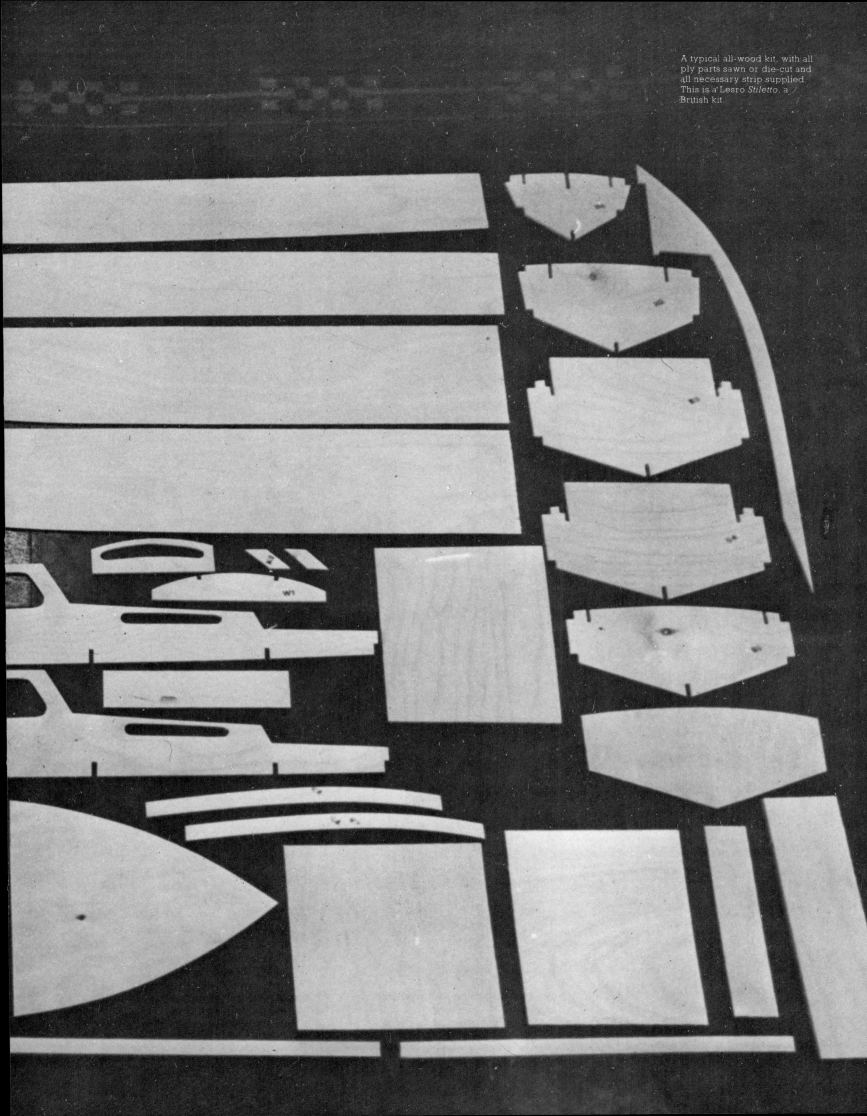

A typical all-wood kit, with all ply parts sawn or die-cut and all necessary strip supplied. This is a Lesro *Stiletto*, a British kit.

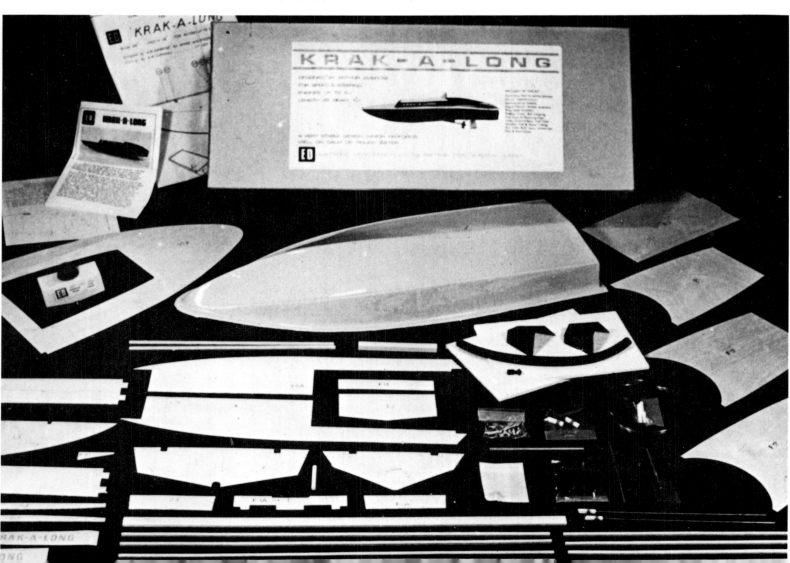

Probably a majority of people receive their introduction to modelling by means of a kit, of which there is a choice from hundreds. Some are excellent, but inevitably some leave something to be desired. Very few kits can be totally complete, particularly with respect to adhesives and paint, partly because of the chance of drying up between manufacture and purchase but also because of restrictions on inflammable liquids and the like in transport. Often, too, motors and other major items are omitted, both to keep the kit price down and to give the purchaser the option of what he will install. In recent years a practice has developed whereby a basic kit is supplied separately with the option of buying a separate pack of fittings; in some instances of quite elaborate scale models, the fittings cost more than the basic kit. This encourages a beginner to buy the kit, but if he is unsuccessful in assembling it, he is spared the expense of buying all the finishing details.

The first step for a potential customer must be to decide what sort of model he wishes to undertake—working or non-working, sail or power, type of power, scale or functional, radio or free running—then how big he would like it to be and how much he is prepared to spend. If he has seen a model he likes at a local pond or club exhibition, he can ask the owner if it is a kit, or if

not is there a kit like it, and if so is it within the capability of a beginner? Or he can study the advertisements in model magazines and short-list models which might be suitable, then send for catalogs and/or, if he knows where enthusiasts gather on a Sunday morning, go along and ask for opinions. Having thus probably narrowed the field, he can visit a model shop to see if his possibilities are in stock and discuss them, with a reasonable chance of being able to examine his final choice before plunging.

People vary so much in ability and, indeed, self-assessment of ability, that it is impossible to give general advice. What may be an over-ambitious undertaking for one beginner may be a simple exercise for another. Virtually all kits follow one or other of the techniques outlined in this book, which may help you to decide whether a particular one is within your capabilities. Basically, if you have trouble knocking a nail in straight, go for something reasonably simple and straightforward, but if you have a reputation for being clever with your hands and you possess patience, you should be able to cope with most kits.

The advantages of a good average kit are that all the timber requirements are provided in the quantities required, so that there is little waste, and that most of

the heavy or tedious work has already been done. Disadvantages are perhaps that your choice of subject is limited by what is available in kit form, choice of material is restricted (unless you substitute something bought separately for any part which you think dubious) and you are, of course, paying for the work which has already been done, plus the cost of boxing, advertising, and so on. Clearly from the number of kits sold, the advantages well outweigh the disadvantages.

Having purchased a kit and got it home, the first step is to read all the instructions carefully, studying the drawings at the same time, and to identify all the various parts supplied. 'When all else fails, read the instructions' is the *cri de coeur* of all designers and manufacturers, a cry which really does spring from experience. Understand the general method and sequence of building as far as possible before starting; do not, however, be too despondent if a late stage in assembly seems unclear, since things often become obvious as work proceeds. Most kits come with concise and understandable instructions, but there may be occasional slips, especially with foreign manufacturers who make a laudable attempt to provide a translation which may not quite come out as intended.

When ready to start construction, with any further requirements such as glue and a building board at hand, lay out the first pieces. Some kits achieve accurate and clean die-cutting in ply, balsa, spruce or whatever but it is not uncommon to have to complete the cuts in order to lift pieces cleanly out of a sheet. A sharp modelling knife is usually best, but if the uncut areas are extensive, a fretsaw may be better. In some cases an impression is made on the surface of ply as a guide for sawing, and of course where the components are printed-on rather than die-cut, a tenon saw for straight lines and a fretsaw for curves will be needed, unless your tools include a bandsaw or power fretsaw. Balsa and other timbers which have been die-cut need the same techniques, but since grain will have more influence on a knife blade, always make a number of light cuts rather

**Above**
Japanese kit for the cruiser *Minegumo* is designed for steam power. Balsa superstructure is basically broken down to boxes; it would be better in thin ply.

**Above right**
The *Minegumo* kit comes with a finished natural grp hull with deck bonded in place. Superstructure fits on one large hatch and a small hatch at rear gives access to rudder mechanism

**Below right**
Completed *Minegumo* makes a handsome model, one of the few available intended for steam power and radio control Length is 47½in (1206mm).

**Below**
One of the bigger kits available is this 52in (1320mm) Vosper Fast Patrol Boat for 10cc engines produced by the British firm of Veron.

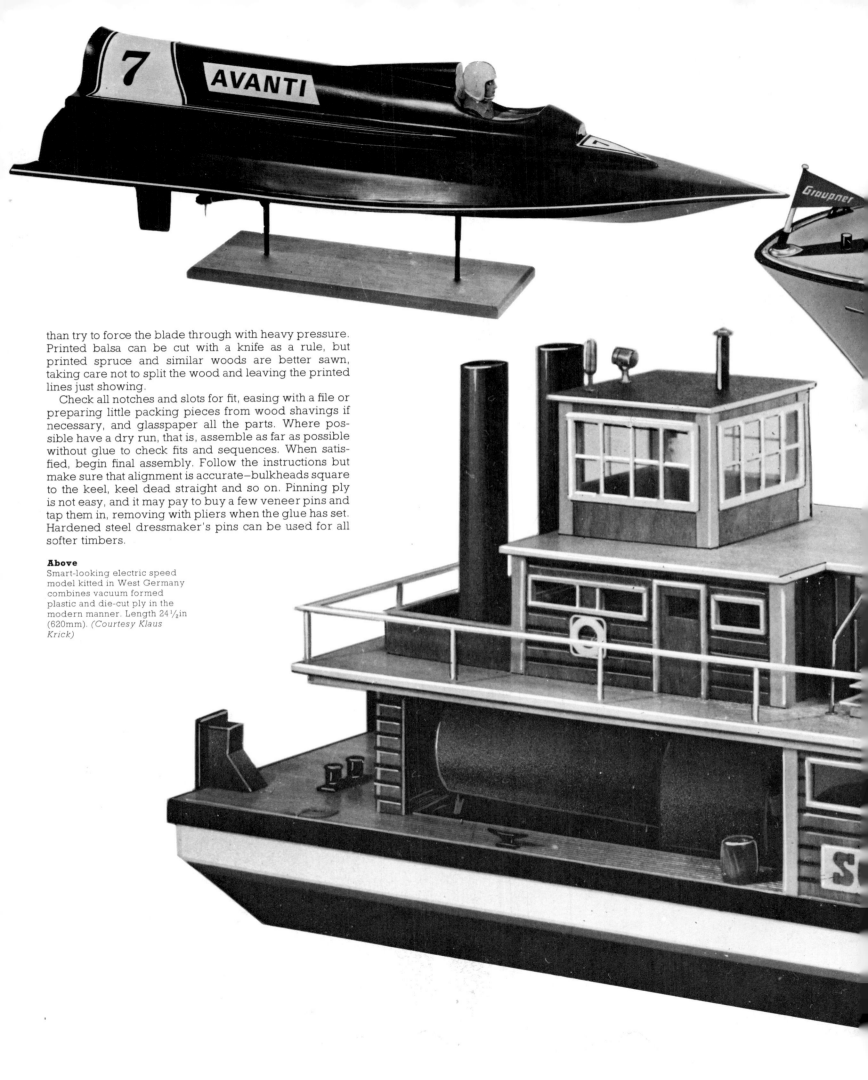

than try to force the blade through with heavy pressure. Printed balsa can be cut with a knife as a rule, but printed spruce and similar woods are better sawn, taking care not to split the wood and leaving the printed lines just showing.

Check all notches and slots for fit, easing with a file or preparing little packing pieces from wood shavings if necessary, and glasspaper all the parts. Where possible have a dry run, that is, assemble as far as possible without glue to check fits and sequences. When satisfied, begin final assembly. Follow the instructions but make sure that alignment is accurate—bulkheads square to the keel, keel dead straight and so on. Pinning ply is not easy, and it may pay to buy a few veneer pins and tap them in, removing with pliers when the glue has set. Hardened steel dressmaker's pins can be used for all softer timbers.

**Above**
Smart-looking electric speed model kitted in West Germany combines vacuum formed plastic and die-cut ply in the modern manner. Length 24½in (620mm). *(Courtesy Klaus Krick)*

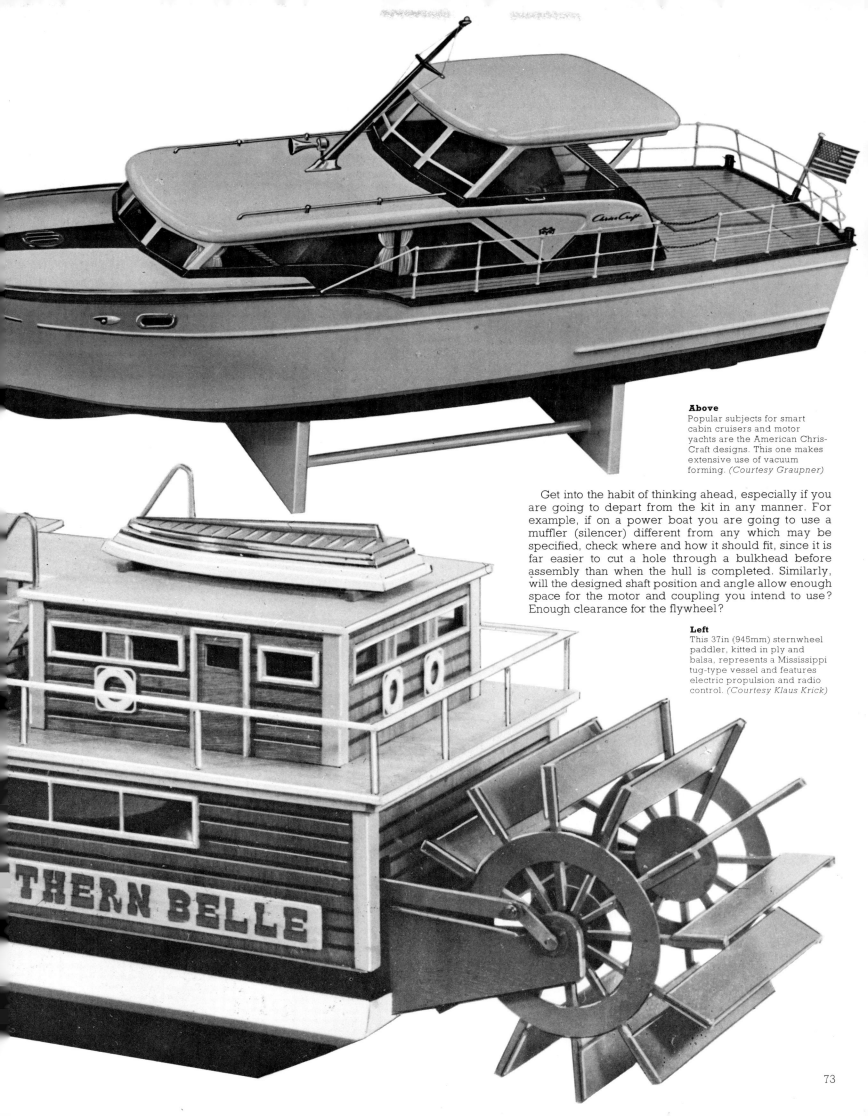

Get into the habit of thinking ahead, especially if you
are going to depart from the kit in any manner. For
example, if on a power boat you are going to use a
muffler (silencer) different from any which may be
specified, check where and how it should fit, since it is
far easier to cut a hole through a bulkhead before
assembly than when the hull is completed. Similarly,
will the designed shaft position and angle allow enough
space for the motor and coupling you intend to use?
Enough clearance for the flywheel?

**Right**
Slightly simplified lines enable
many full-size designs to be
modelled in sheet ply. This
example is a Fairey Marine
Huntsman, produced as an
all-ply kit.

Ponder a little, too, on any areas which will be closed off by later construction, and give them a coat of paint or varnish. Water and oil get into all sorts of nooks and crannies, and a dab of paint to reduce the chances of soakage will prolong the life of the boat.

The most important points are complete symmetry, for any boat, and, for power boats, complete accuracy of line-up of the motor shaft and propeller shaft. More boats are spoiled by misalignment at this stage than by any other fault. For yachts, a truly vertical fin, skeg, and mast must be achieved, and for non-working models, neatness and closeness of fit of all components, thorough grain filling, and delicacy of rigging and details are the main points to bear in mind. In all models, painting can make or break the final result, so a full chapter is devoted to this subject.

As assembly proceeds, a number of little jobs will arise which the manufacturer was unable to prefabricate. On a chine hull, for example, the keel doublers, chines, and inwales will have to be bevelled to angles which change throughout the length of the boat to form a fair seating for the skins. A really sharp chisel and a series of small and light cuts, followed by glasspapering, will take care of this. Pin a sheet of glasspaper to a block of wood long enough to span the two members concerned and the correct angle will automatically appear. Never be satisfied until you are certain that a

particular job is done to the best of your ability, remembering that the whole is the sum of the parts. A minute or two extra here and there while building will hardly be noticeable in total time, but will show in the finished result.

Scale models, or models of scale type, can frequently be individualized by finding out as much as possible about the prototype, especially if pictures can be found. Rarely are even sister ships identical, and you may find that extra fittings or a different color scheme can be applied to your own model. Familiarization with the prototype also goes a long way towards giving a model that indefinable 'life' that distinguishes a good model from an average one.

Once assembly is understood and under way, there are likely to be no great departures from conventional practice as outlined in the relevant chapters of this book. Peculiarities which may occur are almost certain to be explained in the instructions and/or drawings, but if a builder is nonplussed, if possible he should ask someone at the model shop or local club who will gladly advise him. If he is very much on his own, a letter to the manufacturer or importer stating the specific query clearly and enclosing a stamped self-addressed envelope should resolve his problem. The standard of modern kits, however, is such that this sort of situation is rarely likely to arise.

# Building from Plans

A very high proportion of ship modellers and boating enthusiasts build from plans, which may be shipyard drawings, commercially available designs, or plans drawn up by the modeller himself. There are several reasons for this, but the main one is choice of subject. The cost of tooling up for a kit is considerable and the manufacturer must be reasonably certain of a return for his outlay, so that he naturally tends to produce something which he thinks will be popular. This means that kit subjects tend to fall into fairly well-defined groups and many may alter basic shapes to simplify construction, both to reduce manufacturing costs and to appeal to a wider market. There is obviously only a limited demand for an experts-only, possibly 'way-out' model.

As the world market continues to grow, manufacturers are gradually becoming more adventurous and, indeed, more numerous, but the basic financial constraints remain. To produce just a plan requires a very much lower outlay in both money and time, and it is therefore possible to produce designs commercially which would be unlikely to be financially feasible as kits. Plans which may be purchased vary from straight-forward line drawings and general arrangements showing the ship itself with no suggestion of model construction, to detailed constructional drawings showing how to build the model and giving all the necessary structural pieces drawn out for tracing on to timber. Some experience, or willingness to read up construction techniques, is needed for the former, but a plan of the latter type can usually be undertaken by a novice.

A main advantage of building from a plan is, therefore, wider choice, but other benefits are that it is usually very much cheaper, allows selection of material, gives greater satisfaction, and, if it is relevant, has an immediate advantage over a kit model in static judging in a competition. On the debit side, it may take longer because everything has to be traced and cut out, some materials may be hard to obtain locally and fittings and the like may have to be made. Many modellers prefer to make everything themselves, but others prefer to buy all the detail fittings, in which case their choice should be confined to a model of a standard scale with conventional fittings

Someone who wishes to model a particular ship will, in most cases, have to seek out his own information, and in many instances may find his search disappointing. For an older vessel the trail starts by checking lists of drawings offered by the number of (usually) small firms supplying drawings, then by consulting museums

and libraries looking for any sketches, paintings, or mentions of the vessel. Many old technical drawings simply show the hull so the rig and details may have to be surmised by reference to similar contemporary ships of which more details can be found, or by working from one or more of the books on the subject. It can take a lot of time and expense, either visiting possible sources or writing letters (with stamp or reply coupon), not to mention determination and perseverance, and it may well turn out to be fruitless.

More modern ships can be equally frustrating. If the vessel was of particular interest, one of the shipping journals may have carried small drawings or details. This may mean a journey to one of the major copyright or reference libraries and a day spent searching. The shipping line which owned her may still exist and may be able and prepared to help, or the builders may. The problem here is that if archives exist, having staff search through them is expensive and may well lead to a firm saying no. Many British and European firms lost all their archives during World War II, or they were scrapped on closure or amalgamation since then (although in some cases they were passed to museums). The position with warships may be slightly better, since in recent years a number of books and plans have appeared and some help may be forthcoming from such sources as the US Navy Bureau, the Ministry of

Defence, and other related departments.

The ship modeller who has only a specific type of vessel in mind rather than one particular craft, is in a better position, as drawings of a variety of ships are available from several sources and many shipping journals have carried small but detailed plans of many ships in their pages over the years. In most cases, however, a modeller sees a plan of a ship which attracts him and decides to make a model of it, so that the question of a long search does not arise.

Scaling up a small drawing to required size is not too difficult. The easiest, but not always the most accurate way, is photographic enlargement, though this can be a little expensive for a large model. Since it is usually a process involving wet or at least damp development, paper shrinkage can cause distortion and a very high degree of enlargement produces inevitably thick lines. However, if a part of a drawing such as the body plan or a particularly detailed area is enlarged, distortion can be less and the result provides a base from which to produce a good drawing.

Some builders use an episcope or epidiascope to project a drawing on to paper while the essential lines are drawn in, but most simply scale up with pencil and ruler. The simplest approach is to make a scale rule, reduced by the scale factor; for example, for an enlargement $\times 8$, a ruler would be made where $\frac{1}{8}$in (or

**Below**
Unusual early US warship model by English modeller Steve Kirby typifies the out-of-the-rut subjects which can be found in museum archives. This ship was intended to ram opposition.

1.25mm) divisions represent inches (or centimeters) measuring the small drawing with the scaled rule and the large one with a normal rule. Architectural scale rules can be purchased and may include the scale required. Drawing squares over the small drawing and correspondingly large ones for the enlarged one is an old practice; drawing them on the back of tracing paper for the new plan avoids rubbing them off if corrections are made. It is possible to obtain proportional dividers adjustable to the scale factor, measuring the original with one end which automatically sets the scaled dimension at the other.

Working from a shipyard plan or drawing, or from scaled-up drawings of a ship, means evolving one's own structure, but this is not particularly difficult. The

plan which is not difficult. There you are, designing!

Transferring what has been drawn onto timber can be carried out in a number of ways. It is possible to slip carbon paper between the plan and the wood and go over the lines to be transferred, but there are two snags: there is the possibility of moving the plan, giving an inaccurate tracing, and, since usually only half of each section or bulkhead is drawn, positive location of the center line to trace the second half is difficult. It can also be wasteful of material. One answer is to pin the plan to the wood on the center line with two carefully positioned pins, and use the same pinholes when the plan is turned over for the second half.

A development of this idea is to pin-prick through the plan round the outline, joining up the pin-pricks in the

methods of construction outlined in Chapters 3 and 7 cover all the conventional ways to build, and a look through model magazines will turn up models of the same general types and size and give a good indication of material sizes to use. The essential item in every case is a body plan, and even if your drawing does not have one, it should not be difficult to find a similar ship of about the same size and date which includes a body plan, the character of which can be followed to produce a new one for your own model. To prove its accuracy waterlines should be plotted from it. This process is just like plotting out individual planks for bread-and-butter construction, except that they are superimposed on the same center line. Any big wavers must be corrected by adjusting one or more sections on the body

World War II destroyer model is one of hundreds of possible subjects if time is spent researching. Determination to build a particular ship is usually rewarded.

wood with a pencil. A pin or needle held in a pin-vice is more comfortable than holding it in the fingers. Dabbing the plan with a rag damped with turps or light oil will render it semi-transparent, which sometimes helps; the turps or oil will dry out in a few days.

Some builders cut out the pieces of plan to be transferred and draw round them, but as already mentioned, there is danger of distortion, especially with long, narrow curved parts.

The best method is undoubtedly to trace the parts on to tracing or kitchen greaseproof (not waxed) paper, using a sharp but soft pencil. The tracing can then be turned over and positioned on the wood, and the lines gone over with the same pencil from the back. This will transfer a clear if slightly faint line to the wood, which can then be heavied up to be easily visible while cutting or sawing. For symmetrical parts (bulkheads, etc) a strong center line should be drawn on the timber first and the tracing positioned on this; after drawing over the back, the tracing can be turned over again and the backing lines will transfer to the wood when the original lines are again pencilled round. Always strengthen the lines on the wood immediately the tracing is lifted, while, silly though it may seem, your fingers 'remember' the curve; the darker lines are also more easily visible through the tracing paper for positive alignment of the second half, or tracing of the next piece close by to economize on materials.

Some parts may require assembly over the plan, for instance, a center keel assembly with a propeller shaft

Modellers who draw up their own plans for functional models almost invariably have some experience, and their drawings will incorporate their own ideas arising from building and operating previous models. There are, however, some people who want to start from scratch with models of their own design. It is suggested that anyone so inclined reads as much as possible about the particular types of models which attract him, and bases his first effort on a proved successful design—altered in appearance by all means but not too drastically changed in basic hull shape. Originality is to be encouraged, but success comes from an understanding of elementary principles.

The shape of a scale or even scale-type model is more or less determined for a builder. The area which

tube built in. In such a case the plan will be pinned to a flat building board and the temptation to cut out pieces on this board should be resisted. Keeping the plan whole and reasonably tidy ensures that no later vital part is missing or obscured. Assembly directly over the plan usually means the parts becoming stuck to the paper, tearing the plan and needing the paper to be sanded off the assembly. This can be avoided by covering the part of the drawing being used with waxed paper such as is found in many cereal packets, or by rubbing the joint areas on the plan with dry soap or a candle stub. There have been suggestions that soap or wax will be absorbed into the glue and weaken the joint, but this seems unlikely or, at worst, insignificant with the adhesives used in marine models.

Once all parts are traced and cut out, the builder is, in effect, in the same position as the purchaser of a kit, except that his expenditure has been very much less, he has spent two or three hours tracing and cutting out parts, and has had to assess what materials he needed to buy. From this point on construction follows one or other of the procedures explained.

Torpedo boat destroyer of around 1900 makes an excellent scale straight runner (class EK). This example is steam powered.

seems to give the most trouble is in scale *consistency*. Perhaps the commonest faults are grossly out-of-scale doors and hatches when compared with, say, the guard-rails, and dinghies or ship's boats which would barely accommodate one adult. Even if the scale of a model is unknown, an approximation can be established. A scale man cut out of a postcard can be used as a comparison with various parts of a model or drawing. Deck-head heights, access, and details such as lifebelts, hand windlasses and so on can all be checked for feasibility in this way. It does not necessarily guarantee complete accuracy, but glaring errors will be avoided. Probably the commonest dimension among ships and boats, by the way, is rail height, which is rarely far from about 42–45in (106–114cm).

One final word of warning on working from plans. Paper varies with temperature and humidity, and a plan may stretch or shrink from day to day. Always, therefore, measure and check lengths which may be critical. On a model such as a Marblehead yacht a 0.5 percent change in the paper could put the finished model out of rating.

# Plastic Hulls

Over a space of a dozen years in the 1950/60s, full-size small craft production changed from a tiny proportion of glass-fiber boats in a mainly wood market to a tiny percentage of wood boats in a glass-fiber market. The new material made an impact on the model world, but not to quite the same extent, but then part of the attraction for most modellers is building the model oneself.

There are two forms of plastic hulls used for working models, glass reinforced plastic (grp), which is the more correct term for what is loosely called 'glass fiber' or 'fiberglass' and vacuum formed styrene, or similar sheet-form heat-deformable plastics. Grp is well established and almost certainly fully developed, and has the advantage of being workable without special tools by individuals. Vacuum forming, on the other hand, is in some ways still only starting to be exploited for model purposes, despite having been around for a number of years. A drawback from an individual viewpoint is that it needs an expensive machine, although as more machines are installed by small firms, the chances of getting a one-off job done for a modeller will increase.

Glass fibers are long drawn glass threads or filaments woven into cloth, or short lengths loosely and randomly assembled into what is called mat. There are also woven glass tapes, tissues and loose string-like bundles known as rovings. The glass threads are made up into yarns which can be varied in thickness and the weaving or mat assembly can vary to give different thicknesses of cloth or mat, identified by its approximate weight in ounces per square foot or gm/dm². Thus reference is made to '1½oz cloth' or '2oz mat' etc. Mat is the material

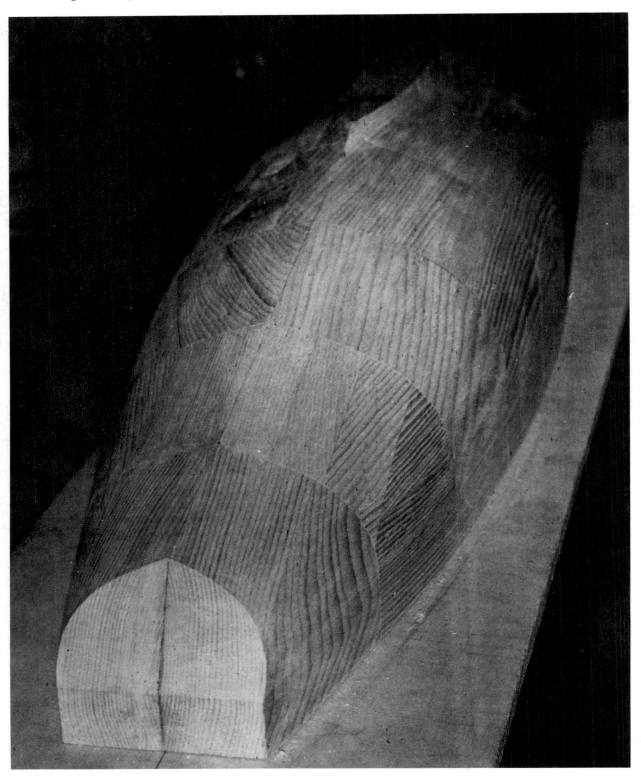

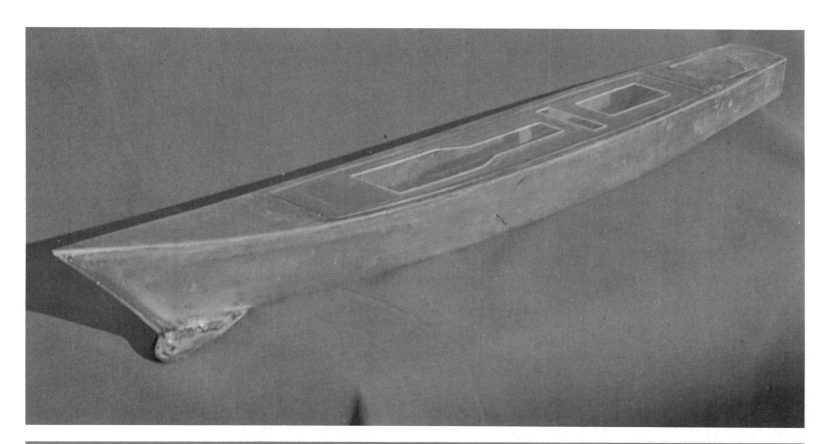

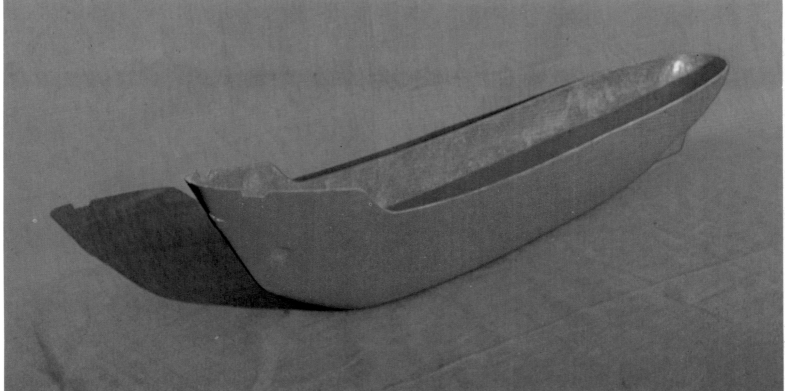

most frequently used in model ship and boat construction; the fibers are held together with a binder (which dissolves into the resin) but it is very much easier to persuade into curves and other shapes than cloth, as well as being considerably cheaper.

The resin used in molding is a polyester mixed with styrene to which an accelerator has been added, so that cold curing (curing without externally applied heat) will take place when a catalyst (hardener) is added. When the hardener is stirred in, curing begins immediately, the resin thickening until after perhaps ninety minutes it has solidified, though still remaining quite soft and flexible; this is known as gelling. Curing and maturing continue over several days; the final

product is hard and stiff. The process throughout is affected by temperature–the warmer the quicker–and also by the amount of accelerator present. Probably most difficulties arise in amateur use by the addition of the wrong amount of hardener; this also affects curing time, but significant variation from the recommended proportion can result in imperfect curing.

Most amateurs will use only two resins. The first is general purpose lay-up resin which will give entirely satisfactory results if the maker's recommendation on the amount of hardener is followed. The amount of accelerator (already mixed in) is determined by the manufacturer, and the only variation in gelling and curing time under the control of the user is therefore

temperature. For better results a layer of gel resin (the second resin) is often used. This is a special resin which forms a tough outer film and is applied to the mold before starting the main lay-up. It is normal to color the gel coat by the addition of pigment, usually bought in the form of a paste from the supplier of the resin, but not to color the lay-up resin. Additives such as fillers for opacity or to render the resin thixotropic (so that it will not drain off vertical surfaces) are also available but not often used for amateur moldings. Do not try to mold in cold or very damp conditions; a dry atmosphere and minimum 10°C temperature are conditions recommended by all experts.

A wide range of commercially produced grp hulls is available covering scale and functional power boats and racing yachts, and most clubs have a 'glass fiber expert' among their numbers. The amount of work needed to produce a single hull is rather more than is required for a wooden boat, but once a mold has been made, additional hulls can be produced for comparatively small amounts of time and effort and at modest

cost. Advantages of grp are very high strength at average hull weight (or average strength for extremely light weight), maximum internal space, freedom from water or oil absorption leading to long life, and the ease with which quite complex shapes can be produced.

The standard procedure for making a hull is first to produce a 'plug.' This is simply a pattern of the required hull incorporating all the external features which it is intended to mold. In most cases it is carved from a solid bread-and-butter block—there is no need to hollow it. Occasionally an existing hull is used as a plug, or one can be made by cutting a keel profile and sections and setting them up on a building board as for planking. Scrap wood blocks or tightly crumpled papers are used to fill most of the internal space, then plaster is trowelled on, smoothed approximately to shape, and scraped to finished contours while it is green, that is, set but not fully hardened. The keel and sections, cut to actual size, should just show on the finished surface.

As with all molding, thought must be given to removing the mold from the pattern and the finished molding

from the mold. For a simple rounded hull with its widest points along the gunwale, a one-piece mold is suitable, but if there is tumblehome (the sides of the hull taper inwards, and the deck level is narrower than lower down) or any raised band on the surface, a two- or even three-part mold may be needed.

It is essential that the plug is brought to a perfect finish, since any faults it possesses will appear in the mold and hence in the finished molding. The surface must therefore be filled and rubbed down as often as is necessary to remove any flaws, then rubbed and polished to a smooth gloss. Polyurethane varnish is excellent for this, but good quality oil paints can be used. The finished surface is then given two thorough coats of wax polish (not siliconized wax) and it is recom-

mended that it is then treated with a release agent. Polyvinyl alcohol (PVA) can be applied with a sponge and dries into a transparent film which normally can be peeled off the finished mold or molding.

If the plug is mounted inverted on a baseboard, it should be packed (or initially carved) to be in solid contact throughout. A scored line will show the sheer-line to which the finished molding will be trimmed, and the mold can be continued down to the baseboard and turned out to form a flange which greatly adds to its strength and rigidity. The above-sheer part of the plug and the baseboard must also have fully sealed and polished surfaces, waxed and coated with PVA.

For a two-part mold, separation is normally along the center (keel) line, and a batten should be held in posi-

tion while a wall of plasticine is built along the center. This should be as high as the center flange is intended to be and must also be treated with release agent. A thick and preferably quick-curing gel coat is now brushed onto the first half and allowed to gel.

For most model hulls two thicknesses of 1½oz mat are likely to be adequate for a mold if some stiffening is glassed on to the exterior. Cut or tear the mat into convenient pieces before starting; there is a tendency for it to get a little sticky later on which makes handling the glass difficult, especially when the resin is mixed and time is felt to be pressing. Apply a coat of lay-up resin to the gel coat, lay the mat in place, and stipple it down, using a stabbing action with the brush (trying to brush conventionally just pulls up the fibers). Overlap the mat as additional pieces are placed, stippling hard on the joint area to consolidate the two sets of fibers. The aim is to wet all the glass thoroughly (shown by the mat turning from white to translucent), and to make absolutely certain that no air remains trapped. Professional moldings are rolled thoroughly, usually with a plastic or metal washer-type roller, but for a one-off hull, modellers often rely just on brush stippling.

The second layer can be applied immediately, if possible staggering joints and again thoroughly wetting and ensuring that no air bubbles remain trapped. Reinforcement in the form of strips of wood, wires, or

lengths of string or rovings, can be added to the surface as soon as the last layer starts to gel. The whole thing should then be left for at least 24 hours.

Brushes and tools, hands too, can be cleaned with cellulose thinners followed by washing in strong detergent and thorough drying. Work should be carried out in ventilated conditions. (The fumes are heavier than air, incidentally, so that a spare bedroom workshop will see them moving downstairs; rotting cabbages or coal gas are two common descriptions of the smell. . . .)

A two-piece mold now needs the plasticine cleaned off, the second half treated with release agent, including the center flange, and the procedure repeated. When cured, the now-double flange is drilled through at intervals to receive bolts to join the mold halves.

Removing the mold from the plug may mean first releasing it from the baseboard. It is then possible to work round the edges to allow air to enter between plug surface and mold, usually by inserting a strip of celluloid or, with care, a thin-bladed knife. Creaking and cracking noises are normal at this stage. Work the knife into the central flange joint and the halves will free; with a one-piece mold, work it gradually deeper, but be careful to avoid cracking the mold surface. In a case of a raked bow and vertical transom, the bow can often be freed first and full release achieved by working back from there.

**Above**
Finished model from Hegi *Stella* kit, believed no longer in production. Ply deck is simply pencil-lined and varnished. Fish boxes and general clutter yet to be added.

**Right**
Grp is very common for racing yacht hulls. This French RM is from an English *Moonraker* kit. Deck is melamine and fin marine ply. *(Courtesy Nylet Ltd)*

The mold will not be fully matured and it is best to replace it on the plug in order that it will not sag out of shape. When it has hardened, lift it off again and if in two halves, bolt them together. Inspect it for surface flaws, as the odd tiny bubble can be filled and polished down. Working on the mold is not easy and it pays to make sure the plug is perfect at the outset.

Making a molding follows much the same procedure, polishing the mold with wax, carefully swabbing with PVA, applying a gel coat and so on. The gel coat will not be quite so thick, and the glass may vary, perhaps a layer of surface tissue (a very fine mat) and one layer of 1 or $1\frac{1}{2}$oz mat, or two layers of 1oz mat, depending on the weight and strength required. Some builders weigh out resin and glass beforehand and stretch it out to make the hull where weight is important. The quantities required can be approximated by aiming for one-third glass weight and two-thirds resin weight (for mat—with glass cloth the figures will be nearer half each) which is not difficult to calculate. Take the weight per square foot of the mat to be used, calculate the surface area of the molding roughly and multiply by the number of layers of glass to be used. The less resin used per square foot of glass, provided it is thoroughly wetted out, the higher the strength/weight ratio. Using more resin than is necessary simply adds weight but little strength.

Leave the molding in the mold for at least one day, preferably two. It should be easier to separate them as both have some slight flexibility. If the hull has to be sawn along the sheer line, the earlier this is done the better as it is easier to do when the hull is cured but not matured. Strip off the PVA film or wash off with hot soapy water, and inspect the surface. Small defects can be made good, or the molding can be accepted as a practice run to learn the technique and work the mold in. Certainly it gets easier after three or four hulls have been made in a mold. Check the weight and, by holding it up to the light, the distribution of the glass. If in any doubt, clean up the mold, repolish, and try again.

Once a hull has matured, the resin forms a hard and shiny inside face which is resistant to water, oils and also to adhesives. To secure anything in the hull is simple while molding but it is not always convenient. Later it is essential to roughen the resin surface to provide a key. The strongest way to fit anything is to scratch thoroughly all round its site and to bed it on wet resin, then apply resin around the vicinity and position pieces of mat or glass cloth to cover or at least fillet the fitting, wetting the patches out thoroughly as normal. Trimmings of mat can be cut into small pieces or shredded and stirred into resin to form an immensely strong adhesive. Metal plates or feet should, if possible, be drilled with a series of holes to key them too, as resin will not grip quite so well on smooth, hard surfaces. If epoxy resin is used, score the hull surface with a sharp point or file end through to the glass strands to achieve a really good bond.

Fitting inwales is straightforward. Once again ensure that the surface is roughened. If possible, these and deck beams should be fitted with the hull in the mold, to ensure retention of shape. There is sufficient flexibility in a hull for a springy inwale to change the shape slightly. If bulkheads are required, card templates

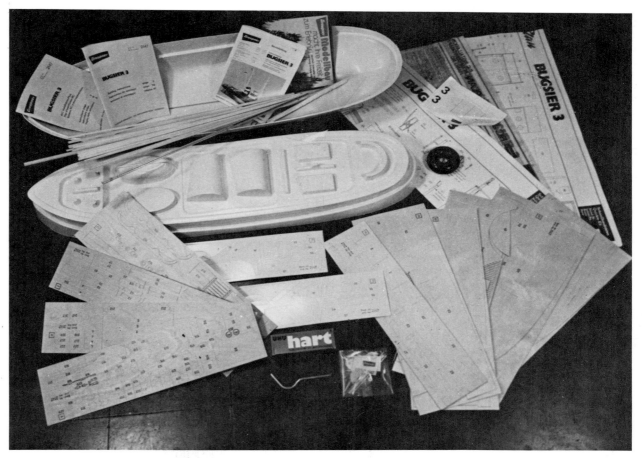

**Above**
Early kit containing vacuum-formed hull. Trimming lines can clearly be seen on the hull molding. Other parts are die-cut styrene and ply sheets.

**Left**
Fitting the inwale to a grp *Pacemaker* hull using epoxy adhesive and lots of clothes pegs. Opposite inwale is pegged in place to prevent asymmetric distortion.

**Below left**
Inwale part fitted in tug hull. Glue-filled sawcuts make bends at bow easier, stern will have a shaped block fitted before attaching deck.

**Right**
One of the most universally popular models, the tug *Bugsier 3* from Graupner, who were among the pioneers of acuum-formed kits.

should be made and the shapes transferred to ply. They can be glassed in with scraps of mat, as can any wood blocks for equipment mounting. Propeller shaft tubes can be slid through holes drilled and filed as necessary, and held in place by blobs of plasticine while the joint area is matted. A fine-tooth saw, a file, and ordinary metal drills are the only tools needed if any cutting or shaping of the hull is necessary.

If it is desired to paint the hull, it should be thoroughly degreased, wiped over with cellulose thinners, then lightly rubbed all over with very fine carborundum paper to give a key for the paint.

## STYRENE HULLS

Most vacuum-formed hulls are molded from styrene or ABS sheet, which can also be bought in flat sheets as plastic card. In a vacuum-forming machine the plug is stood on a perforated or wire-mesh screen and the plastic sheet mounted above it. Electric elements above the plastic heat it, and as it reaches softening point the machine is closed, bringing the plastic down on to the plug and at the same time exhausting the air round and beneath the plug, so that atmospheric pressure forces the softened plastic into intimate contact with the plug.

**Below**
Australian champion R10R uses a commercial *Pacemaker* grp kit. The detachable fin and bulb is in the foreground; note too, the deep and narrow spade rudder. *(Courtesy Nylet Ltd)*

Thus the inside surface of the formed molding faithfully reproduces the contours and details of the plug; details will appear on the outside surface, but their crispness is affected by the thickness of the plastic sheet.

This type of plastic is dense and quite heavy, but need only be thin for adequate strength. Thus, apart from a slight rounding of corners, external detail is normally of acceptable quality, though any small parts are better added separately. Thicknesses vary according to the size and purpose of the molding, for model boat hulls from about .01in (.25mm) or 'ten thou' up to perhaps .060in (1½mm), the latter for a large- or a medium-sized

**Below right**
Despite the strength of grp or vacuum-formed hulls, details are still fragile, and a carrying case is the safest form of protection. Rubber block holds model firmly.

one intended for an internal combustion engine. A hull may require stiffening by the addition of a wood or plastic strip inwale, and possibly by the insertion of ply or plastic sheet bulkheads.

The material may be sawn, filed, drilled etc but is subject to a build-up of static electricity from any work involving friction. Where possible, the best method of shaping is to cut a continuous line to a modest depth with a sharp blade and to flex the plastic, until it snaps cleanly through along the line. Scissors can be used on thin sheet. There is a tendency for a knife-blade to slip and score the plastic if too much pressure is used, so

two or three light cuts on the same line are safer than trying to cut deeply in one stroke.

Kits incorporating hulls and other moldings usually come with the shapes molded into sheets and the first step is to cut all parts from the sheets, or, if the hull is supplied rough trimmed, to cut the sheer line to final shape. Sometimes the cutting line is in effect a small radius, part of which will remain on the cut-out item, in which case a file or fine glasspaper will clean it up. Avoid scratching the plastic as far as possible, as scratches are almost impossible to remove or disguise satisfactorily.

Adhesives used are solvents, and therefore need to be applied carefully. There are two customary types, one in thin liquid form applied by means of a fine paintbrush, and the other a thicker but still runny liquid supplied in tubes. Both melt the surface of the plastic, enabling parts to be bonded together, but neither adheres very well to other materials. For small plastic-to-plastic detail jobs in particular, the brush-applied adhesive is recommended, since capillary action draws it into all cracks and there need be no sign of adhesive. A stronger joint is easier to obtain with the tube type, but for right-angled joints with the thin plastic sheet, it is not easy to ensure a good continuous bond without some of the cement remaining visible.

Wood-to-plastic joints are best made with the adhesive sold by builders' merchants for use with plastic plumbing. This will make a very strong plastic-to-wood bond and can be obtained from some model suppliers in tins from 125ml. It is also suitable for plastic-to-plastic joints. Most other adhesives will not stick well to styrene or ABS; even epoxy resins cannot be guaranteed, though a fair joint will result if the plastic is roughened beforehand. Metal fittings are best trapped under patches of plastic, and a little ingenuity will suggest other answers. The hard, smooth and non-porous surface makes for excellent adhesion of double-sided sticky pads or tapes, for example. New plastics coming into use for vacuum forming include some with which cellulose cements can be used, so the instructions supplied should be read carefully or one or two experiments made with scrap pieces from the waste sheet surrounding the moldings.

Though few working models are scratch-built from plastic card, it is a reasonably easy and clean material for such purposes. Although it is heavier than wood for similar rigidity, it is waterproof and needs very little finishing; any design intended for ply or other flat sheet construction can easily be adapted.

Most use has been made of it for scale superstructures and details where clean, square edges, the absence of grain and the need for minimal painting are advantages helping towards more convincing reproduction. Use is also made of its thermoplastic qualities for simple moldings, and of the range of sections made primarily for professional architectural models and, to some extent, for model railway trackside buildings.

Molding of small details usually entails making a male plug to the shape required, less the thickness of the plastic, and cutting a corresponding hole in a piece of thin ply or metal. A sheet of plastic is pinned or clamped to the ply and warmed in front of an electric fire until it softens. The plug is then pressed against the plastic to force it through the shaped hole. Two or three warmings may be necessary, depending on the depth of 'draw' required. The plug should be pushed through a fraction further than the depth of the molding so that any distortion can be trimmed away. A little practice is required to get things absolutely right, but as a means

the high density very thin paints produced originally for model railway work since these have a very high covering power but are so thin that they will not obscure the tiniest detail; it is not necessary to prepare the surface for these other than to ensure that it is clean and dust- and grease-free.

**Below**
Commercial vacuum-formed hull to author's design fitted with bulkheads and superstructure cut from flat styrene sheet. *(Courtesy I Peacock)*

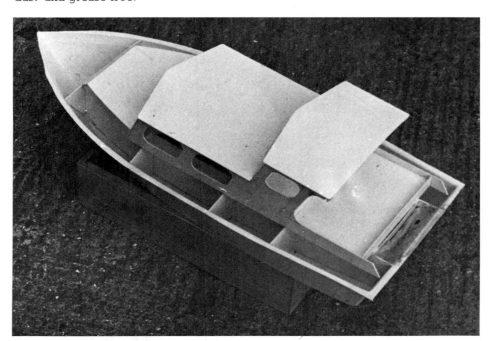

**Below**
The same hull as adjacent right, this time fitted with a vacuum-formed deck and cockpit-cum-hatch to make an attractive little beginner's radio model.

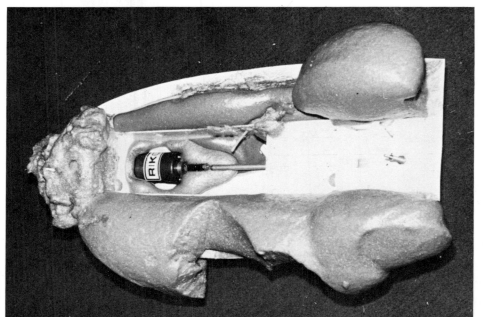

of producing light and neat ship's boats, gun turrets or covers, radar blisters and such it has no equal.

Molds may not be necessary in some instances. If hemispheres are required for cowl vents, liferaft ends, and the like, steel bearing balls of the appropriate diameter can be heated and placed on a sheet of plastic lying on a piece of soft foam. Slight pressure will produce the molded shape required. Other possibilities, such as an old-fashioned fat metal curtain ring for molding half lifebelts, will occur with a little thought.

For painting styrene or ABS, any conventional paints are suitable, except any which are cellulose based. Normally no undercoat is needed, but some builders take the precaution of rubbing the surface lightly with fine steel wool, crocus paper, or whiting on a damp rag to take off the high gloss and provide a microscopically keyed surface for the paint. Cellulose may attack the surface of the plastic unless sprayed on in very light coats which are virtually dry within a second or so of contact. For details and small areas the best paints are

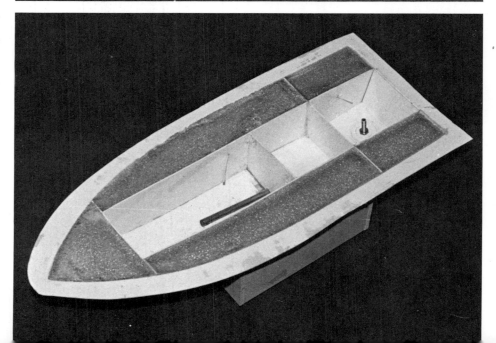

**Right**
Finished parts on a *Bugsier 3* give no indication that they started life as a flat sheet of plastic. Crisp overall effect is noticeable. *(Courtesy Ripmax Ltd)*

**Center left/bottom left**
Since styrene has no natural buoyancy, chemical foam is mixed and poured into unused hull spaces. Once it has foamed up and set, surplus is sawn away ready for decking. Boat is now virtually unsinkable. *(Courtesy I Peacock)*

**Below**
This working model is made of plain white card (Bristol board) by card expert G H Deason. It could equally well have used plastic card.

# Steam Power

**Left**
Twin cylinder oscillator engine
built with hand tools only by
J E Jane (except flywheel)
showing that elaborate
equipment is not essential for a
workmanlike steam plant.

**Right, above and below**
Freelance tug model by M
Sriver of Florida, 46in
(1170mm) long and 50lb (24kg)
weight. Stuart Turner Double
10 engine with reverse, center
flue boiler, propane fired, radio
controlled. *(Courtesy M Sriver
Esq)*

Model power boats were recognized from about the 1880s, and it is safe to assume that, with the possible exception of an occasional clockwork model, steam engines provided the propulsion for all power craft before then. Steam predominated for a further fifty years, while gasoline and electric motors were struggling to develop, but it declined very markedly during and after World War II. At its lowest probably in the 1960s, less than one percent of model power boats employed steam, but as is so often the case, the pendulum swung and steam power started to enjoy a revival from the mid-1970s onward.

Steam engines have always had a magic of their own, possibly because it is fascinating to perform work from an action so simple as boiling water. And there are usually so many exposed parts that can be seen moving, and the smells of hot oil, damp metal, and flame combine to be distinctive and somehow attractive to many people. A simple engine is also quite straightforward to understand, so that people feel more at ease. As a power unit for a boat, a steam engine is comparatively cheap to run, quiet, and easy to operate.

Disadvantages are the bulk and weight of the plant necessary, of which probably only one eighth is the engine itself, the heat, and the tendency to distribute oil and condensate around rather freely. Speed control and reversing are not easy to achieve with single-cylinder engines in particular, without fairly complex valve gear.

The simplest and cheapest form of engine uses an oscillating cylinder, the cylinder being pivoted through a flat face provided on one side which mates with a flat face on the fixed engine standard. The piston is rigidly secured to its connecting rod which engages on a crank at its lower end. Rotation of the crank thus swings the piston and rod, and since the piston is inside the cylinder, the cylinder must oscillate. Steam is piped through to a port on the flat face of the standard and, at one position, a port on the cylinder flat face registers,

admitting steam which drives the piston down and rotates the crank. At the opposite angle, the cylinder port registers with an exhaust port on the standard face, allowing the rising piston to expel the steam. Thus there is one port in the cylinder and two ports on the valve face of the standard; the size of these ports determines the periods in which steam can enter or leave the cylinder. Light spring loading is usually applied to the cylinder pivot to keep the flat faces in intimate contact and reduce the chance of steam leakage and the crank

**Above**
A small commercial steam plant
with an oscillating engine and
simple spirit lamp pot boiler.
Small extra cylinder is
displacement lubricator, yet to
be fitted.

**Top right**
V-twin slide valve engine
installation. Boiler lagging
reduces heat loss and increases
efficiency. Note pressure
gauge, manual steam-control
valve and steam whistle.

**Below**
Very nicely made in-line twin
engine with return-tube boiler.
Cranked uptake is to bring flue
gases up through scale-
position funnel.

is attached to a shaft carrying a flywheel to provide sufficient inertia to carry the piston onward from bottom dead center (BDC).

To increase power, the unit may be made double-acting by sealing the bottom of the cylinder and introducing steam to push the piston back up. This simply entails providing a cylinder port in the bottom half, and two more ports, inlet and outlet, in the lower part of the standard face. A gland must be provided in the cover which seals the bottom of the cylinder, to allow the piston rod to slide up and down without steam leakage.

Further development is to use two or more cylinders on a common crank. Twin cylinders are usually horizontally opposed, but in-line configuration is possible by linking the crankpin of the second unit to the flywheel of the first. Triple cylinders disposed radially using a single crank are occasionally seen.

Greater efficiency at the cost of more complexity and accuracy is achieved by a slide valve engine. Here the cylinder is fixed and the piston rod (or connecting rod) must be articulated. The cylinder incorporates a valve chest, in which slides a cupped valve; steam is admitted

to the chest through a port in its wall and exhausted through a central port under the sliding valve. Two ports allow passage of steam into and out of each end of the cylinder. The valve is moved by means of a valve rod driven by an eccentric mounted on the crankshaft, and the slide is of such a length that when one cylinder port is covered by it and thus linked to the exhaust port, the other is open to the steam pressure in the valve chest. Thus steam enters one end driving the piston along, which expels the steam from the opposite end. As the piston nears the end of its stroke, the slide valve has moved to the opposite end, reversing the steam flow and thus driving the piston back in the opposite direction.

Pressure from the steam entering the chest holds the slide into the valve face; a totally flat and smooth face together with a well-made valve are essential to avoid steam leakages. In order to take advantage of the extra power available if the steam is given time to expand, the end faces of the slide are wider than the cylinder ports, the extra width being termed the lap, so that the timing of steam admission is controlled. There is little

point in feeding steam in, once the piston is about two-thirds of the way along its stroke, as the amount of work it would do is slight, so steam admission is cut off by the valve lap. Valve movement is arranged so that steam starts to enter the cylinder just before the piston reaches the end of its stroke, so that there is time to absorb the full power; this is called lead.

An alternative to a flat slide valve is a piston valve in which a small piston performs the function of the slide, moving in its own cylinder attached to the main cylinder and ported in a similar manner.

One other form of valve arrangement is sometimes seen. It is called a clapper or sometimes poppet valve and consists of a ball resting over a hole in a steam chamber in the top of the cylinder. A spigot in the center of the piston lifts the ball off its seating to admit steam, the steam is exhausted through ports low down the cylinder wall which are uncovered as the piston nears the bottom of its stroke. This can obviously be only single-acting, but is a simple form of engine to construct and should be at least as efficient as an oscillator.

The steam to power any of these engines can be dry

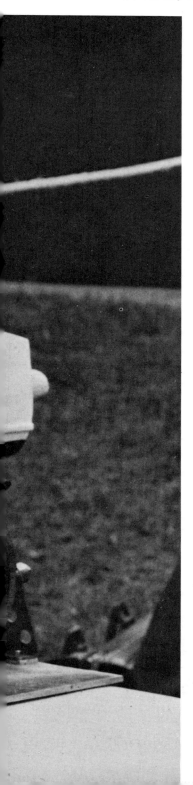

**Below**
Piston valve steam engine shows central steam inlet via displacement lubricator and exhausts at either end of valve cylinder. *(Courtesy Model Boats)*

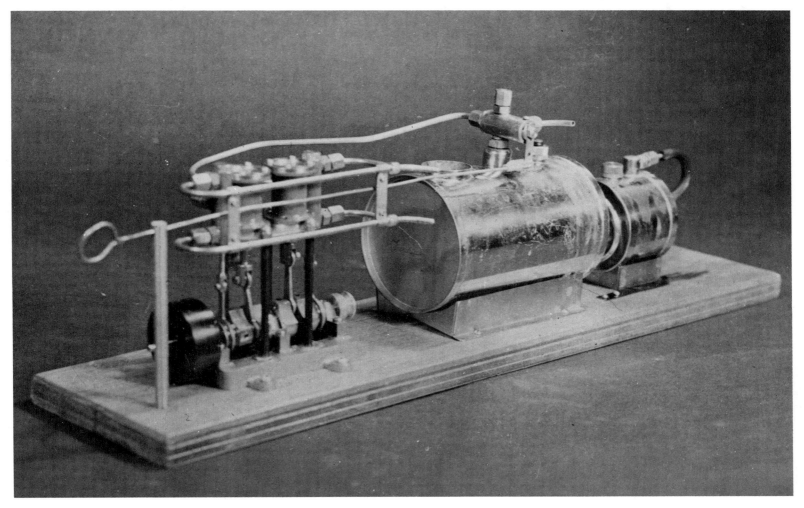

or saturated. Steam from a kettle is saturated, containing water droplets which give it the familiar white color. Increasing the steam temperature evaporates the droplets, 'drying' the steam, and the higher the temperature of the steam, the more work it will produce. Dry, or superheated, steam is produced by heating the pipes carrying saturated steam from the boiler, usually by passing one or more loops through the flame of the boiler's lamp.

Steam pressure also affects the amount of work of which the engine is capable, and this is dependent on the rapidity with which steam is produced compared with the rate at which it is cooled and/or exhausted by the engine. In turn, the rapidity of generation depends on how much and how quickly heat is conveyed to the water. Apart from basic strength, boiler design is mainly a question of ensuring maximum heating surface and minimum radiation in order to absorb as much of the available heat as possible into the water.

The simplest form of boiler, known as a pot, is a cylindrical tank set over a basic heat source such as a methylated spirit lamp or a block of solidified alcohol-type fuel. The heat will play on the bottom of the pot and then fade away upward, while the pot itself will radiate heat to atmosphere. By surrounding the pot with a fairly close-fitting casing, the hot gases will be held in contact with the pot, and radiation will be cut down especially if the casing is insulated. A flue is required in the top of the casing, and holes must be drilled along the lower sides to allow entry of adequate air for combustion. Such a boiler could reasonably be expected to supply steam at up to say 30lb/sq in (2.1kg/cm²), enough for an oscillator or small slide valve engine.

The weakest parts of such a boiler are the end plates, which should be flanged and silver-soldered to the main tubular body; an improvement would be to dish the end plates, or better, fit a solid stay through from one end to the other, the stay ends being threaded and nutted. A safety valve should be fitted, and this is

often combined with a filler cap. A sight glass showing water level is desirable, though this can be omitted if the burning time of the fuel is observed and the amount of water gauged so that the burner will extinguish itself before the water is all boiled away. Usually the collection pipe for the steam is carried inside the boiler at the top and the boiler never filled more than about three-quarters full. The steam pipe is passed back over the burner before leading to the engine to give some degree of superheat.

Increase of heating area can be achieved by silver soldering solid rods along the bottom of the boiler or in vertical rows beneath it, or by bringing water-tubes out of the boiler and running them from one end to the other directly through the burner flame, or by fitting vertical fire tubes through the boiler through which the hot gases from the burner will pass.

The next step is to provide the heat in the form of a blowlamp flame using bottled gas, paraffin (kerosene) or gasoline. For smaller boilers use a vaporizing spirit burner. The flame can be directed beneath the boiler through coiled water tubes (a Scott boiler) or through a large fire-tube passed through the boiler (a center flue boiler). If the flue is situated at the blowlamp end and a space left in the casing at the opposite end, tubes to bring the gases back to the flue can be placed above the center flue (a return tube boiler). Smaller water tubes or solid rods placed across the center flue increase the heating area still further (a cross-tube center flue boiler). There are many variations of greater or lesser difficulty of construction, but in all of them the aim is to increase heating area without increasing bulk and without too severely restricting the flow of hot gases. Most, matched to an engine of the right size, are capable of sustaining a flow of steam at about 60psi (4.2kg/cm²) which is the sort of pressure at which most steam boats operate.

Burners operate on the same self-pressurising principle as the lamps (torches) used for paint-stripping or

plumbing work, where the fuel is vaporized before ignition by passing through a coil surrounding the burner tube. In the absence of Primus nipples, now not easy to obtain, a needle valve can be used to control the very fine aperture required for the emergence of the pressurized gas. Bottled butane or propane gas is replacing gasoline and paraffin, as they are cleaner and easier to deal with and, indeed, much less trouble, since it is possible to adapt a conventional gas blow-lamp simply by cutting off the burner and extending it as required with a length of tube which is curved to allow the gas container to be stowed upright. Butane is commonly available for picnic stoves and although it is believed not to produce quite as much heat as the liquid fuels, it is adequate for most steam models.

Model boilers are pressure vessels and are quite highly stressed so they must be made carefully and be more than adequately strong. Many clubs insist on formal boiler tests–pressurizing to twice working pressure and issuing a test certificate without which a boat is not permitted to run.

Where a boat is likely to be kept in steam for some time, and may take ten or fifteen minutes to come up to working pressure, having to release pressure to refill with water is inconvenient. A hand pump is therefore fitted, capable of forcing fresh water into the boiler, through a non-return valve, against boiler pressure. Many boats also have a feed pump driven off the engine, which continually replenishes the water supply; the hand pump then is an emergency stand-by should blockage of the feed pump or some similar circumstance allow the water level to fall. A boat regularly run on a clean fresh water lake can take its feed water from the

lake through a filter, but for salt or dirty waters a reservoir may be carried in the boat; this reservoir may be topped with water condensed from waste steam.

High powered steam craft, capable of more than 60mph (100kph) employ a system known as 'flash steam,' where no water is carried in the boiler. A blow-lamp heats a single or double coil of, usually, stainless steel tube, and water is pumped into this, flashing instantly into high pressure steam. Initially to start the engine running, the water is hand-pumped, but once running the automatic feed pump takes over. Metering the exact amount of water to match the coil temperature and engine steam consumption is only one of the problems associated with this exciting but difficult aspect of steam propulsion.

Lubrication of any steam engine is important and the methods can vary from a simple needle-valve controlled drip on, for example, the valve faces of an oscillator, to quite sophisticated circulation by an engine-driven pump. Oiling between runs is often enough for the crankshaft and crankpin, though for the shaft it is simple enough to provide a drilled oil hole and a small reservoir in the form of a countersink or a Gits fitting, and an oil groove round the crankpin is a help against running dry. A common means of lubricating the valve faces and piston is to use a displacement lubricator, which is a tall narrow reservoir of oil interposed in the steam pipe between boiler and engine. A small amount of condensate gets left in the reservoir, and this sinks to the bottom, displacing an equal amount of oil which is carried by the steam into the working parts. A drain plug at the bottom of the lubricator allows the condensate to be drawn off periodically, and fresh

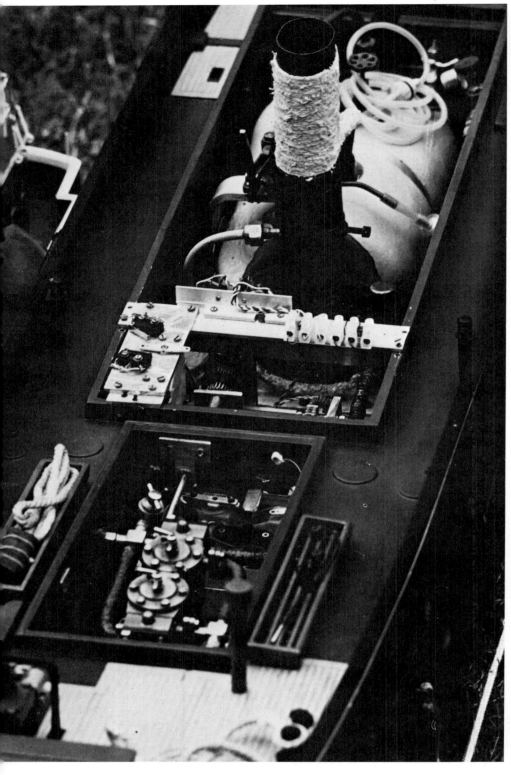

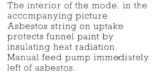

oil is added to top up through a removable screwed cap. Most people use ordinary motor oils, but special steam oils are available.

Traditionally, steam-tight glands have been packed with graphited yarns, often of square section, and this has sometimes been used for packing the piston. Recently, however, silicon rubber O-rings have become widely used for these purposes and these, made to a suitable specification, are available together with many other steam engine requirements from a growing number of specialist suppliers whose enthusiasm for steam is helping its quite remarkable revival. Addresses are listed in appropriate modelling journals.

Choice of boat for steam power is affected by the bulk and weight of the plant, including the space needed to insert and remove the burner, and by the height of the center of gravity of the boiler, which is the heaviest part. The depth of hull below water combined with

The interior of the model in the accompanying picture. Asbestos string on uptake protects funnel paint by insulating heat radiation. Manual feed pump immediately left of asbestos.

generous beam makes a tug the favorite subject; a similar combination of depth and beam in most other vessels is likely to mean considerable length. This is undoubtedly why distortion of scale was accepted forty and fifty years ago when most model power boats used steam engines and transport of a lengthy model was more of a problem. Nowadays, besides tugs, one sees reasonably true-scale small steamers such as inter-island passenger-cargo vessels, Clyde pleasure steamers, trawlers, and the like.

Adequate boiler insulation, usually in the form of asbestos millboard, reasonable airspace round the plant, and occasionally a coat of heatproof paint on the interior surfaces, plus adequate ventilation ensure safe installation of steam plant in wood and grp hulls, though few owners of steam engines care to risk their engines in thermoplastic hulls such as styrene. It is sometimes necessary in a shallow hull such as a paddle steamer,

to use a disguised metal deck immediately above the boiler; wood decks have a tendency to warp in the rising heat. Early radio equipment was frequently temperature-sensitive, but modern gear offers few problems provided that the receiver and servos are sited in cooler areas of the hull.

While rudder control offers no difficulties, engine control is not always straightforward. Ideally, a two-cylinder engine is required with the pistons phased so that the engine will not stop, or remain stopped. A double-acting slide valve engine will normally be controllable. For reversing, a fairly complex valve gear is usually needed, and most such gears operate through a die-block sliding in a link, the link being moved by two eccentrics (one for ahead, one for astern) to drive the valve. The die-block is moved from one end of the link to the other by an arm, to be influenced by one eccentric or the other, and it is this arm that can be

Attractive large R/C tug model, the *Cervia*, on a London pond. Short, wide, and deep, tug hulls are ideal for steam plant, and *Cervia* is one of the most popular designs.

operated by radio. Engine speed will be affected by the position of the die-block, which is a more reliable control than attempting to vary steam pressure.

Two-cylinder engines are occasionally of the compound type where high-pressure steam drives in one cylinder, and the exhaust, which is still at reasonable pressure, drives in the second, larger bore cylinder. A further step is a triple-expansion engine, with high, intermediate, and low pressure cylinders. This type of engine was widely used in full-size ships for maximum economy, but its use in models is more for scale realism.

A very few coal-burning models exist, the coal (or sometimes charcoal) being burnt in a firebox or occasionally in the main flue on a conventional grate drawing air through the fire from beneath. Keeping a clear fire, with minimum clinker build-up, and regular cleaning of sooty deposits from the fire-tubes contribute to the limitation of this form of firing to a very few enthusiasts.

# Internal Combustion Power

SA 27

It is necessary to use the somewhat cumbersome 'internal combustion' term because there are three basic types of ic engine used in models; glowplug, diesel, and gasoline or spark ignition. The last has the longest history, and examples built between 1900 and 1910 survive; one, in the original boat, still runs on special occasions.

Early engines were hand-built by enthusiasts and almost every one could be described as experimental. There are still keen amateurs building engines from raw materials, experimenting with new ideas, and much of the continuing progress in miniature engine performance is due to them. In the 1920s development had evolved a reliable standard approach to design, and sets of castings became available for home constructors, mostly for engines of about 15–20cc (.9–1.2cu in) capacity, considered quite large today.

By the early 1930s the fourstroke cycle was beginning to give way to the two-stroke, a trend which was strongly accelerated by the introduction of commercially-made small gasoline motors in the USA. These were all two-strokes, light and powerful compared with the slower, heavier four-strokes, and they became available in amazing quantities and varieties over a space of four or five years. America was gripped by an upsurge of air-mindedness, a phenomenon shared by other developed nations, and the demand for engines for model aircraft resulted from this. For some thirty years, engine development revolved round aircraft, motors for model boats being more or less a spin-off. Although specialized marine motors appeared during this time, and more research has recently gone into specific requirements for boat use, there is still considerable aircraft influence in the design of engines intended for marine use.

Gasoline-engined model flying ceased in Britain and most of Europe between 1939 and 1945, but during this period two important advances were made. In Switzerland the first commercial compression-ignition (so-called 'diesel') engine appeared, and in America the glowplug was developed. Both these innovations dispensed with the weight and bulk (and sometimes temperament!) of the conventional ignition system, and when mass production restarted after the war, almost all engines followed the new principles, mostly diesels in Europe and glow motors in America. In time, the glow engine proved to have greater development potential in terms of engine speed and power output, and has gradually taken over the lion's share of the market.

**Spark Ignition** A four-stroke engine, used in the majority of cars etc, relies on a timed spark to ignite the fuel, since combustion takes place only once in two revolutions. At its simplest, a mixture of atomized fuel and air is drawn into the cylinder as the piston makes the first downstroke of the cycle, through a valve opened in the cylinder head. On the second stroke while the piston is moving up, the valve is closed and the mixture is thus compressed. Near the top of the stroke the spark occurs, igniting the mixture which burns and expands, driving the piston down for the third or power stroke. As the piston returns, an exhaust valve opens in the cylinder head and the burned gases are thus expelled on the fourth or exhaust stroke.

Obviously there are two valves requiring a mechanism to drive them, and something to trigger the spark, and each of these functions is required only once in every two revolutions. Further, each of them should be adjustable in order to get the best possible performance from the engine, although in practice the adjustment of valve timing is carried out on prototype engines and no, or only limited, adjustment is possible on production examples. Spark timing is easier to alter, and this and the richness of the fuel/air mixture are the controls usually available to the user, plus, of course, a throttle to regulate engine speed. Fuel is normally gasoline but methanol (methyl alcohol) is occasionally used.

Lubrication is usually by the splash system, where

the depression occurring in the crankcase on the rising piston is used to draw in a small amount of oil from a reservoir (often controlled by a needle valve) and the rotation of the crank etc splashes the oil onto the cylinder walls for the piston to pick up an adequate supply.

The two-stroke cycle is very much simpler. As the piston rises, crankcase depression draws in the fuel/air mixture and as the piston descends, it compresses the charge and drives it through transfer passages into the cylinder. The spark occurs as the piston rises again, the piston is driven down and uncovers the exhaust port(s) and fractionally later the transfer ports; the inflow of fresh gas helps to expel the burned gases. Combustion occurs on every revolution, there are no valves, and the contact-breaker creating the spark is easily mounted on the crankshaft since it operates once per revolution. Engine aspiration is fixed by the port positions and sizes, so the controls are spark advance/retard, mixture, and throttle.

The same fuels can be used in two-stroke as in four-stroke, but lubrication is normally by 'dead loss.' Oil is mixed with the fuel and passes through the engine with it, is partially burned with the gasoline and expelled with the exhaust gases. This accounts for the marked difference in the smell of the exhaust. With fewer moving parts and firing on every revolution, it is to be expected that a two-stroke engine will be lighter and faster-running than a four-stroke. On the other hand its low-speed performance is less reliable and it is susceptible to occasional snags such as plug fouling.

Model gasoline engines have been made in all sizes, the upper limit being regarded as 30cc (1.8cu in) and the smallest commercial example being $1\frac{1}{2}$cc (.09cu in) though smaller ones have been made by individuals. There have been twin and four cylinder engines, in line and horizontally opposed, and five, seven and nine cylinder rotary and radial engines. Some of these are still made by skilled enthusiasts, but commercially there

**Above**
Starting a four-stroke spark ignition engine at a regatta. Waders are common at old-established English clubs, and starting the boat in the water has advantages.

**Extreme left, top**
There are vintage enthusiasts in model boating, too. This petrol engine and boat were built in 1935, though the accumulator and ignition coil are modern. Runs once or twice each year.

**Extreme left, bottom**
A four-cylinder in-line ohv four-stroke engine. This particular one is in a Belgian boat, but model engineers building these are found in most boating countries.

is very little activity with ignition engines specifically built for model purposes. Most engines offered nowadays are conversions of small industrial units, made originally to drive chain saws, water pumps, generators and the like, and are nearly all in the 20–25cc (1.2–1.5cu in) size range. Two-stroke and four-stroke examples are available.

One major change in recent years has been the virtually universal adoption of magneto ignition, usually by the inclusion of magnetic bars in the flywheel in place of the battery, coil, and condenser which used to be standard. It may be that development into electronic ignition timing and other technological innovations will see a return to popularity of this type of engine. Four-strokes in particular are clean, controllable, fairly cheap to run, and comparatively quiet, all desirable points.

**Top**
Converted two-stroke chainsaw and other industrial motors are frequently used, though not often as installed in this Italian multi-racing catamaran.

**Above left**
Gasoline-engined fishing boat by G Caird, Bromley Club. Hand-built engine is slow-revving and makes authentic pomp-pomp-pomp noise associated with such craft.

**Above right**
Warming up and adjusting a 15cc hydroplane engine. A good indication of the power produced is given by the degree of water disturbance.

Use of spark ignition engines is confined chiefly to larger tethered hydroplanes, scale models, sport models of moderate speed (up to 15mph, 25kph) and multi-racing models in the specific classes set aside for them. Because of engine size, boats tend to be slightly larger than average, but operation presents few problems providing the ignition system is kept dry. The exhaust gases are at high temperature, so any manifold or muffler (silencer) joints need to be brazed or silver soldered; contact breakers and plugs need to be kept clean and adjusted to the specified gap. Plugs used are 10mm, or the special model sizes of $\frac{3}{8}$in ×24 and $\frac{1}{4}$in ×32, which, together with ignition coils, were difficult to obtain for a number of years but are now more easily available due to a growing interest in reviving vintage models.

**Above**
Two views of the 3½cc (.21cu in) *Sea Otter*, designed for marine use as opposed to a converted aero engine. Note drive is taken off opposite end from flywheel. *(Courtesy E D Ltd)*

**Diesels** To be accurate, the diesel engine injects a metered amount of fuel directly into a cylinder at the point where a spark would occur in a gasoline (petrol) engine. Model 'diesels' do not operate in this way, but on the normal two-stroke cycle, and are more correctly termed compression-ignition engines. If you have pumped up a bicycle tire, you will have felt the pump body grow hot, and this heat comes solely from compressing the air. The same thing happens in a diesel cylinder and if the air contains a fuel which will ignite at the temperature reached, the engine will run. Model engines use a fuel which is a mixture of ether, paraffin (kerosene), and lubricating oil, and this is atomized by a spraybar set across the flow of air being sucked into the crankcase in the conventional two-stroke cycle outlined earlier. A needle valve controls the amount of fuel

**Above left**
A good example of a small rear-induction diesel, the 1½cc (.09cu in) *Super Fury*. Compression adjustment screw has anti-vibration locking bar. *(Courtesy E D Ltd)*

**Above right**
The 2½cc (.15cu in) *Racer* diesel. Rear induction incorporates throttle, annular exhaust collector has two angled outlet pipes. Upper smaller pipes are water jacket inlet and outlet. *(Courtesy E D Ltd)*

entering the airstream.

The point at which the critical temperature is reached in the cylinder will be related to the compression ratio, and the critical temperature may alter slightly with variations in the fuel mixture or even as the whole engine grows hot. This is taken care of by varying the compression ratio by having, in effect, an adjustable cylinder head. A small inverted piston is fitted into the top of the cylinder which can be moved by means of a screw in the head proper. Thus the operator has two controls, the fuel needle and the compression screw; getting the *right* relationship between these two is something that has to be learned.

All engines carry a flywheel to smooth running and to provide inertia to carry the piston up to continue the cycle. The traditional method of starting is to insert a

cord or leather thong into a groove round the flywheel, or a pulley formed on its face, and to pull the engine over by a strong pull with one hand while the other hand retains some tension on the other end of the cord. Usually an assistant holds the boat firmly on its stand and is available to choke the engine by covering the air intake with a thumb or finger as required to allow neat fuel to be drawn into the crankcase. Recently electric starters have made an appearance, operating from a car battery. A rubber belt is positioned in the boat when the engine is installed (in a majority of installations, the engine flywheel/coupling/propeller shaft form an unbroken line, so the belt must be left permanently in place) and this is engaged in the flywheel groove and in a pulley on the end of the starter motor shaft. By switching on the starter and pulling it upward to tension the belt, the engine will be turned over fast and continually, with little physical effort.

**Above**

Barrel type throttle showing how the rotation of the barrel gradually reduces the flow through the venturi inlet tube. The needle valve controlling fuel is on the right. *(Courtesy Ripmax Ltd)*

**Right**

Selection of throttles by HP Screw on body limits rotation of barrel or butterfly to adjust slow running. Smallest item is needle valve for adjustment by radio control. *(Courtesy Ripmax Ltd)*

**Below**

The difference between aero and marine versions of an engine is shown here—just a water-cooling jacket and a flywheel added to the basic design. Engines are *Meteor* 40s (6.6cc). *(Courtesy Micro-Mold Ltd)*

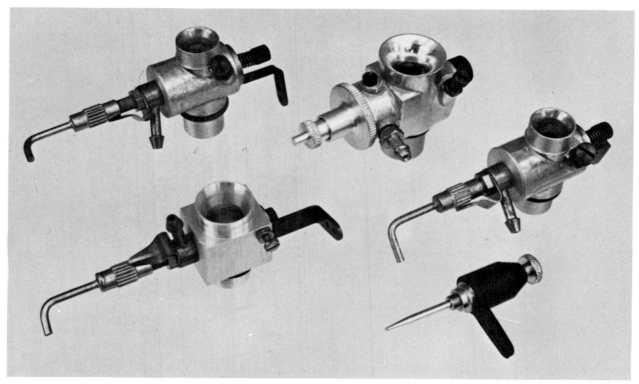

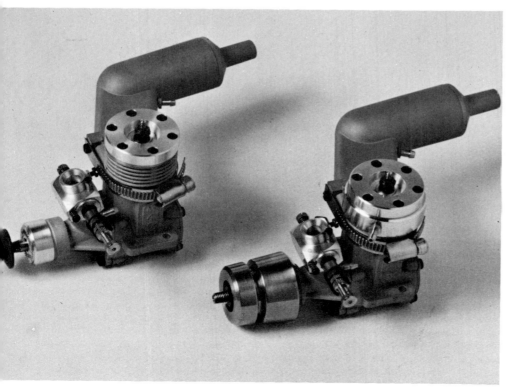

With so small a space left between the piston at TDC and the contra-piston due to the high compression ratio, a hydraulic lock can occur if the motor becomes flooded with fuel and this can cause damage. It is therefore always advisable to turn the engine over by hand before pulling on the cord or belt. If locked, unscrewing the compression screw will allow the contra-piston to rise, and the engine can then be pulled over to clear the surplus fuel, advancing the compression slightly between pulls until the engine fires and clears. Diesels are normally built stronger (and therefore heavier) than other ic engines because the fuel tends to detonate rather than burn evenly, imposing greater strains.

On the whole, diesels run slightly slower than glow engines but will usually drive a slightly larger propeller. The largest now made is of 5cc (.29cu in) capacity, and marine engines (or marine conversions of aircraft engines) are available in sizes of .5, .8, 1, 1.5, 2.5, and 3.5cc. Conversion is usually a matter of fitting a water-cooled jacket to the cylinder and a flywheel; in an aircraft engine the relatively large diameter propeller gives flywheel effect. The smallest sizes of engine are not usually available equipped with a throttle.

Exhaust is cool, so that soft-soldered joints and rubber tubes can be used, but usually much oilier than other engines, thus making the use of an oil trap highly desirable. This is a tin or box with a removable lid, with the exhaust pipe leading into it and an outlet pipe (of the same or larger diameter) fitted at a different level or angle to the exhaust pipe. The gases swirl while changing direction, giving an opportunity for oil droplets to fall to the bottom, from where the residue can be syringed or swabbed out from time to time.

**Glowplug Engines** The glowplug is rather like a spark plug with a fine coil of wire joining the electrodes. This coil glows white hot when a small current is passed through it and will ignite the fuel charge in the cylinder. It loses heat slowly, relative to the milli-seconds between one revolution and the next, and once the engine is running, absorbs and retains enough heat from the combustion of one charge to remain glowing long enough to ignite the following charge. Thus once running the battery supplying the initial current can be disconnected. Plugs are available operating off either 1.5 or 2 volts, but the current drain is fairly heavy and an accumulator supply is really necessary, especially in view of the cost of dry cells.

As the plug is glowing all the time, no ignition timing is possible and a smooth-burning fuel is needed. The temperature rise due to compression will affect the point at which combustion begins, and this point may also vary with the exact fuel blend and the plug temperature. Hot plugs with increased insulation and therefore slower heat dissipation are needed for cool engines, cold plugs for hot engines (to avoid burning out) and often, for slow-running engines or ones used throttled down, an idle-bar plug is desirable; the bar helps to store heat and prevent the glow from dimming too rapidly. The physical position of the coil can also affect combustion.

The fuel used is methanol (methyl alcohol) and lubricating oil, frequently castor oil. To this can be added oxygen-releasing constituents, the usual one being nitro-methane, and here arises a major snag. Adding 'nitro' to the fuel can considerably increase power output, and many American and Japanese motors will not run without a proportion of it unless the compression ratio is increased. However, throughout Europe and in other countries including Britain, nitro-methane (or any similar additive) is banned for competition use on the grounds that it is very expensive and not freely available in all countries. In the interests of fair competition, therefore, only 'straight' (methanol/oil) fuel is permitted, and in major events the organizers actually supply the fuel ready mixed. It is interesting that many of the top American speed models use Italian

engine will clear and fire after a pull or two. Major flooding has to be cleared by removing the plug and spinning the engine over fast. Throttle control is available or even standard on most engines over $1\frac{1}{2}$cc, often designated by the inclusion of the letters 'RC' in the engine title.

Glow engines can be quite lightly constructed and this is one reason for their faster running. Some do not achieve peak power output until they are running at perhaps 23,000rpm, and in the smallest competition size ($2\frac{1}{2}$cc) it is not uncommon to gear them down so that the propeller is turning at 16–18,000rpm, when it is

and Austrian engines running on sixty percent nitro!

For sport running there are no such restrictions, and several commercial fuels contain small amounts of nitro, perhaps five to ten percent. Experimenting with different fuels and plugs will usually overcome any starting or running problems and may result in enhanced performance.

Starting procedure is much the same as other engines, except that there is only one control, the needle valve, and one must of course be certain that the plug is glowing adequately. Minor flooding can often be identified by hearing the plug sizzling, and normally the

more efficient. Several sophisticated engines are built to 'ABC' specification (aluminum, brass, chrome) using an aluminum piston running in a chromed brass cylinder liner. These are usually stiff to turn over when cold, but differential expansion means that when running the clearances are exactly correct for maximum performance. In addition the inertial forces of the very light piston are low, which, since it is changing direction nearly 800 times *each second* is extremely important.

Early model engines used what is called 'sideport induction,' where the rising piston uncovered a port in the cylinder wall through which a fresh gas charge was drawn into the crankcase. There is, however, a limit to the time the port can be open and thus to the amount of gas which can be drawn in. Attention was switched to rotary shaft induction, which uses a hollow crankshaft with a port registering with the fuel/air inlet pipe as the shaft revolved; many early glow engines used this system and, in fact, a lot still do. To increase admission time without weakening the crankshaft, a rotary disk and, later, a rotary drum were introduced, driven by the crankpin, extended beyond the length necessary for the connecting rod big end and engaging in a hole in the disk·or drum. The term 'rear induction' covers both these systems and a third, the reed valve, where a thin metal plate covers the induction pipe inlet, opening on crankcase depression and closing on crankcase compression.

To move the increased volume of mixture in the crankcase, the single transfer passage and port gave way to 360° passages and ports, that is, passages disposed circumferentially round the cylinder, milled into the cylinder wall and leaving only a minimum of bearing surface for the piston, and to ensure maximum clearance of exhaust gases, 360° exhaust ports were sited immediately above the top of transfer passages. The fastest engines, however, have resulted from returning to the basic single transfer passage and exhaust port, but of considerable size, and so designed as to retain a directional flow to the gases.

Carburetion relies basically on the needle valve, which is incorporated in, and adjusts the fuel issuing from, a spraybar set across the air intake. Air being sucked into the crankcase passes the spraybar at high speed and reduced pressure, and atomized fuel is drawn off and mixed with the air as a result. Some sophisticated installations use a pressurized fuel feed system, so that fuel flow is consistent irrespective of how the boat may be thrown around by rough water or abrupt maneuvers. This is most commonly done by tapping off pressure from the crankcase or from the exhaust system and piping it directly into a sealed fuel tank.

Most throttles use a drilled barrel fitting across the air intake, often incorporating the spraybar, which when

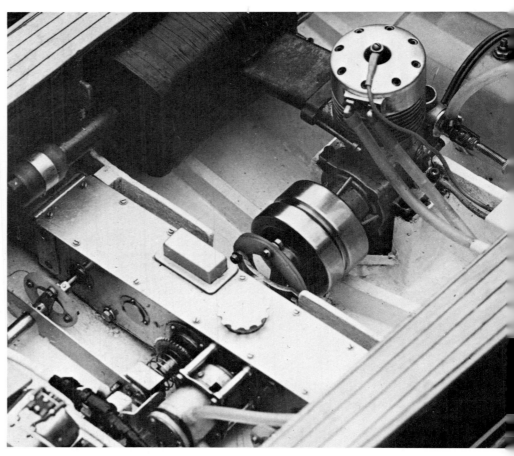

open offers no obstruction to the airflow but which can be rotated to blank off the intake gradually. The difference in engine speed between flat out boat speed and 'tick-over' is much smaller than is generally realized; one popular sport engine capable of running at about 14,000rpm in air (that is, with the boat held out of the water) runs at 8000rpm flat out in water, giving a speed of 12–15mph (19–24kph) in a good typical hull and drops to 4000rpm and about 4mph (6½kph) when throttled back to its slowest reliable running speed.

The drop in engine speed when a boat is placed in the water after starting up on the bank naturally reduces air and gas flow velocities, affecting the fuel mixture, which is the usual reason for engines stopping as soon as the boat is placed in the water. Reduction of the venturi effect in the induction pipe means that less fuel is drawn off, and because it is a square effect, the fuel mixture becomes too weak. It is therefore necessary for the engine to be running over-rich as the boat is lowered into the water. With a diesel it may also be necessary to back off the compression. In general the larger the engine, the more latitude there is in this respect as they will often keep running, albeit erratically, when a small engine would stop dead.

Propeller size is an important factor but one on which it is almost impossible to give practical guidance since

so much depends on the size and power of the engine, the speed at which it delivers peak power, the shape and weight of the hull, and other factors. Reading current magazines will usually turn up a similar engine in a reasonably similar hull, and the propeller used will be a good starting point in the absence of recommendations by the manufacturers of the hull or engine. It is advisable to try the next sizes of propellers up and down, and/or the approximate equivalent in a different pitch. This is what is done by all the experts, and also by full-size racing craft. There are excellent and relatively inexpensive plastic propellers available; metal propellers can be superior, but good ones are much more costly than plastic, and if they hit an obstruction such as a floating twig, there is a greater possibility of damage to the engine.

Pitch is the distance moved forward by a point on a propeller during one complete revolution, and it can be theoretical, which is what the distance should be in ideal conditions, or effective, which is how far it actually moves when slip is taken into account. A 20% slip factor is usually allowed, but it is empirical and the true slip may be much more or much less.

Theoretically it is possible to work out the pitch required, allowing for slip, for a given boat speed at given engine rpm, but there are so many variables that

**Bottom center**
Ambitious geared twin-prop installation from one 10cc engine, not recommended unless you are expert. This model also includes a radio-controlled clutch and other refinements.

**Bottom right**
Selection of marine glow engines from Enya, just one of the Japanese engine firms. Sizes usually run from .09 (1½cc) to .60 (10cc). Note no plugs fitted. *(Courtesy Ripmax Ltd)*

**Below**
Competition kit model for multi-racing or steering, showing relationship between propeller, water-scoop, and rudder. Shape of rudder can have considerable effect on performance. *(Courtesy E D Ltd)*

**Left**
Changes in load on propeller are considerable on choppy water. This glow-engined Fairey Marine *Swordsman* is participating in an offshore race, particularly hard on boats and engines.

**Below far left**
Smaller glow motors (under 5cc) are often geared down for greater propeller efficiency. Gears are incorporated in engine mounting, as here. Tuned pipe exhaust and trim tabs also visible.

in practice the trial and error system has been found to give better and quicker results, except with very slow-revving engines where a reasonable approximation can be made. Unless very high speed is the object, there is usually sufficient excess of power available for satisfactory performance even without the best possible propeller. Ultimate speed in any sphere is expected to be expensive in both time and money, and in model boating the practitioner can face additional problems such as aeration, loading in turns, propeller stall, etc, all of which require experiment to cure, but none of which is likely to afflict the average model.

One propeller effect that is common to all models is torque reaction. A propeller meets resistance to its rotation from the water, and this resistance is transmitted through the shaft and motor to the boat, trying to rotate the boat in the opposite direction to the propeller. In a normal set-up with the propeller rotating anti-clockwise (viewed from astern), the effect is to heel the boat to starboard and, with the rudder straight, the extra resistance of the more deeply immersed starboard side will cause the boat to turn to starboard. The effect varies depending on hull, propeller, beam, engine power, and so on but it is always there. In a particular boat, it will naturally change with engine speed, though not necessarily in a constant relationship. Permanent application of rudder means continual extra drag, and the most satisfactory cure is to mount a small wedge under the starboard side of the stern which tends to lift that side; the faster the boat moves, the more lift is produced to counter the increased torque. The wedge must be trimmed by experiment to produce just sufficient lift.

Fast boats frequently employ trim tabs mounted on the transom, adjustable individually to control torque reaction, and also to trim the running angle of the hull to its most favorable. They are also used to balance out turn diameters, since torque and the manner in which the spiralling waterstream from the propeller impinges on the rudder together can have the effect of allowing a very tight turn in one direction but preventing a tight turn in the other. Trim tab adjustment can help, but in extreme cases it may be necessary to change the shape of the rudder. A dagger plate (a small fixed fin projecting downward about halfway along the hull bottom) is also used to make turns tighter, by checking the tendency of a boat to skid outwards in a turn thereby providing a pivot point round which the rudder forces act.

With any boat, one of the most important points is accurate alignment of the engine to the propeller shaft. Failure to achieve this is a common fault and causes more disappointment than anything else. The braking effect of friction caused by even slight misalignment can halve the power available at the propeller, and in the case of small engines can prevent them from running at all. Most engines nowadays are bolted to a metal or ply plate, which in turn is screwed to cheek blocks securely glued into the hull, so that by adding thin packing, or paring away the block tops, alignment can be adjusted before the screw holes are marked and drilled. It is possible to buy rigid connectors to which both engine shaft and prop-shaft screw, simplifying alignment and being replaced by a ball-and-socket coupling of identical length once installed.

Couplings of several types are used, the commonest being a cross-pinned ball and a slotted socket, or a slotted socket on each shaft with a connecting piece having a cross-pinned ball at either end. Carden types, with two plates bolted to a common leather or fiber center disk, are popular for bigger engines, and some engines are supplied with two parallel pins projecting from the flywheel, engaging in notches or slots in a dog or disk screwed on the prop-shaft. Other less common types may be seen, such as a grooved rod sliding into an internally grooved cup, the drive being transmitted by bearing balls located in the grooves.

Shafts are usually of stainless or other alloy steels, ranging from 3mm for small engines to 4 or 5mm for

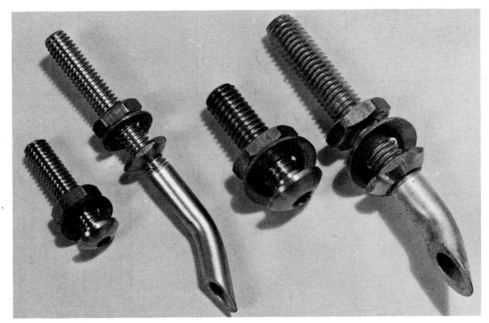

10cc. Normal practice is for them to run inside a brass tube which is bushed at each end with a sintered bronze bush. Ball races are fitted at each end in some instances, the one at the lower end usually being a thrust race. Separate thrust races are available for plain bushed shaft-tubes; propeller thrust should be taken on the tube end rather than the coupling or engine crankshaft. Some builders incorporate a thrust block inside the boat, against which the thrust is exerted through a larger ball-race than could be used externally. Hydroplanes and some fast monohulls use a separate short horizontal tailshaft running in a stern bracket, with a bare shaft emerging from a short stuffing box in the hull and driving the tailshaft through a universal joint.

Water cooling is achieved by siting a pick-up tube just aft of the propeller, or sometimes incorporated in a hollow rudder stock, and connecting the top of the tube to one pipe on the engine jacket by means of neoprene tube. The second jacket pipe is connected to an outlet in the side of the boat, sometimes at the transom, or occasionally into the exhaust system. Water flows through the system as soon as the boat is put afloat with the engine running. Too much water is to be avoided; it should be very near boiling point at the outlet, other-

**Top**
Water scoops or pick-up tubes and outlet bushes. Connection to the engine jacket is usually by neoprene tube. Outlet bush can fit in hull side or transom. *(Courtesy Ripmax Ltd)*

**Above**
One of the top motors for power output is the Italian OPS. Central exhaust on aft side of engine makes installation of pipe simpler; silicon rubber coupling tube withstands red heat.

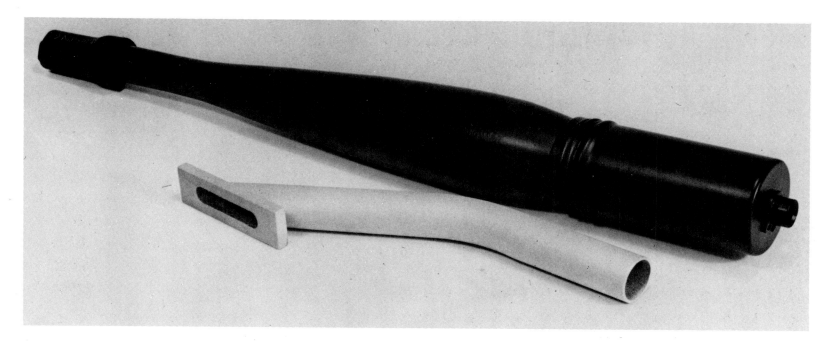

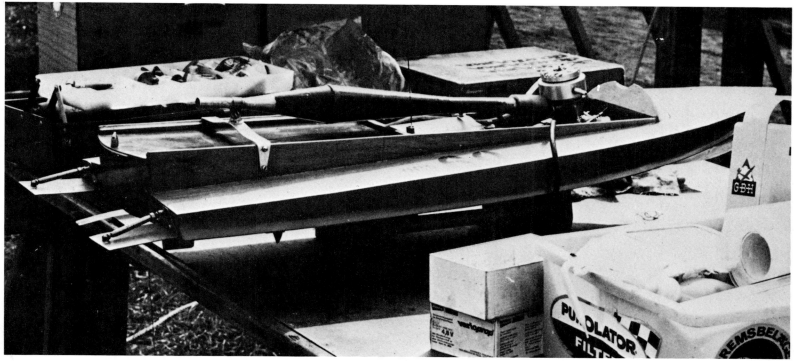

**Top**
Tuned pipe exhaust, with manifold to fit engine. This E D exhaust is fitted with a muffler (silencer) canister and results in a noticeable increase in power and a reduction in noise.

**Above**
F1V speed model showing tuned pipe exhaust and large trim tabs on transom. Layout of boat is typical, though additional muffling (silencing) on exhaust would be needed in many countries.

**Left**
Neat home-built muffler (silencer) on tuned pipe. Reduction of exhaust aperture area cuts noise markedly, but also tends to reduce rpm of engine. Noise is taken seriously by modellers.

**Left**
Flexible shaft outdrive is used in America but rarely elsewhere. Rudder and water scoop are also carried on the outrigger which supports the lower shaft bearing. *(Courtesy Dumas Products Inc)*

**Below left**
Not likely to be an acceptable form of exhaust nowadays, but this picture shows clearly a typical engine mounting and also cooling by winding a copper tube tightly round the cylinder head.

**Below**
Starting procedure. Assistant holds model firmly on stand while starter operates cord. Electric starters are becoming more common, especially for bigger engines.

**Right**
An early two-cylinder outboard engine marketed in the USA for a short time in the 1960s. Each cylinder is .049cu in (.8cc) and as can be seen they are glowplug ignition.

**Below right**
Outboard motors are not yet common, but the very powerful 3½cc K and B is competitive. *Hot Shot 21* is a tunnel hull design, 27in (685mm) for this or similar engines. *(Courtesy Dumas Products Inc)*

wise the engine will be overcooled.

Model-size two-strokes are extremely noisy, and legislation exists in many countries to control their noise. Silencing, or muffling, is required by most national and all international rules, the usual figure being 80 dB at 10m, or sometimes 84 dB at 7m. Initial reaction to any form of noise control was hostile, on the grounds that it must involve interference with the free passage of exhaust gases and reduce engine performance. Limiting noise means, in general, reducing the output of high frequency sound waves, which travel furthest, and by changing the direction and speed of the exhaust flow, the offensive frequencies can be damped. Baffling the gas flow creates back pressure, resulting in

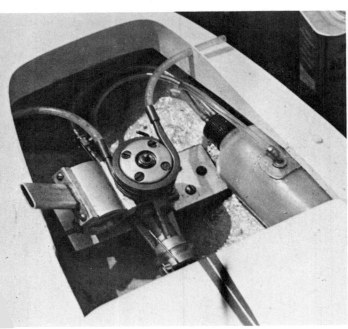

incomplete scavenging of the cylinder and can reduce top rpm by 1000–1500 or so in a high-performance engine.

A tuned exhaust system, on the other hand can actually increase power while reducing noise and, even with additional silencing stages added on, can still produce a net power gain. It consists of a pipe expanded in the center so that initially the exhaust is led into an increasing diameter, then a reducing diameter; it is basically two cones joined at their bases. The second cone reflects sound pressure back towards the first, more sharply tapered one, setting up pressure waves or pulses which can be tuned to a limited speed range of the engine. Negative pressure timed to coincide with

the exhaust port opening sucks exhaust gases out so forcibly that part of the fresh unburnt charge is drawn through, and the pulse of positive pressure immediately following pushes much of this charge back into the cylinder after the transfer passages have closed, as the exhaust port is closing. Thus the charge is boosted and engine power increased. Timing involves adjusting the distance of the cones from the exhaust port to match the engine speed, moving it a fraction of an inch at a time until a sudden increase in engine speed occurs, when the engine is said to be 'on the pipe.' Silicon rubber tubing, capable of withstanding almost red heat, makes this adjustment easy to carry out, but since the engine speeds up when the boat is moving, finding the critical length involves several runs.

Exhaust noise is only a part of total noise output, which also includes engine clatter, intake roar, and vibration transmitted to the hull, which, especially if grp, can act as a sounding box. Clatter and roar can be muffled to some extent by covering the engine bay with a hatch, preferably one with absorbent padding covering its underside. Vibration can be reduced by introducing polyurethane foam filling to large empty spaces or, better, by mounting the engine and propeller shaft in rubber mountings now made especially for the purpose, avoiding any metal-to-hull connection. Boats with rubber mountings are often faster than similar models with rigid mountings, and are barely audible at 50m.

Before leaving the subject of internal combustion engines, some mention should be made of the effects of fuel and/or exhaust residue. Most engines blow raw fuel out of the air intake, or throw it off the flywheel from the crankshaft bearing and leaky exhausts are not unknown, though silicon bath caulk is a help in the last respect. Gasoline and gasoline exhaust are not particularly difficult, and apart from excessive oiliness,

diesel fuel and exhaust are not too troublesome, although if left in contact with ordinary paint or enamel for some hours, some attack is possible. Thorough painting to avoid oil soakage is essential, and a coat of fuel-proof varnish is recommended.

With glow fuel and methanol exhaust residue, particularly with nitro-methane added, ordinary paints are quickly attacked. Polyurethane or epoxy paints are therefore recommended, though thorough fuel-proofing over conventional paints can be satisfactory. Grp is reasonably safe if untreated, but a coat of fuel-proof paint or varnish makes the interior of a hull easier to wipe clean, and any exterior paint trim also needs to be fuel-proof.

# Electric Power

Surveys have shown that at least seventy percent of all working model boats are electric powered, without including the many thousands of battery-operated toy boats sold annually. For the average modeller who just enjoys an occasional quiet afternoon's boating, this form of power has many advantages—clean, reliable, no starting problems, quiet and easy to handle. Perhaps the chief disadvantages are limited running time as the batteries run down and the inability to achieve planing performance without some expense. In fact, technological progress in the last few years means that elec-

efficiency, all of which are not easy to measure except under laboratory conditions. Measuring the actual voltage at the motor brushes and the amperage of the current being drawn forms the usual basis for comparison, the two measurements being multiplied to give the wattage. Performance can be approximately compared with ic engines for which horsepower is quoted in magazine tests since 1hp = 746watts.

Most motors used in models are of the permanent magnet type, in which an armature rotates in the field of the magnet. The current is supplied to the armature through two brushes rubbing on a commutator which acts as a switch to reverse the current flow through the armature windings every 180°. The armature may have any number of poles over three, usually an odd number

**Below**
Electric power does not have to produce a slow and stately performance, as is evident. Fast electrics are a comparatively recent and fast-growing area of competition running. *(Courtesy Ripmax Ltd)*

tric speed models are only a little slower than their glow-engined counterparts, and as a result of these developments it is possible to run a boat at planing speeds for perhaps twenty minutes or so, or a slower boat for a couple of hours, for a similar outlay to that required for a diesel or glow installation.

At one time electric power was discussed in terms of developed torque, measured in oz/in or gm/cm, but nowadays it is normal to talk of watts. This usually means watts input, which is fairly simple to measure with a meter; watts = amps ×volts, so that a motor drawing 4 amps from a 6 volt power supply has an input of 24 watts. Watts output to the propshaft depends on the efficiency of the electric motor, and total output depends on this together with friction losses and propeller

to ensure self-starting, and the commutator has one segment for each pole. Permanent magnet motors are simpler and cheaper, and may be reversed by changing the polarity of the current fed to the brushes. Cheap motors usually employ stamped sheet phosphor-bronze brushes which tend to wear through; better quality motors have copper-carbon rods. Light spring-loading is usual to ensure a good rubbing contact.

Electro-magnetic motors, where the magnetic field is produced by passing a current through a wire-wound field coil, were at one time widely used for larger motors, but advances in permanent magnet technology have reduced the need for field-wound types of motor in model sizes. Disadvantages are increased bulk, and more complication for reversal, since the current flow

**Left**
The boat in the picture opposite, the Graupner Mini-Speed, the first commercial kit for a fast electric model. Typical installation is a *Bullet* motor and 18 1.2 nicad cells. *(Courtesy Ripmax Ltd)*

**Above**
Range of Japanese-made moderately priced motors suitable for scale models or, in the bigger examples, competition F3E and quite fast electric boats. *(Courtesy Ripmax Ltd)*

**Below**
A permanent magnet motor (foreground) compared with a field-wound example. Power output and current consumption for motor weight are similar; only disadvantage is more complex astern switching.

has to be reversed in either the field or the armature windings, not both. Further, in those motors available in the model sphere which are shunt wound (the field coil and armature windings are wired in parallel) the current through the armature must be switched off if the field is switched off or there is a chance of damage. Thus reversing direction of rotation is not accomplished by a simple change of polarity; the usual method is to employ a double-pole change-over relay.

Dry batteries (primary cells) used to be the commonest power source, but their vastly increased cost coupled with the introduction of alternative storage (secondary) cells at relatively modest prices has seen their use diminish, though for small motors and lowest possible initial outlay they still have a place. Early electric boats used glass or pottery-cased lead-acid accumulators, but dry batteries were fairly extensively used in the 1930s. After World War II there were innumerable government-surplus motors, ex-bomb sight, camera, etc and heavy lead acid (still glass-cased) and nickel-iron accumulators. In the 1960s the search for higher power/weight ratios produced expensive installations using silver-zinc or salt cells, but the average model still used dry batteries or lead-acid cells, now plastic-cased. Nickel-cadmium cells, available for some years in button form suitable for radio control equipment, began to appear in sizes suitable for main pro-

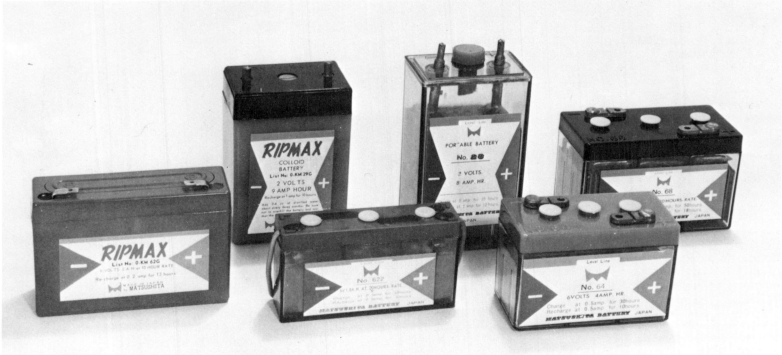

pulsion power around 1970, and since then have established themselves as first choice for average-sized model boats.

The problem with dry batteries is that the current demand made on them by a boat motor is far in excess of what they are intended to supply, so that a battery which will last for many months in a flashlight (torch) or an electric doorbell will be flattened in a few minutes in a model. The flashlight and doorbell require an intermittent drain and demand only a few milliamps rather than a couple of amps or more. Heavy discharges cause polarization (hydrogen bubbles on the internal electrodes) reducing the activity and causing a drop in voltage. After standing for a few hours to allow depolarization, much of the original capacity is restored, though less each time the cell is used. Battery life can be extended by using two sets alternately, never allowing them to discharge completely, and resting them for a day or so between outings.

It is not generally appreciated that halving the current drain will more than double life. If a battery gives, say, ten minutes running at full speed, it will normally give over half an hour at cruising speed. Alternatively, using two batteries wired in parallel (positive to positive and negative to negative) will give over three times the running time of a single battery. Always use as big a battery, or as many cells wired to give the necessary voltage, as possible. Weight is the main objection, but is not often too critical with a displacement hull. Getting planing performance from a suitable hull using dry cells is improbable. High power (HP) cells are superior to standard ones both in the initial voltage delivered and the time for which current can be supplied, and are well worth the extra cost.

Quite a lot of radio equipment is available for dry cell use, at a lower price than if fitted with nickel-cadmium

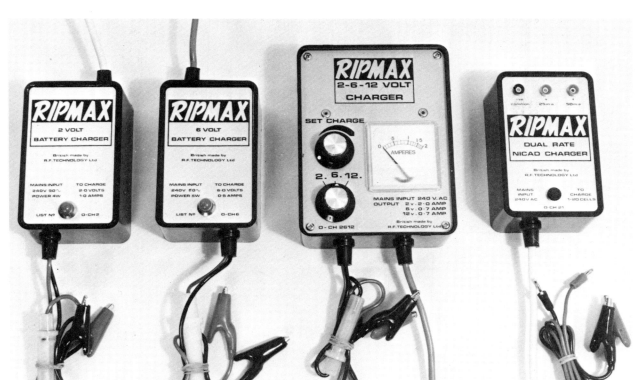

**Left**
Range of chargers for different cells. Obvious choice is the largest, which does everything the others can do, though naturally requires a larger initial outlay. *(Courtesy Ripmax Ltd)*

cells. In the case of the transmitter, dry batteries are reasonably economic, but rechargeable cells are a better proposition for the receiver under average conditions of use. Since this means that a charger will be needed, the transmitter may as well be equipped with nickel-cadmium cells. However if initial outlay has to be restricted, there is nothing wrong with dry cell operation; a transmitter battery will last perhaps a whole season, and dry cells for the receiver/servos will give at least two or three hours normal use. Nicads can always be added when finances permit.

Lead acid accumulators will be familiar to car-owning readers, since car batteries are lead acid, though larger than those used in average models. Motor scooter batteries, incidentally, are excellent for larger models. Neglect of such a battery has familiar consequences, and it is true that in model sizes, lead-acids need more attention than other batteries. They must always be kept topped up (by adding distilled water) and never left in a discharged condition, or they will deteriorate rapidly. On the other hand, they are comparatively inexpensive and give a good output for their weight; as they deliver 2v per cell, three cells will supply 6v against four silver-zincs (1.5v) or five nickel-cadmium or nickel-iron cells (1.2v). Further, they will retain the ability to deliver 2v per cell even when discharging heavily, whereas some of the other forms of cell exhibit a marked voltage drop.

The electrolyte in these cells is normally sulphuric acid in liquid form (specific gravity, 1.26) but sealed cells using jellied acid are available, and recently sealed 'dry lead-acid' cells have been introduced. Either type gives 2v per cell, so that fewer cells are needed to produce a total nominal voltage, which compensates for the higher weight per individual cell. These too must not be left in a discharged state.

All rechargeable cells have an amp/hour rating based on a discharge over a period of 10 hours. Thus a 6v 4a/h battery will deliver 400 milliamps (.4amp) at 6v for approximately 10 hours. At the one hour rate, the capacity would fall; that is, it would not be possible to draw 4 amps for one hour, and at, say, the 15 minute rate, the capacity would fall to about half, 2a/h, delivering 16 amps for around 7½ minutes rather than 15 minutes. At this sort of current, intermittent discharge of perhaps not more than a minute at a time would probably be needed because of the battery heating up and the possibility of permanent damage.

The capacity of the battery as expressed in the amp/hour rating also indicates charging rate, which should be at the 10hr rate at a maximum (except for cells specifically designed for fast recharging) and is often recommended at the 20hr rate, that is, in the example given, 400 milliamps maximum or 200mA normally. The lower charge rate contributes towards longer overall life, but the greatest effect on life is the degree to which the battery is regularly discharged. Running down only to half discharge will mean the cells lasting four times as long as if they are regularly completely flattened. When charging, one third is normally added to the nominal charging time to take care of losses due to heat and chemical change, so that in the same example, it would be customary to charge at 400mA for 13.3hr (10+3.3) or 200mA for 26.7hr if the battery was completely flat. Overcharge at the low rate will not really cause harm, but the faster the charge rate

**Above**
One of several charger/discharger units available. Fast charging of cells makes previous discharge to standard basic voltage desirable, and this device does it all automatically. *(Courtesy Ripmax Ltd)*

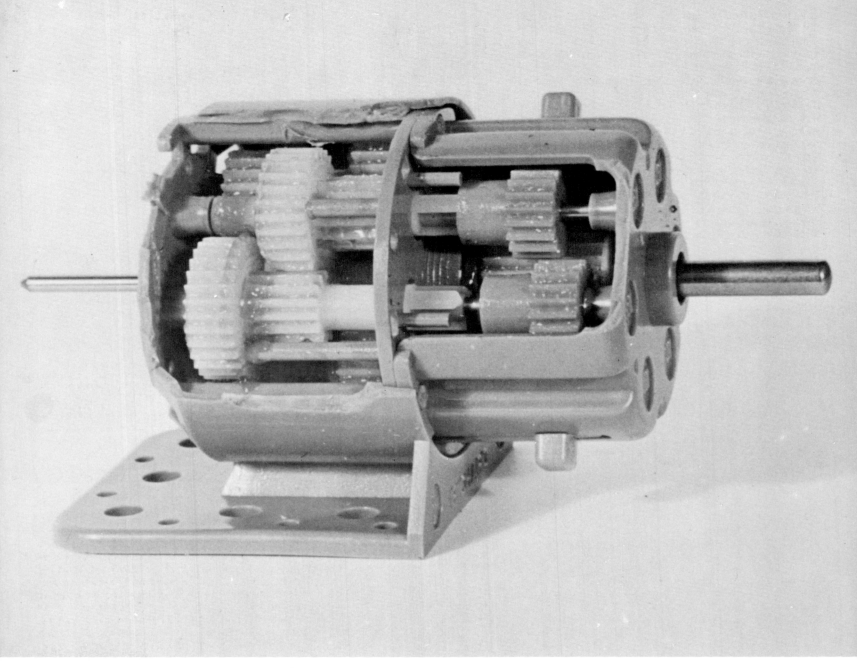

The Richard gearbox in cutaway form. Ratios are engaged by sliding the appropriate knob on the narrow end, thus moving the Delrin gears. (Courtesy Ripmax Ltd)

the more accurate the charge should be.

Silver-zinc cells are little used nowadays because of expense: not only are they much more costly initially but they have a very much shorter life than other types of cells. If every care is taken, life might be stretched to two seasons' use. They must never be left partially discharged, even for a day or two, but recharged after use at the 10 or 20hr rate till a reading of 2.1v per cell is achieved. Output drops to a standard 1.5v within seconds of coming into use. Their advantages are very light weight and small size, offering weight for weight about four times the running time per charge as lead acid.

Salt cells are in a category by themselves, and consist of a small plastic envelope containing salts and a pair of electrodes. Introduction of water activates the cell, which produces 1.5v at an equivalent of five or more amps, for a period of three or four minutes, after which it is thrown away. It is not used nowadays except possibly experimentally.

Nickel-cadmium (nicad) cells are very much the present-day batteries. They are not too expensive, simple to use, will withstand considerable neglect and abuse, and can be rapidly discharged without ill effect. Five or six years of service can be expected, which makes them the cheapest form of electricity supply in terms of total cost per hour's running. Modern cells are sealed and metal-cased, and should be kept clean and free of rust or other corrosion. Ideally they should be discharged to 1v per cell for storage, and they can be left in this condition for months. There used to be concern that if a pack of cells was discharged completely, some would reach 0v quicker and would be receiving current from those still discharging, which was thought to cause a permanent reversal of polarity in the flat cells. Experience has shown that two or three charge/ discharge cycles will correct any such condition and return the cells to normal power.

Nicads are available in several capacities (all 1.2v per cell) and in sizes corresponding to dry battery dimensions. There are also fast recharge versions which can safely be fully recharged in a few minutes, either from a mains source or from a car battery. Button cells, often called Deacs, used in radio equipment, should on the other hand be charged slowly, not faster than the 10hr rate. Careful users log the time for which the cells have been used and charge for only a corresponding period, but at low charge rates overcharging does not appear to be harmful, and, indeed, some makers of equipment recommend a full charge before operation irrespective of when or for how long the equipment was last used.

For fast recharge nicads, many experts prefer to work in amp/minutes, (amp/hours ×60). Thus the common 1.2v 1.2a/h cells become 1.2v 72a/m, from which it is easy to see that a current of 1 amp can be supplied for 72 minutes, 2 amps for 36 minutes, etc, bearing in mind that the faster the cell is discharged, the greater the disparity between the theoretical time and the actual time in practice; the 4a for 18 minutes of theory would more likely work out at 13–14 minutes. The amp/minute figure is also convenient for charging, since if the charger output is known, it is simple to calculate how many minutes are required to bring the cell back to full charge. It is safest to discharge the cells to .8v each by connecting up a 12v 24 watt car bulb before fast charging, so that the charge starts from a known point. With charge rates of up to 10 amps, it is vital to ensure that no overcharging occurs. If the cells are not fully discharged, it is better to use a 5 or 10hr rate, where charge time is less critical.

When banks of cells are to be made up, always use thick wire and ensure good contacts. If soldering is required, tin the wire and the cell contact with a large hot iron and make the joint as quickly as possible. Prolonged heating is one of the quickest ways to ruin any type of cell. Wire leads to the motor should also be of generous size and anchored to the structure so that they cannot be inadvertently tugged. Taping packs of cells together is sensible provided that they are not totally covered by tape which can hide early traces of corrosion. In most boats it is possible to mount the batteries in trays or open-top boxes just clear of the boat's bottom, to avoid them getting wet from any water weeping into the hull via the propeller tube. *Never* leave batteries in the boat between outings.

Most motors are provided with a mounting plate, enabling them to be screwed to a ply plate supported by cheek blocks. Some, however, may be simple cylinders, and these may be strapped down with an aluminum or brass strip shaped to fit over the motor casing and screwed down either side. A piece of rubber sheet between strap and motor is worthwhile, and wood strips can be glued to the mounting plate each side to locate the motor positively. It is possible to strap the motor in place with rubber bands between hooks on either side, but the bands should be renewed frequently.

Couplings can be much as described in the previous chapter, and if anything alignment is even more vital; misalignment can drastically reduce power output and increase current consumption (it is, after all, like running with a brake on) and can cause overheating and much reduced motor life.

Occasionally a case of electrical interference arises, a radio failing to perform properly when the boat's

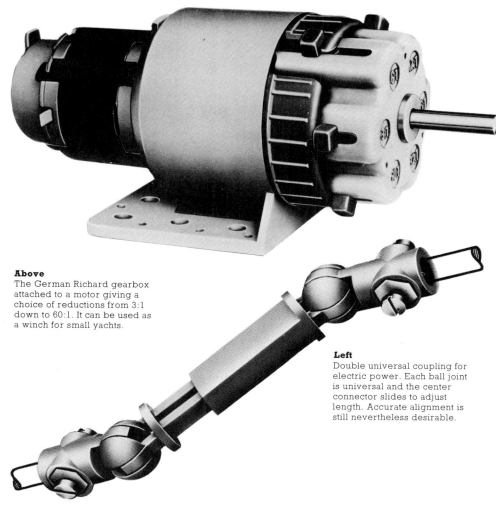

**Above**
The German Richard gearbox attached to a motor giving a choice of reductions from 3:1 down to 60:1. It can be used as a winch for small yachts.

**Left**
Double universal coupling for electric power. Each ball joint is universal and the center connector slides to adjust length. Accurate alignment is still nevertheless desirable.

**Below**
Pile gears. Each of the four laminations visible is a separate gearbox engaging its predecessor and so increasing the reduction. As many as needed can be used.
*(Courtesy Ripmax Ltd)*

motor is running. This is due to sparking of the brushes on the commutator in almost all cases, as any spark discharge emits radio waves over a wide band, and although the range is limited, the radio receiver cannot be mounted sufficiently far away. Most modern radios reject this type of interference, but there are times when some form of suppression is called for. A capacitor of between .01–.05 microfarad between each brush and the motor case is the first step, followed by a similar capacitor directly across the brushes. A choke of 5–8 microhenries in each battery lead, as close to the motor terminals as possible, is another measure. Ensure that the aerial is kept as far from the motor as possible, and that it is the recommended length. If all else fails, a screen of balsa or ply, faced with aluminium kitchen foil can be interposed between motor and receiver, or the receiver placed in a tin box. Earthing the motor case to the propeller tube sometimes helps.

Gears are sometimes advantageous with electric power, but only if the gears are well mounted and friction is very low. It is possible to buy some motors already equipped with gears, or separate gearboxes which can be interposed between motor and shaft. With a single propeller, gears are used to allow a larger and more efficient propeller to be driven while still allowing the motor to turn at the rpm giving highest power output or lowest current drain. The gear ratio for a main drive of this type can vary from say $1\frac{1}{2}$ to 1, up to about 3 to 1, and it is rarely necessary to exceed the latter figure unless a very large-scale propeller is to be driven, in which case belt or pulley drive may be a better proposition. With modern propellers, however, it is now uncommon to see single propeller geared drive.

Where two or more propellers are to be driven by one motor, a simple gearbox can be used, and the opportunity may be taken of introducing a reduction.

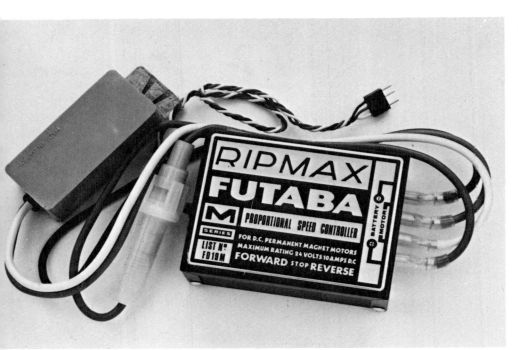

**Above**
Easiest form of electric motor
speed control is one which
plugs straight into the radio

system. This Japanese one will
handle 240 watts, enough for
most motors. *(Courtesy
Ripmax Ltd)*

**Figure 11**

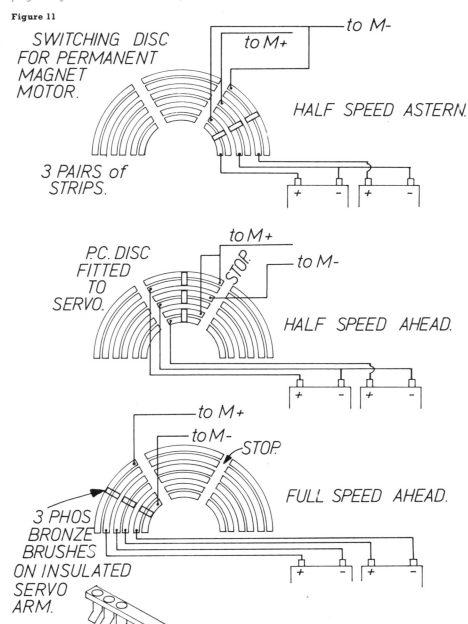

SWITCHING DISC
FOR PERMANENT
MAGNET
MOTOR.

3 PAIRS of
STRIPS.

to M–

to M+

HALF SPEED ASTERN.

+ – + –

P.C. DISC
FITTED
TO
SERVO.

to M+

STOP.

to M–

HALF SPEED AHEAD.

+ – + –

to M+

to M–
STOP.

FULL SPEED AHEAD.

3 PHOS
BRONZE
BRUSHES
ON INSULATED
SERVO
ARM.

+ – + –

A sealed oil-bath box is not really necessary if the gears and shafts are regularly oiled or lightly greased, and the usual practice is to use two brass plates bolted together at the corners with spacing tubes between the plates. After marking out and center popping one plate, the other should be soldered or clamped to it for drilling, to ensure true alignment, and care should be taken to make the spacer tubes square-ended and identical in length. An old trick for marking out was to mesh the gears tightly together with a strip of tissue paper between the teeth, marking through the center holes accurately. The tissue gives just the right degree of clearance. If an idler gear is included (for opposite-handed propellers) it can be smaller and mounted above the other gears, enabling them to be brought close together and reducing the amount by which the motor must be mounted off center.

The size of the gears should be selected so that twin shaft spacing is achieved by five gears (six with an idler) since this produces propeller rotation in the same direction as the motor. Although electric motors can be reversed, they may be manufactured with a slight lead so that they will rotate faster in their intended direction. Gears used can be nylon, brass, steel, etc, depending more on what can be obtained than on the likely loading. For most purposes a gear thickness of $\frac{1}{8}$in (3mm) is the most suitable. A flexible coupling between the motor and drive gear, and the same between driven gears and prop-shafts, produces the likelihood of least losses.

Although an arrangement of bevel gears and cross-shafts can be used for widely spaced prop-shafts, it is probably better to use separate motors on each of the shafts. Any variation between motor speeds, as is not uncommon, can be offset by rudder bias, or the faster motor used on the starboard side to counter the torque effect of the propellers, although this is less noticeable with multi-propeller installations. Independent motor speed control eliminates any problem, and also helps the boat's maneuverability. Long, narrow hulls with scale-size rudders are normally slow-turning, and with twin motors help can be given. The simplest improvement is to arrange for the tiller when hard over to operate a micro-switch which breaks the circuit to the inside motor, stopping it; the obvious development is to switch it astern. Rudder operation remains normal for most of the time, and the inside motor is only affected when full rudder is applied. It is possible with most radios to centralize the trim lever and use full rudder without switching the motor, but when switching is required, it can be achieved by moving the trim lever to the appropriate side, thus giving an extra fraction of movement sufficient to operate the micro-switch.

Twin propellers do not guarantee higher speed *per se*, incidentally, since propeller interaction often reduces the efficiency of both propellers. Some builders have been surprised to find that their model travels as fast on one prop as it does on both. A central propeller with two smaller wing ones further forward is probably the most advantageous layout for scale models, the wing props having an area of hull between them to limit interaction and the center motor being switched off for low speed evolutions.

Motor control can employ an adjustable resistance of some type, which although wasteful, since the resistance dissipates surplus current in heat, is simple to arrange and acceptable when large capacity batteries are carried. Possibilities are a series of switches bringing in car or motorcycle headlamp bulbs, or a sliding contact driven along a length of electric heater element. Microswitches operated by a servo could bring into circuit fixed resistors of, say, 1 ohm and 3 ohms each side of center, or, simplest of all, the servo can be provided with a contact arm which wipes over a piece of circuit board so arranged as to activate a series of circuits, each carrying a different value of resistor which would have to be established by reference to Ohm's law or by experiment.

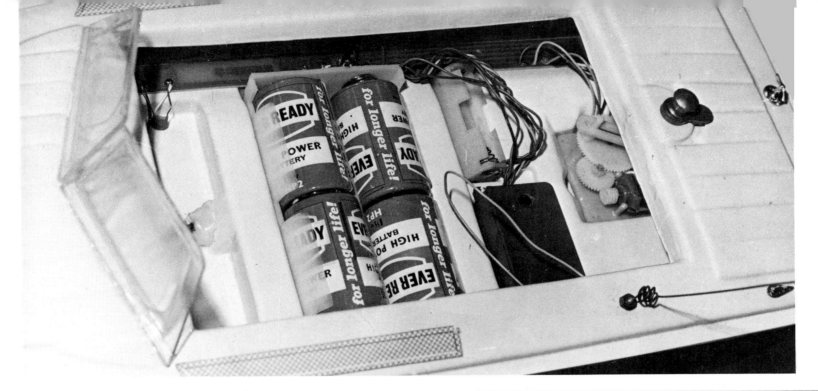

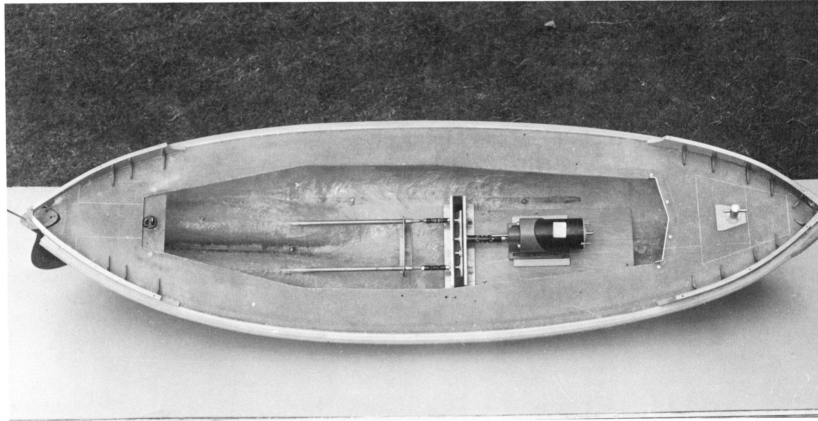

A better and equally simple scheme would be to use a similar circuit board switcher to bring in all or only part of the battery supply; current consumption is approximately proportional to voltage supplied, so that halving the voltage will produce about a quarter of the power, and because hull resistance approximately relates to speed squared, a quarter power will give in the region of half speed. Such a switcher is sketched diagrammatically (Figure 11) providing half astern, stop, half ahead, and full ahead very simply from a conventional servo. The wiring for each function has been separated to make it easy to follow, but in practice duplication can be avoided, for example by fitting short links from the half ahead joints to the half astern strips. The only important point is that the two half batteries should be equal in voltage and capacity, for example, two separate 6v 4a/h lead acids or two

sets each of three 1.2v 1.2a/h nicads. This system is all that most people require for control.

Transistorized proportional controllers may be bought, or circuits have been published in model magazines for those who wish to build their own. These quite sophisticated gadgets give smooth proportional speed control right through from stop to full ahead or astern, normally using a multivibrator circuit which feeds pulses of current to the motor, the pulse duration being controlled by a potentiometer operated by a servo.

Electric power always tends to sound rather technical, but there is really nothing that requires more than basic electrical knowledge and common sense, plus, if possible, the use of an inexpensive multimeter or a voltmeter and an ammeter, and, of course, the ability to make a neat soldered connection.

**Top**
Vacuum-formed tray fitted in commercial model houses battery holders and radio equipment above any water which may have leaked into the boat, and positions everything firmly.

**Above**
Open-frame gearbox driving twin shafts in lifeboat model. Note universal couplings on driving and driven shafts. Light occasional greasing is all that is needed. *(Courtesy J B King)*

# Sailing Models

One truism that applies to all boats, full-size or model, is that they always look a great deal bigger out of the water than when afloat. This seems particularly true in the case of a yacht; a 36in Restricted model, the smallest racing class, looks huge in the living room to someone used to small toyshop yachts, but on the water it appears quite small. It is also true to say that, in general, the bigger the yacht the better it will sail, and the easier it is to sail it properly.

There are experienced sailing enthusiasts who say that nothing under 3ft (915mm) will sail well, but this is not strictly accurate. The longer a yacht's waterline length, the faster it will sail (all other things being proportionate) so that a bigger yacht will sail faster. Both are subject to the same wind and will blow sideways the same distance in the same time, but the bigger, faster yacht will have covered a greater forward distance and therefore has made a better angle to the wind. In other words, it is not necessarily sailing better, just faster. Nevertheless, the first advice to a would-be model yachtsman is do not be under-ambitious–build

and a long thin cylinder with the ends tapered by carving and filing is often used for external ballast on a scale-type hull or along the bottom of a false keel.

Simple molds can be made by cutting out the required shape from blockboard or thick ply and nailing the resulting frame to a backing board. The well thus formed is filled flush and the lead allowed to cool. There is a little charring and, as the lead cools, the exposed surface will hollow slightly with contraction, but it can be planed (lubricated with turpentine) or filed flat. Such flat-sided panels are suitable for screwing to fin keels and do not have any noticeably adverse effect on performance. Some modern racing yachts use ballast with a flat top and bottom rather than flat sides.

More elaborate ballast bulbs of circular or kite shaped cross-section require proper molds. They can be cast in molding sand (see books on foundry work) or, as is usual in modelling, in plaster molds. A carved or turned wood pattern is required, and this should be smoothly finished, painted and polished with wax. A box just large enough to contain it is made, open-topped and split along the horizontal center line. The bottom half is filled with liquid dental plaster or plaster of Paris; the pattern is pressed into it up to its center line; and the plaster is allowed to set. The exposed

**Right**
Scale-type full-keel design with vacuum-formed hull kitted in Germany by Graupner. Rudder pivoted on aft edge of full keel is not used for racing models.

**Left and below**
Casting leads the simple way described, and the leads mounted on the model's fin ready for final cleaning up. Note the slight hollow caused by contraction.

a rather bigger model than you first intended and you will be glad you did.

Perhaps the most off-putting aspect of any sailing model is the need for ballast and the need to use the ballast in a concentrated form, that is, as a casting. In fact casting lead is extremely simple; it requires something in which to melt the lead, a heat source, and a mold of some sort. Lead can be obtained in sheet or pipe form from scrap-metal yards and an old discarded saucepan will suffice for melting. An iron pot is best, but thick aluminium will do for melting up to 15lb (7kg) as long as the handle is secure and strong. An ordinary gas or electric element is quite able to provide the heat but it is worth mentioning that scrap lead may be dirty or greasy, and tends to smell a bit as it is melted.

The mold will depend on the individual model but can often be quite simple. *It must be dry*–this is important, as hot lead hitting even a slightly damp mold will create instant steam which can blow molten lead into the air. If one is casting ballast 'pigs' to place in the bottom of the hull, simple wooden trays are all that is needed; one modeller uses dry housebricks and fills the frogs with lead, giving about 5lb (2¼kg) per pig, for internal ballast in large models. Cylinders can be cast in cleaned scrap iron pipe firmly mounted vertically for pouring,

plaster is now sealed with two or three coats of shellac, and waxed, and the open top of the box stood in place. Keys in the box sides or cut into the set plaster will enable the top to be replaced in exactly the same position later. More plaster is now poured in to cover the pattern. When set, the box top is prised off, complete with the upper half of the plaster mold, and the pattern removed.

A pouring hole should now be cut in the highest part of the mold and fine vent holes drilled through each end to allow air to escape. Extra vent holes halfway between pouring hole and each end may be helpful. The complete mold must now be allowed to dry out thoroughly, either by leaving it on a radiator, in the airing cupboard, or even baking it for half an hour in a low oven.

This procedure would produce a solid casting, and if a slot is required to fit on the fin, this would have to be drilled/sawn/filed in the finished lead. However, a piece of material identical to the fin can be screwed into the mold box and the pattern mounted on it (a loose fit) before pouring the plaster, which saves a lot of work later, since the slot will be cast in.

Cut the lead into pieces with shears or an old pair of scissors in readiness for melting and allow 15–20% extra weight. Drop the lead pieces in the saucepan and heat; once the first few pieces have started to run the rest follows quite quickly. Do not overheat–a stick should just scorch when immersed. Scoop off the dross with an old spoon, or hold it back with a stick while pouring. Wear gloves as the pan handle gets hot, and have the mold standing on a piece of wood or hardboard, ready for the pour immediately after all the lead has melted. Pour steadily and reasonably quickly until lead rises in the pouring hole; some of this will be drawn into the mold as the casting chills round the outside and contracts. Molten lead poured on solidified lead will not bond, so make sure there is enough melted to fill the mold in one pour.

When cool, castings can be cleaned up with a file and any blowholes on the outside filled with an epoxy filler as used for car repairs. Check the weight, which can be reduced by laborious filing or by drilling holes and tapping in dowel to fill them. Lead is naturally greasy so care should be taken to roughen the surface if the casting is to be epoxied in position. One or two fine brass or stainless steel woodscrews are recommended for security, or brass or stainless steel rods can be epoxied in holes that are drilled right through the lead and the fin.

Alternative methods of ballasting are to use a hollow fin and fill it with lead shot or chopped lead, or to mold

**Left**
Patterns and plaster two-piece mold for keel casting. Symmetrical patterns can be turned on a lathe, but otherwise hand carving is necessary.

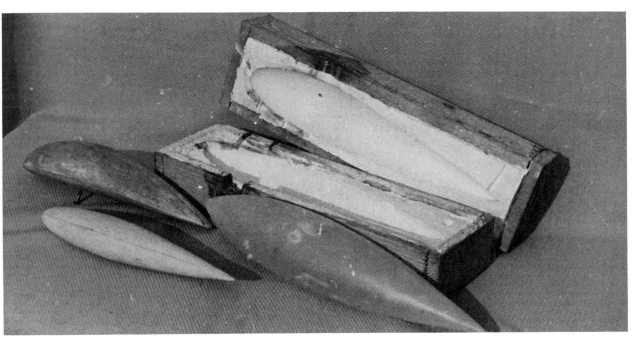

a grp bulb and fill this. Sheet lead can be carefully flattened, sanded and laminated with epoxy to build up the required shape, carving with a sharp knife and filing to finish, then drilling and screwing for security.

Fins for racing yachts are usually made from marine ply or one of the cloth-reinforced laminates such as Tufnol. As a rule they are fixtures, but it is possible to make a ply or grp box in the hull into which the top of the fin slides. A bolt epoxied into the top protrudes through the deck to receive a securing nut. Sometimes part of the fin projects above deck to form a handle, or two bolts are embedded in the fin top and a metal handle engages on these.

Some recent yachts employ a grp fin, or one made from two pieces of melamine-faced plastic, with a metal (usually dural) strut firmly mounted inside the hull and passing down through the fin into the lead, which may be detachable. In the case of A and RA yachts, where the fin is limited in depth by the rules and may include 50lb (23kg) or more of lead, greater thickness is normal, and many boats are fitted with a detachable fin separating just outside the hull. Two screwed rods pass into the hull, often through tubes, and are held by wing nuts. The fin thickness helps to make a firm assembly. This type of fin is traditionally carved to shape, then that portion which is to be lead is sawn away and used to make the mold, the rods being cast into the lead and passed through the remaining timber (called the dead-

wood). Grp shells filled with lead are used quite extensively today, as are bulb keels with massive lead bulbs externally mounted.

The necessity of mounting the fin square, straight and vertical to the hull cannot be overstressed, and its symmetry is also most important. Thick fins tend to be shaped to airfoil sections such as NACA 0018, but thin ones are brought to a sharp leading edge and a finely tapered and sharp trailing edge.

In radio yachts, spade rudders are normal; these are all-moving surfaces with no fixed areas. By using a pivot line giving up to thirty percent of the rudder area ahead of the axis of rotation, the load on the servo is reduced, as the waterstream pushing on the area ahead offsets much of the pressure on the after part of the blade. For other yachts, the rudder is usually hung on a fixed vertical skeg, which increases the directional stability of the boat. The use of a full-keel layout, where the rudder is mounted on the aft edge of the fin, is rarely seen; models have used the fin and skeg arrangement since the 1930s, and it is interesting to see that most new full-size designs are now adopting this layout.

To reduce friction, the tube through the hull (the trunk) is of greater bore than the diameter of the rudder stock, and the rudder is mounted between a pintle secured to the bottom of the skeg and one at deck level, so that it has complete freedom of movement. A spade rudder, however, is equipped with either a close-fitting trunk or a larger tube fitted with bushes top and

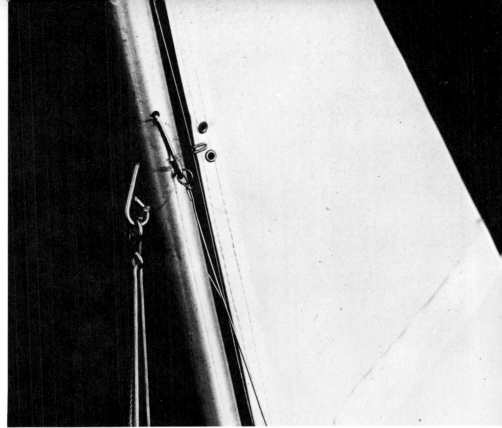

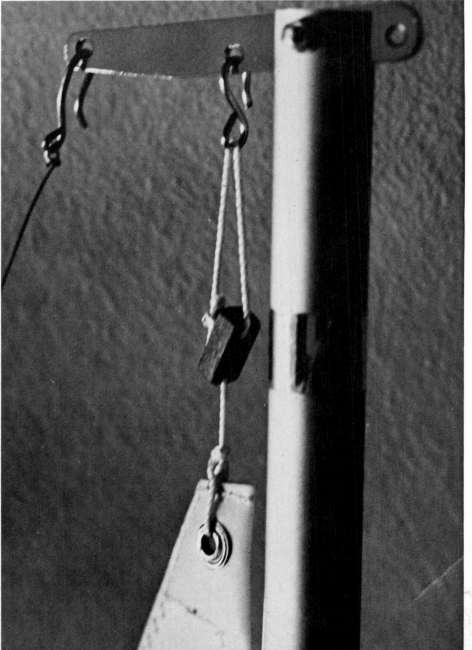

**Above**
Metal tube masts allow simplification of rigging, which can simply hook into drilled holes. Note sail hook formed from opened-out dressmaker's hook riveted in luff hem.

**Left**
The mast-head with jumper strut. The wire is the backstay, and the head of the mainsail is drawn taut by the cord and bowsie uphaul. Note method of reeving bowsie.

**Above right**
End of main boom with internal screwed flow adjuster. Mainsail clew hooks to projecting lug which can be moved fore and aft by turning knurled wheel.

**Right**
Deck stepped mast on an RM yacht. Radio is stowed in waterproof sandwich box. Rotary switch on edge of hatch is to select receiver crystal frequency.

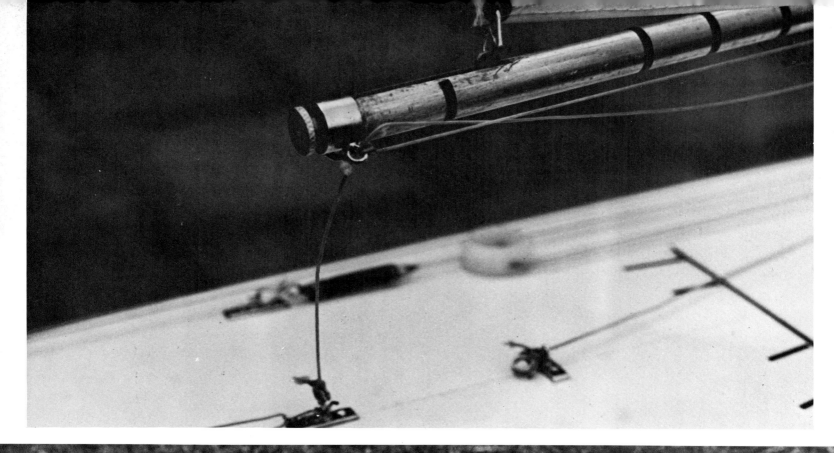

bottom, and it may pass through the deck for an external tiller or terminate above the waterline below deck.

Another major difference with radio models is that a deck-stepped mast is common, whereas other models usually employ a mast step mounted in the hull bottom, the mast passing through a slide at deck level, allowing adjustment of position and rake. The advantage of the latter is that the mast is held rigidly at two points and its shape can be more easily controlled; bends in the mast affect the set of the sails and by adjusting and balancing tension in the rigging, the sails can be made to set perfectly. With a deck-stepped mast, additional rigging, perhaps in the form of diamond stays and angled spreaders, may be needed to achieve the same result, but, on the other hand, by avoiding a mast slide, the main cause of water leakage into the hull is eliminated.

Racing models usually use aluminium alloy tube for masts, though special extruded section can be obtained and wood masts are occasionally seen. The extruded and the wood masts are usually provided with a luff groove, a slot up the after face into which the luff of the sail is drawn. Giving the slot a keyhole section allows a cord in the sail luff hem to lock the sail into the slot. Tube masts normally have a fine wire jackstay secured to them, the sail being fitted with small hooks which engage on the jackstay. Recently the old method of attaching the sail by means of wire rings round the mast has reappeared, probably because this method allows the sail to adopt its correct position more easily when the yacht changes tack in very light winds.

In order to control the sails and set them to maximum efficiency, racing models use booms for both jib and

**Left**
Another RM showing fairly standard control arrangement of above-deck tiller and push-rod, and drum winch with tensioned sheets. Handle is for carrying and lifting out of water.

**Right**
The *Santa Barbara* model which was the first popular one-design radio class in the USA. Hull is 72in (1830mm) long, about R10R size. *(Courtesy Vortex Model Engineering)*

**Below**
Race meetings are run by an Officer of the Day (OOD) who addresses skippers before starting, to advise of any special requirements. This race was for 36R vane yachts.

mainsail which are made from smaller diameter aluminium tube or planed up from wood. Adjustment is provided to vary the length of the foot of the sail by hooking the clew in one of a row of holes, by a screwed adjuster, or perhaps by a cord and bowsie outhaul. This is to increase or decrease the amount of flow (curve) in the sail: the lighter the wind, the greater the flow required. The booms are also provided with kicking straps (called *vangs* in the US) or other means of holding their outer ends down while still allowing them to swing freely. If the outer ends lift too far, air is spilled from the sail or the sail can twist out of shape, much of it adopting an inefficient angle. Pivots for the booms must allow easy swinging through almost 180° and a certain amount of lift in the outer end, more or less a universal joint arrangement. The main boom always has a form of gooseneck which allows this, usually a horizontal pivot pin which engages with a vertical pivot, but the jib can vary from a simple swivel hook to quite elaborate radial fittings, as shown in photographs (opposite center and below).

The sails themselves are normally made from hot-rolled dinghy nylon (or terylene or dacron) and since they provide the power unit of the model, need to be very carefully made. Most racing skippers have their

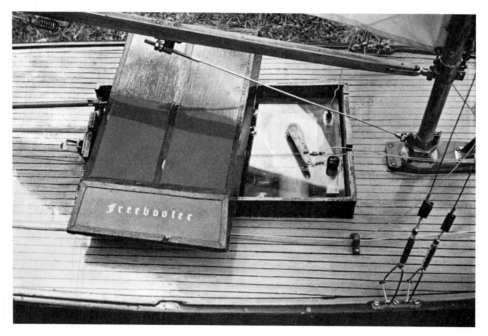

sails made for them by expert sailmakers—an indication of their importance and also the skill required. Cut may vary, but basically if a slight curve is cut into the luff and this is then sewn into a straight folded tape, the sail will have a belly. How much belly and where it is positioned will depend on the degree of curve, the rate of curve, and where the point of maximum curvature occurs. The leach of the sail must be parallel with the selvedge of the cloth—this is vital—and it is essential that the tape and thread used for sewing are as similar as possible to the sail so that any stretch or shrinkage does not wrinkle the sail. The foot of the sail may or may not be taped, but the leach is normally cut with a heated knife or sharpened soldering iron, which seals as it cuts, and does not have a hem or a tape.

Small triangular reinforcement pieces called tablings are stitched into the corners, and tape pockets (to accept thin ply or plastic battens to prevent the leach from curling) are stitched perpendicular to the leach. The number, positions, and lengths of battens allowed are controlled in most rules. In most cases, a curved area is allowed on the leach, called roach, and is unmeasured except for a maximum width from a straight line connecting head and clew. The roach tends to curl, hence the battens. (See Figure 12.)

A headboard, of plastic or metal, is sewn or eyeleted

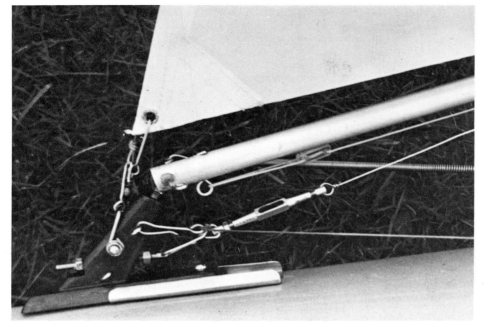

to the head of the mainsail (size limited by rules) though the jib head normally has a plain eyelet. Eyelets are also positioned at the tack and clew of each sail. These bottom eyes slip over fixed hooks or have hooks fixed in them which engage in wire loops or holes in the booms etc. The head eyelet (or headboard) has a short adjustable line so that the luffs may be drawn taut. Hooks may be fitted to the jib luff to engage on a jibstay, or the jibstay may be threaded through the luff tape. This stay must be absolutely taut in order for a model to sail properly, so it needs its own tensioner, and the sail itself needs a separate uphaul to draw it taut in turn.

Basic support for the mast normally involves shrouds, which are a pair of wires from the level of the upper jibstay attachment point down to the deck-edge slightly aft of the mast. These wires together with the jibstay form a trihedron holding the mast upright. A backstay, which can be cord (braided terylene fishing line), runs from the masthead to the hull stern; usually the masthead has a jumper strut to move the backstay far enough aft to clear the roach of the sail. A forestay, from the masthead to the bow, is frequently but not always fitted. Other standing rigging depends on the rigidity of the mast and, to some extent, personal taste.

Turnbuckles, or bottle screws, which consist of a

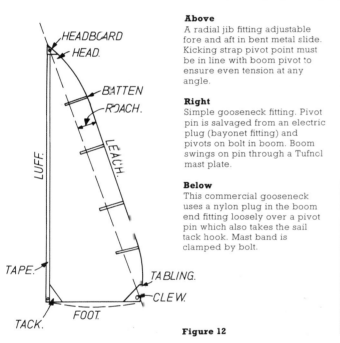

**Above**
A radial jib fitting adjustable fore and aft in bent metal slide. Kicking strap pivot point must be in line with boom pivot to ensure even tension at any angle.

**Right**
Simple gooseneck fitting. Pivot pin is salvaged from an electric plug (bayonet fitting) and pivots on bolt in boom. Boom swings on pin through a Tufnol mast plate.

**Below**
This commercial gooseneck uses a nylon plug in the boom end fitting loosely over a pivot pin which also takes the sail tack hook. Mast band is clamped by bolt.

**Figure 12**

body accepting a left- and right-hand threaded rod so that rotation of the body lengthens or shortens the unit, are usual for the shrouds and the kicking strap(s). Otherwise most adjustments are made with flat or round bowsies, made from, respectively, thick sheet plastic or thick-walled plastic tube. The correct way of reeving a line through these can be seen in the various photographs.

Sheeting lines, controlling the swing of the booms, normally run along each boom and back, finishing in a bowsie; the free end is turned through an eye and ends with a hook. This hook can be engaged in a central eye on the deck or to a traveller (a sliding block) on an athwartship rail called a horse. An alternative arrangement is to position the boom eyes exactly equidistant from their respective boom pivots and to carry the sheets from these eyes through deck eyes directly beneath them to a single large bowsie sliding on a sheeting jackline stretched along the deck aft. Moving this bowsie will allow both booms to swing to the same angle at any position of the bowsie; this system is called synchronous sheeting.

This arrangement is used on the great majority of radio yachts, except that instead of a large bowsie, the sheets feed on to a winch drum operated by the radio, or hook to a plate or an endless line moved by the winch.

In the case of a plate, light elastic tensioning is used to take up any slack when the winch pays out, to avoid any possibility of tangling. An alternative system, used more in the USA than anywhere else, is to attach the sheets to the end of a lever which describes an arc of about a third of a circle in a matter of two to three seconds; the radius of the arm is sufficient to provide the required sheet movement to allow the booms to move from hard in to fully out and, of course, vice versa.

Although the foregoing details are concerned primarily with racing yachts, the basic principles apply to all forms of fore and aft rigged sailing models. Masts and spars might be all wood instead of tube, depending on size; it is better to plane a mast from square timber than to use dowel, especially if the timber has been split from a board so that it is certain that the grain runs straight. Sitka spruce or Oregon pine are excellent for this. Smaller models, too, might have the sails attached by spiral sewing, ensuring that the tension is nicely balanced between too tight and too loose.

Lightweight sailcloth is available, though difficult to buy in ordinary shops. An acceptable substitute is tarantulle, (sometimes called nurses' veiling) or boiled-out draftsman's linen, or in fact any lightweight cotton or linen cloth which is so close woven as to be in effect airproof. As before, the leach must run along the warp (or straight grain) of the material, parallel to the selvedge, and the tape and sewing medium used must match, that is, cotton for cotton, or linen thread for linen, etc. Pre-war sails were made from 'union silk,' which was actually Egyptian cotton, and were sometimes treated with banana oil or other flexible fillers to ensure that air could not pass through.

Square sails are more difficult to rig for easy control and adjustment. They can be spirally sewn to a yard, or hooked to a jackline on the yard using the hook part of the tiniest of dressmakers' hooks and eyes. The yards can be slung with parrels (wire loops threaded all round with tiny beads) and suspended by lifts through tiny holes drilled across the mast above them. Braces to the mast ahead or abaft, or down to the deck aft, can be used to control their angles; cheating a little, yard arms can be linked to those ahead so that adjustment of one yard swings the corresponding one on the next mast. Another way is to secure the clew earings (loops of 'rope' in the bottom corners) to hooks on the yard below, so that when the lowest sail (the course) is turned, the sail above follows. For this to be effective the sails have to be pulled fairly tight which makes them flat, but the model will sail better with the sails rather flatter than might be absolutely correct.

It is not easy to make a square-rig model sail at much less than 90° to the wind unless the square sails are almost all removed or furled and the model sailed on headsails, staysails, and spanker only. Just as in full-size, a barquentine, brigantine, or topsail schooner, with a majority of fore and aft sails, is easier to handle. Though square rig looks magnificent on the water, rerigging to sail to windward and then to leeward is very time-consuming, especially when fingers are cold and wet.

## Sailing

Sailing is a matter of balance and although there are various automatic steering aids and, of course, radio, initial trials and tuning must be carried out with any such devices disconnected or at least inoperative. To achieve maximum efficiency the boat must as nearly as possible sail itself, and tuning is the process of adjustment to bring about this condition.

A pair of vane boats beating to windward in a race at Gosport. These are Marbleheads, far and away the most popular class in both vane and radio worldwide.

**Right**
A German model of the barque *Gorch Fock* showing an increase in keel area for greater stability and better sailing. Also has auxiliary electric motor and is carrying full staysails.

**Below**
R10R models approaching the starting line. Six or seven boats are normal in Europe, but up to 13 are raced together in USA. Fewer boats mean less confusion, Europeans feel.

**Left**
Nice scale appearance of the biggest of the Graupner vacuum-formed hull kits, the 41in (1040mm) *Optimist* which, though non-class, makes a pleasing radio yacht.

**Below**
Attractive little scale sailing brig. Absence of main course (lowest sail on second mast) is probably to balance sail plan and would have little effect on overall speed.

**Bottom**
Topsail schooners make a good compromise between having square sails while retaining the better performance of fore and aft rig. This model has radio control.

Any vessel under sail will make leeway, ie, it will be blown downwind, and its resistance to sideways motion concentrates on a particular point, the center of lateral resistance. Wind pressure on the sail plan concentrates on the center of effort, and it is not difficult to see that if the center of effort (CE) is ahead of the center of lateral resistance (CLR), as the boat moves sideways, the bow will be blown round away from the wind. Similarly, if the CE is behind the CLR, the stern will be blown round until the model faces into wind and stops sailing. Balancing the opposing effects of these two centers is best done with the boat sailing as close to the wind as possible consistent with reasonable speed, on a course termed a beat.

Considering first a yacht which has only two sails and is therefore simpler, the rudder should be wedged amidships (a piece of rubber under the tiller?) and the sails set at about 8–10° to the center line. The boat should now be held at about 40° to the wind and examined from astern. Adjust the kicking straps until the sail leaches form matching curves, and set the sheeting lines so that the jib is at a fractionally greater angle—say 8° on the main boom and 10° on the jib. Place the boat afloat in the center of the downwind bank of the lake, point it about 40° to the wind, and ease it gently away. Ideally a steady breeze of 6–7mph (9–11kph) is needed.

Watch the boat carefully to see whether it comes up to the wind or falls off. The reason for a movable mast will now be obvious: if the boat bears away from the wind the mast can be moved aft a notch; if it comes up to the wind, shakes, drifts and pays off, starts to sail, and comes up again, the mast can be moved forward a notch. Try it again, and try it on the opposite tack, adjusting until there is just the faintest tendency for it to turn towards the wind, but it never quite does so. This is the mast position required, and it should be marked carefully.

A scale-type model is unlikely to have movable masts, and so the sailplan must be adjusted until the balance is achieved, or the area of the false keel can be modified to move the CLR. To achieve this latter modi-

Radio Marbleheads (RMs)
racing. These particular boats
are well spread out, but tight
bunching is not uncommon;
knowledge of the rules and
quick reflexes then count.

fication a few trimmings of plastic card, scissors, and a roll of plastic insulation tape should be carried. Discovering how the area of the keel should be altered in this way enables a more permanent job to be made back in the workshop before the next outing. It is better to have the visual effect of the full sailplan and adjust the CLR, since appearance on the water is one of the primary incentives for building such a model.

Sailing courses are divided into three general groups, the beat (towards the wind), reach (across wind) and run (downwind), with modifications to the basic terms (close beat, free beat, close reach, free reach) to indicate more precise courses where necessary. Fore and aft sail settings vary from boom angles of 5° or 6° to the center line on a close beat, to perhaps 40° on a full reach and through to nearly 90° for a full run. When sailing, one must always be aware of the precise wind direction, or the mean direction if the wind is swinging or curling round local obstructions using observation of flags, smoke, and any other indicator which may be convenient. Many radio skippers use a light tell-tale on the masthead to show the direction of the wind affecting the model, which may be

**Left**
A pair of Marbleheads leaving the bank simultaneously having both been retrimmed. In a close race such as this a fraction of an inch in adjustment can win or lose.

**Bottom left**
The topsail schooner from page 135 has a false keel and low-mounted ballast, as can be discerned here. Copper plating is reproduced.

**Right**
Using the pole to turn a vane boat. There are a few lady model power boat or yacht enthusiasts and in most cases they are very competent and competitive.

**Below**
Very few scale sailing kits are available, but an attractive one is the *Emma C Berry* schooner, 49½in (1257mm) which is suitable for radio. *(Courtesy Sterling Models Inc)*

different from that felt by the skipper himself on the bank.

A major difference between free-sailing racing yachts and other sailing models is that spinnakers are used for running. A spinnaker is a sail extending from a boom rigged to the mast, on the opposite side to the main boom, right across the boat to a sheet-line attachment on the opposite side, and usually up to the jib-hoist. For light winds spinnakers are enormous, heavily curved sails (sometimes called bags of wind) made in very light polythene sheeting, which may more than double the sail area of the yacht. For stronger winds, heavier polythene or sail cloth may be used, and the sails get progressively smaller. When the wind is quartering rather than dead behind, flatter spinnakers are used.

With this extra sail, speeds can be very high, the yacht often planing in a fresh wind and requiring skill and timing to stop it before it crashes into the lee bank of the lake. With the wind behind, the high center of effort of the sails tends to push the bow of the boat under, which is a first step towards broaching (slewing suddenly sideways, out of control) but a spinnaker can be so rigged as to lift the bow. So far no practical method of rigging and striking a spinnaker by radio control has been evolved, and radio yachts are not therefore as fast on the run as free-sailers; they also can be troubled by bow burying, cures for which can adversely affect performance on other courses.

Burying the bow–or the lee bow–is a considerable problem with model catamarans and other multi-hulls, as, indeed, it is in full-size. Catamarans can be fast, with their narrow hulls and light weight (keel ballast is not strictly necessary) but apart from small fun models they have never really caught on in the model world. Plans and kits for models up to about 40in (1m) are available, but efforts to establish an official racing class have failed due to lack of adequate support.

A fundamental rule for sailing vessels which is not always understood is that the course of the vessel is (or should be) decided by the sails, and the rudder is only used for minor course corrections or major changes of course. The drag created by the rudder when applied is tantamount to putting the brakes on on a bicycle, hence the importance of tuning the model to sail without the influence of the rudder.

### Steering Gears

Methods of applying small course corrections have exercised the minds of model skippers for well over a century. The established technique for many years was to use a weighted rudder, or a selection of differently weighted rudders according to wind strength. A yacht

**Below**
The simplest form of vane steering gear fitted on a 20in *Wind Rider*. Black object is the sheeting bowsie for synchronous sheeting, made from a glue tube screw cap.

**Bottom**
Six RM yachts at the start line. Boat on left has been forced the wrong side of the buoy and must turn and start again. Lake is at Gosport.

**Right**
Lunch break. Skippers enjoy a chat over sandwiches during a breather in a race. Yachts are Marbleheads.

would be trimmed with a tendency to come up into wind, but its heel caused the rudder to drop and apply helm to turn the boat off the wind. With skill and experience, a balance could be struck. In a lull, the heel came off and the yacht was then free to luff up, but by sheeting in the jib (or one of the jibs, since there were often two) harder than the main, the head of the boat could be forced round as the mainsail lost its drive.

This was not the most efficient way to sail, and in the early 1900s George Braine invented the quadrant steering gear which bears his name. Sailing to weather (beating) was carried out on sail balance alone, but for reaching and running, the mainboom sheet was led across the deck to a pulley and returned to hook into a quadrant attached to the rudder stock. An essential part of the method was an adjustable elastic tensioner on the tail of the quadrant tending to hold it central; the sheet hook could be engaged in any of a series of holes drilled along the fore edge of the quadrant. Thus sail pull could be balanced against centering tension for any wind strength and corrective rudder would be applied the instant that the pressure on the sail eased or increased, either by the boat being deflected off course or by a lull or gust in the wind.

There were some refinements developed, but the basic principle of Braine gear remained in use for around fifty years. In the 1930s, however, vane gear came to the fore, and within a few years had superseded Braine. The vane principle had occurred to famous American full-size designer Nat Herreshoff in 1875, but he did not use it until 1925 when he was experimenting with models after his retirement. The first identified vane was published in *Model Engineer* in 1903, but not until a vane was used by a Norwegian entrant in a major international race in Britain in 1935 were its advantages perceived. Much of the early development took place in the USA during World War II, but within a few years of the resumption of sailing in Europe most boats were equipped with this type of automatic steering.

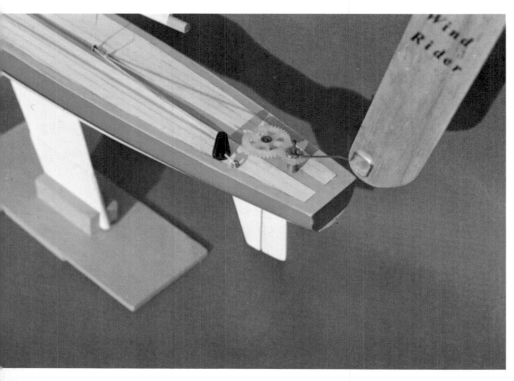

there are on the gear, the more accurate can be the setting, but this simple mechanism will add a new dimension to sailing a small yacht, even if courses must be in 10° steps.

More usually the vane feather is adjustable by friction in relation to a pivoted block or bar which carries an arm engaging with a fore-and-aft tiller, so that wind on the feather moves the block and, by means of the extension arm, the tiller. Complications arise when other functions are incorporated in the mechanism, the most important one of which is self-tacking. A vane yacht beats to weather in a series of tacks, being turned by pole as it comes into each bank, but with vane steering it would be necessary to stop the boat to reset the vane each time. The answer is to place the feather on a secondary pivot and provide independent beating stops, so

The principle is simple and uses a light flat vane feather, usually made of balsa, which can be friction-adjusted through a full circle, and which is linked to the rudder. The yacht is placed in the water pointing in the required direction and the feather moved till it is aligned edge-on to the wind. Now when the boat is released, should it turn away from the desired heading, one side of the feather will be presented to the wind and it will be subjected to a force tending to blow it straight. This moves the linkage and applies rudder to turn the boat back on course. The boat will therefore sail a constant course in relation to the wind; if the wind changes direction, so will the yacht.

Perhaps the easiest way to grasp this is to study the very simple Draper gear photographed. Here a gear wheel is secured to the rudder stock and has a very light elastic centering line attached. The vane feather is epoxied to a second gear wheel engaging with the first and rotating on a pivot long enough to allow it to be lifted out of engagement. The feather wheel can thus be lifted and turned to line up the feather, then dropped back into mesh. Any light force on the feather will then rotate its gear, in turn rotating the rudder gear and correcting the boat's course. Obviously the more teeth

**Above**
A self-tacking breakback vane gear. Rubber bands are part of the gying system and pivoted lever (center top) is the lock. Knurled wheels on curved rod are self-tacking stops.

**Left**
A moving carriage vane gear which incorporates sun and planet gears. It all looks very complicated, but is simple to use once the purpose of all the gadgets is understood.

that while the block remains central, the feather is perhaps at a 30° angle and can still move the block positively one way and, by the geometry, gently the opposite way. Strong movement, such as changing tack, will allow the feather to swing over to the opposite stop and provide control on that tack. For reaching or running, the feather arm is locked central.

The ability to exercise control on either tack leads to the gye. If a light rubber band with adjustable tension and leverage is hooked on one side of the unlocked vane, the boat can be put off on one tack and will sail until a lull or a wave allows it to decrease its angle of heel, at which point the rubber will take effect, snapping the vane over, and the boat will gye, that is, change tack and sail back to the bank it had just left. How far it sails before this happens depends on wind strength and

rubber tension and leverage, plus other factors such as angle of heel, wave height, etc, so that nice judgment is required to make it happen exactly where it is wanted. Gying can be tactically advantageous in a race where the wind is angled across the lake and the yachts are sailing long and short legs, and it is also very useful if one is practising sailing single-handed.

At first, a vane gear looks extremely complicated, largely because of the self-tacking and gying additions, but once its functions are understood, it can be seen to be a straightforward and clever mechanism. Full-size self-steering mechanisms are simplified versions. Chichester spent time with a model yacht club before making the one he used on his round-the-world voyage, which set rather a fashion for them on single-handed yachts.

**Right**
Lever type sail control units are widely used in American R/C yachts. Jib and main sheet can go to one end or opposite ends. Servo or self operating.
*(Courtesy Sail Engineering)*

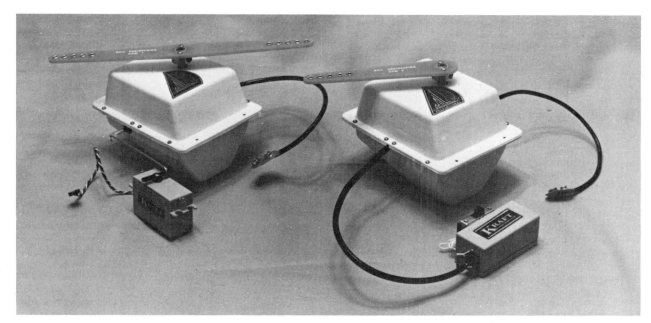

**Below**
When the wind gets fresh, stopping a boat weighing 60lbs or more (30kilos) can be difficult. If it hits the concrete it can be wrecked, so. . . .
*(Courtesy J Browne)*

# Painting and Finishing

Rushing the last stages of a model to get it finished is the surest way of spoiling it; painting can take almost as long as building and requires at least as much patience and care. Good results can be achieved in many ways, but all of them take time and any can be affected by trying to cut corners or to save money. Expenditure at this stage is relatively small once a basic set of tools has been acquired, tools being good quality brushes and/or a reasonable spray outfit. A bad job can be done with good equipment, but it is very hard to do a good job with bad equipment.

Whether to brush or spray depends a lot on personal attitude as well as the job in hand. Either can produce a top-class result, but for large areas (in terms of models) it is probably easier to get a good result by spraying. On the other hand, it could be difficult to spray small details. Some paints lend themselves to spraying, while others are better brushed, and there is little doubt that spraying is more expensive, both in the amount of paint and solvents used, not to mention the initial outlay. Perhaps a resumé of materials likely to be used is the most useful starting point.

*Primers* are specially formulated, usually thin paints designed to bond more strongly to the natural surface being treated than the fuller-bodied paints proper. Different ones are produced for metal and wood, and the vehicles may differ in either case but are usually

cellulose or oil based. It is very important that all the various preparations are compatible—oil paint may be used over cellulose bases, but most paints other than oil will attack oil bases.

*Sealer and fillers* may be similar to primers, applied over or sometimes instead of them, and containing chalk or similar inert powders which help to fill or bridge cracks. Frequently oil undercoats have sufficient body to fill grain etc, but cellulose paints are thin and need a sealed surface. The most familiar to modellers is probably cellulose sanding sealer which is easy to apply, rapid drying, and easy to sand; however, while cellulose will bond to it because of the solvent, oil paints will not. Better sealers for an oil finish are either gold-size (available from art shops) mixed with powdered whiting or thinned undercoat into which is mixed filler powder as used in home decorating; either of these will provide a non-greasy surface. Large gaps or depressions are best filled with one of the two-part epoxy pastes as used for car body repairs.

*Cellulose paints and lacquers* are not extensively used in model ships and boats mainly because for non-working models they are not easy to apply by brush and for working models they do not appear to be so abrasion-resistant as other paints, especially over wood surfaces. Their very quick-drying time means that they must be flowed on with a brush, and if they are thin

enough to dry without brush marks, several coats are needed to produce reasonable density and thickness. They are, however, ideal for spraying, and a wide assortment of colors is available in aerosol cans at car accessory suppliers. Celluloses are hard and excellent for rubbing down and polishing. Thin and clean brushes only with cellulose thinners.

*Oil paints and enamels* are best suited to brush application, though enamels are available in aerosol cans and can be used in a spray gun. Either can be obtained in glossy, eggshell, or matt finish, and should be applied over oil undercoat. Some of the 'one-coat' paints tend to dry in a film which does not bond very strongly to an undercoat. For rubbing down, even the quick-drying types are best left for 24 hours. Always strain part-used tins of finish paint. Thin and clean brushes with white spirit (turpentine substitute) or clean brushes in gasoline.

*French polish and button polish* are basically shellac crystals dissolved in methylated spirit, and can be used for spars and superstructures. They are usually applied with cotton wool, though initial coats can be brushed. Sufficient coats are applied to bare wood to fill the grain and bring the surface to a smooth luster. Clean up with methylated spirits.

*Polyurethane paint* may be one liquid with a fairly low resin content, or two-pot, to be mixed, with high

145

**Below**
The importance of crisp edges
to superstructure parts and
details is demonstrated in a
model such as this. That '5,'
however, does not look right
for a naval vessel.

resin content. They do not normally need a filler or undercoat, but successive coats are applied and rubbed down until grain etc disappears. The two-pot type is infinitely superior, though fairly expensive and not usually available in very small packs. Excellent for rubbing down and polishing, it produces a very hard, fuel-proof and abrasion-resistant surface. It should not be applied over oil bases and is good for either brushing or spraying. Thin and clean up with special thinners of same brand.

*Epoxy paints* come as a paint and hardener, requiring mixing. They are quick-drying and are best sprayed (avoid inhalation) but can be brushed if the ambient temperature is not above about 18°C, otherwise drying is too quick to allow brush marks to flow out. Very tough and totally fuel-proof, this type of paint is not cheap but is available in model-size quantities. Needs its own thinners, and can be applied only over cellulose bases or its own grainfiller.

*Acrylic paints*, sold by art shops for artists' paintings, can be applied very thinly but are very dense. They are water-based resins, so that brushes can be washed in water, but once dry they are waterproof. For small deck details they are excellent, providing one-coat coverage without obscuring detail. Different makes dry to different finishes, from a slight gloss to completely matt. Suitable for plastics, metal, card, close-grained woods and so on.

*Water colors* are sometimes used for miniature models, because they can be worked with a brush damped in water to achieve desired effects and varying depths of color and opacity, again without filling or filleting detail.

*Other paints*—emulsion, poster paints, inks etc may very occasionally have an application in non-working subjects; Indian ink is sometimes used for lining decks, but needs to be varnished over.

*Varnishes* used are usually oil type or polyurethane; the former is available in gloss or eggshell and the latter is available in gloss, eggshell and matt. Experience has shown that either type can safely be used over any other painted surface, except possibly two-pot polyurethane (which however is the best choice for a bright varnish finish).

*Fuel proofers* are generally similar to one-pot polyurethane varnish, are available in gloss or matt, and usually can be safely applied over other finishes.

Where there is any doubt in a builder's mind, one

**Left**
Flash bloom on this model of
HMS *Victory* reveals just the
right surface–not completely
matt, but not glossy. Wet shiny
patches should, however, be
shown in a sea setting.

**Below**
Tiny detail such as that
magnificently reproduced on
the torpedo tubes of this
destroyer model can very
easily be ruined by clogging
up with paint.

**Bottom**
Matt paints look absolutely
right on this model. Rivets on
cowl vents and tank are PVA
glue applied with a hypodermic
syringe; these and deck texture
could easily be spoiled by bad
painting.

147

or two test pieces can be prepared; they need only be scraps of ply and are painted stage by stage with the model. Departures from normal can then be tried in advance to check that there are no ill effects, rather than ruining the work already put in on the model.

Brushes should be of the best quality you can find; although they are expensive, with a little care they will last for years and do a good job every time. Never begrudge an adequate amount of time and solvent to clean them thoroughly. Professionals usually grease

brushes after cleaning, and smooth them into shape, washing the grease out in an eggcup of gasoline and drying the brush immediately before further use. The best brushes are usually sable hair, and writing brushes are better for general model purposes than water-color mops.

Good spray results can be obtained with an inexpensive spray gun using a can of propellant gas or even with expensive aerosol spray cans, but for top class work a good quality gun with a small compressor is desirable. Cellulose and epoxies are better sprayed, but whatever paint is used, make certain that the gun is thoroughly cleaned with the appropriate solvent. Whether to invest in a spray gun is a decision influenced by personal attitudes and the amount of model-building one does.

Functional models are invariably finished in high gloss, miniatures and smaller non-working subjects in matt. There are differing opinions for working scale and larger non-working models as to whether gloss, eggshell, or matt finish should be used. One view states that the prototype would be painted with gloss paint and the opposite claims that a ship seen at a short distance does not glitter. Close acquaintance over many years with judging panels at national and international level leads the author to recommend the following. Large-scale models (1/10 or 1/12) of highly finished prototypes such as luxury motor cruisers may reasonably be glossy. For large glass-case models and working models of merchant vessels etc over about 48in (1225-mm) in length, eggshell (semi-matt) is acceptable; all other models, including all warships, should be matt.

Two objections to matt paint for a working model are that it does not wear well and that it is much more easily fouled by operation on a dirty lake; most lakes have an area where the wind has propelled floating debris and decaying vegetation. The answer is to coat the hull with thin matt polyurethane varnish, which is harder than matt paint and thus resists wear better and is easier to wipe clean.

The secret of a good finish with any paint is thorough preparation of the surface to be painted—this can be messy and time-consuming in the case of wood construction in particular. First the bare wood must be sanded to a first-class finish and dusted off; often the fingers will detect a bump or other irregularity at this stage better than the eye. Any pronounced gaps or cracks should be filled and, for oil paint, a coat of primer applied. This can be lightly rubbed down with fine garnet paper or carborundum paper (about no 240) used dry, then two or three coats of undercoat applied and allowed to dry hard.

A bucket of water, a sponge, and a supply of wet-or-dry carborundum paper are now needed, as the hull is rubbed down wet and sponged off frequently. The shine of the wet hull will help to show irregularities, and the paint will wear through on high spots. Wiping the paper on an old bar of soap will help to prevent it becoming choked with paint particles, and swishing it in the water will clean most of them away. Leave the hull to dry thoroughly, then rub over lightly dry with a piece of worn wet-or-dry, to remove any fuzz or proud grain, and undercoat again. Rub down, and repeat until a flawless surface exists. Try to ensure a dust-free atmosphere for the finish coat—no wind, and no one entering the room while the paint is left to dry. Just before the final coats wipe the hull over with a lint-free cloth dampened with turpentine or a painter's tack rag to remove any dust from it. Use a reasonable size and perfectly clean brush and follow the paint manufacturer's recommendations, but remember that two coats applied adequately but sparingly will produce a better result than one thick coat.

In the case of cellulose, sanding sealer can be used and rubbed down dry; when satisfied with the surface, go over it with a tack rag or cloth dampened (not too wet) with thinners. If brushing on the finish, apply the color without brushing back over more than is essential, and apply two or three coats. If an oil enamel is to be used over the sealer, use a turpentine dampened rag to remove dust and reduce the slightly greasy feel.

Polyurethanes and epoxies are usually used directly

**Left**
Warships are often thought of as a drab gray, but in fact they can have quite a lot of color. Modern ships often have green or brick-red decks which contrast well with gray.

**Below**
More color. The blue and green of this tug are authentic and quite different from the usual tug colors. In the foreground, a naval steam picket boat shows how bright some service craft can be.

**Left**
A corvette model by Tom Andrews being demonstrated at a Model Engineer Exhibition. Rust-stained and salt-caked, the model also shows battle scars.

**Below**
Close-up of the corvette. One naval visitor commented that with the ship in that condition, the first mate would be carpeted, but the model gave other builders many ideas for realism.

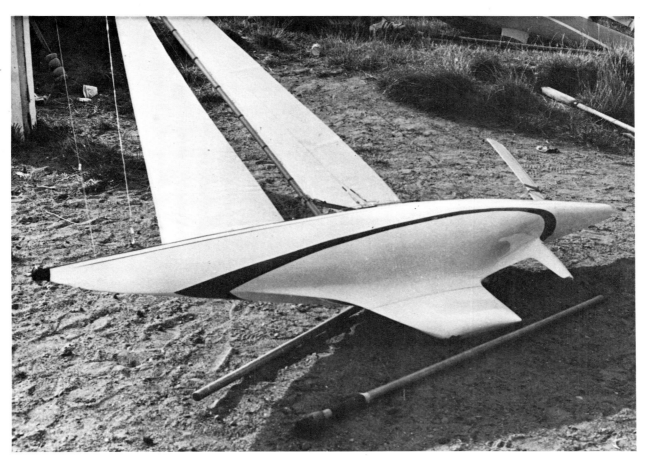

**Left**
Waterline stripe on an A Class model, showing the widening which occurs as the hull angle shallows at the ends. Marking out is just a question of two lines rather than one.

**Overleaf left**
A straight-running liner model (Class EH), the *Kaiser Wilhelm der Grosse*, demonstrates the importance of alignment of masts etc. Out-of-true masts are surprisingly common.

**Overleaf top right**
This aircraft carrier model was planked with 1/16in (1.5mm) ply panels over a basic frame, but such a method leads to angular lines requiring extra work to fair. Full-length narrow planks are recommended.

**Overleaf bottom right**
Fine F2B (radio scale) model of *Ruhr* by G Rudolph of West Germany, photographed at a European Championship where this boat placed second in the class.

onto bare wood, applying sufficient coats (and rubbing down between) to fill the surface. Specially produced filler and undercoating are available from some makers.

Where a grp hull is to be painted, it should be lightly sanded all over with the finest grade of paper available to give the surface a key, and it should then be wiped off with thinners, a fairly wet cloth in this case, to ensure complete removal of any wax or release agent. No undercoat should be necessary, and polyurethane or epoxy are the best paints to use, though oil enamel or cellulose will produce a satisfactory result. Spraying is likely to be better than brushing. Styrene hulls have been discussed, but again, polyurethane, epoxy, or enamel is recommended and cellulose should be avoided. Plastic kit models (polystyrene) are best painted with enamels or acrylics, and certainly never cellulose.

Time and weight can be saved with balsa or other open-grain timber by applying a layer of model aircraft tissue to the bare wood using clear cellulose dope or even sanding sealer as an adhesive. This covers the grain and bonds the surface fibers together; producing a tougher surface and one requiring fewer subsequent coats of paint to fill. Where small balsa deckhouses etc are used, covering with thin card will produce crisper corners and a grain-free surface which is much easier to paint.

Gloss finish coats when allowed to get completely hard can be polished with crocus paper (using soap), liquid metal polish, or even toothpaste or powdered whiting on a damp cloth. Any of these treatments will tend to dull the surface, but two or three coats of furniture wax and plenty of buffing will bring a deep lustrous shine. It takes time and patience, but the result is worth it. The same procedure can be followed with unpainted grp. Naturally, wax should not be used until all painting is completed.

Most hulls require a waterline or boot-topping, and marking this puzzles some beginners. The requirement is a large flat area, giving space all round the model, and a means of holding the hull steady. Yachts with fins are usually chocked upside down, and this

can be helpful with a ship hull, though not completely necessary. The waterline endings are marked at stem and stern, by measurement from the plan or if necessary by eye, and the hull blocked up so that it is firmly held with the marked points at exactly equal heights from the work top. A soft sharp pencil is now mounted, either rubber-banded or stapled, on a fair size block of timber, the pencil preferably angled downward, slightly, and with the point exactly on the stem mark. If the hull is right way up, it should be angled upwards. Now by sliding the block round the model, a pencil line will be drawn right round at constant height.

The reason for angling the pencil will be apparent when the stern is reached. Some builders make a slight indentation with the pencil point, every two or three inches, to give a more permanent guide, the indentations being hard to see unless their presence is known.

**Above**
The arrow-headed effect of a king-plank into which curved deck planks are joggled shows up on this yacht. Note the neat boom markings and spinnaker boom rigged.

Normally the lighter paintwork of the hull is finished first and taken down to just below the approximate waterline, which is then marked on. Masking is applied over the finished color, exactly up to the marked line. The safest masking is gummed paper tape which will have to be soaked off, but unless oil paints have been used over cellulose sanding sealer, no difficulty should arise if clear Scotch tape (cellotape) is used. Proper masking tape can be bought, and it is easier to negotiate curves with this, but care must be taken to see that its edge is sealed down firmly; it has a rather wrinkled surface, and paint can creep up under the wrinkles. Clear tape can be positioned over the pencilled line and a sharp blade run lightly along the line, the surplus tape then being peeled off. For spraying, paper should be trapped under the far edge of the tape to shield finished paintwork.

The overlap of finished paint should be carefully rubbed down, both to key it and ensure that no hard edge remains, and the painting completed. Leave the paint until touch dry before peeling off the tape, or until fully dry if gummed paper has to be soaked off. Any paint which may have crept under the edge of the tape can usually be softened with a touch of solvent on a fine brush and wiped away with a clean cloth.

A colored boot-topping line separating the hull top-side color and the bottom color will need masking at top and bottom after the other paints are dry, but the procedure is the same. Where the hull makes a shallow angle to the water, for example under the stern, a boot-top line will widen considerably, but this is produced automatically by the method of marking out described.

When considering color schemes and painting procedures, the treatment of the deck must be an early consideration. If it is to be natural varnished wood or stained with a water or spirit stain and then varnished, this must be done before any paint is applied to the hull topsides. Otherwise paint tends to encroach on the bare deck edge and cannot be completely removed. If a painted waterway or cover board is to be used, it is not quite so important.

Decks can be planked with separate strips, and indeed have to be, if marked compound curves exist, or they can be false-planked with veneer planks laid on a ply deck. Frequently, however, planking is represented by pencil or ink lines, especially where only part of a deck is planked, the remainder being steel or one of the mastic anti-slip surfaces. Full-size planks are

usually caulked with a black bitumastic or similar compound, but the caulking is not likely to be more than about ½in (1.27cm) wide. Thus even in a ¼in (1/48th) scale model, lines representing it should not be more than about 1/100th of an inch (.025mm) or the

effect will be rather overpowering. This can be improved by using, say, charcoal instead of full black, especially if the plank color itself is light.

On large ships the planks run fore and aft and are butt-joined over frames, the butts being staggered though often symmetrical. The plank ends may lodge on a flange on a steel waterway, giving a curved line round the deck-edge, a scale 9–12in (23–30cm) in from the edge, or a curved plank may be sawn to fit round the edge and the planks joggled into it (see Figure 13). Joggling involves cutting the end of a plank square at about one third of its width and cutting a taper back to leave full width where the next plank ends; the sketch explains it. Small luxury vessels may have the planks laid to the curve of the gunwale, the ends joggling into a straight central king plank. Around hatches or cabins etc appears a constant-width plank, mitered at the corners, the main planking butting to this.

To reproduce a planking pattern, first stain the deck as necessary, remembering that varnishing will darken it; it is worth practising on a scrap of the same material. Apply two coats of varnish (matt–decks are not glossy) and rub down with fine wet-or-dry. Try a pencil mark and check that it can easily be rubbed off with an eraser, if not, apply more varnish. Now pencil in the pattern (a simply-made gauge like a miniature T-square is useful for drawing curved planks) and when satisfied, ink in using a draftsman's pen and ink. Slips can be eased off with a sharp knife point. Allow to dry,

**Figure 13**

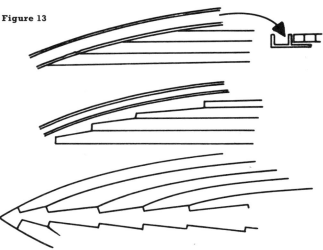

then add two more coats of varnish. For functional models, a glossy varnish is acceptable, but otherwise use matt.

It is advisable to paint deckhouses and fittings before finally securing in place in order to get an absolutely clean separation of color, unless you are very good with a brush or are proposing to dirty a scale model to give an authentic air of use. Spraying dirty thinners (turps for an oil-painted model) over it all is a good start, since this adds a patina which deepens in corners which might be expected to be grimy. Signs of rust and wear can be applied with paint on a brush or on a piece of fairly dry sponge. Producing a convincing model requires imagination and artistry, but the result when well done has much more character than a bandbox-fresh vessel which looks too good to be true.

For any painting of a model, look at other models at the local pond, club exhibitions, museums etc and study them carefully with a critical eye. See what mistakes are made, where sub-standard work shows, and make sure you do not fall into the same traps. For scale modellers, take every chance of studying full-size vessels and envisage yourself painting a model of one. Photographs and a notebook help in recording colors of detail parts, and it is often authenticity of detail painting that adds that 'touch of class' to a model. Above all, remember that your paintwork can only be as good as the surface beneath, and that matt paints require just as good a surface as glossy ones.

# Radio Control

Model radio control has been with us since the 1920s, when a spark transmitter and a coherer receiver were used. The 'coherer' referred to a tray of iron filings which formed into lines on receipt of a radio signal, thus being able to pass a current. It was a crude form of remote control switch, in other words. It was necessary to have a clockwork or electrically driven tapper which tapped the tray every second or so to break up the lines of filings ready for the next signal.

The first commercially made R/C equipment, around 1950, was in principle just a remotely controlled switch; the control exercised over a model depended on the ingenuity with which the current through this single

**Right**
One of the most inexpensive transmitters uses a plug-in crystal on the front of the case (bottom right). Pair of crystals shown with cigarette in front.

**Far right**
Case must be opened to change crystal in many transmitters (yellow tag lower left). Receiver crystal accessible through watertight hatch in radio box.

**Below**
Sliding hatch is fairly waterproof for functional models. Rx and batteries in box on port side, servos for throttle and rudder to starboard. Tube in center is water-cooling feed.

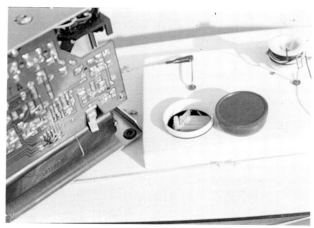

switch was used. Soon reed and filter equipment followed, giving effectively up to six separate switches which could be selected at will and as a result much more comprehensive control, but it was not until the mid-1960s that sets became generally available giving the opportunity of operating more than one model at a time. It seems remarkable to recall that transistors were not widely known when the early sets appeared, and valves (tubes) were standard for the first few years.

Present-day radio is almost exclusively fully proportional—that is, control movement at the model is precisely proportional to the movement of the transmitter control sticks—and crystal controlled, giving the opportunity of operating at least six models simultaneously. Controls available vary from one function (eg. rudder) to, usually, a maximum of six functions, each with trimming adjustment. But in most boats, two functions are normal. In a power boat these are for rudder and motor speed, and in a sailing model, rudder and sail sheeting.

The range of model radio equipment is normally not less than $1\frac{1}{2}$ miles ($2\frac{1}{2}$km) but so long a range is, for normal models, no more than a safety factor, since at distances greater than say 250yd (228m) it becomes

**Top far left**
The radio installation in a yacht in which the winch, tiller mechanism etc is all below deck. Absence of radio waterproofing indicates faith in watertightness of model!

**Far left**
A freelance oil rig tender which includes among its functions the ability to pump water through its fire monitors. Demonstration on an indoor swimming pool.

157

impossible to see clearly what a model is doing, particularly whether it is heading away from or towards the operator. It is rare for a boat to travel much more than 100yd from the transmitter.

Power supply is usually 9–12v for the transmitter and 6v for the receiver, and may be either dry cells or rechargeable nickel-cadmium button cells, usually referred to as Deacs. About two hours use per charge is a minimum, and a set of dry cells gives the same, so that despite the initial cost of rechargeable cells and the charger for them, it is an obvious economy to use them. The cost is likely to be recovered in only 20–25 hours of use, and they will last for at least three years with minimum care and attention.

Basically, the equipment consists of a transmitter (Tx) with an internal power supply, and, in the model, a receiver (Rx) with a separate power supply, and servos. The servos, which are electro-mechanical devices which convert electrical impulses into physical movement, draw their current from the same battery pack as the Rx, except in the case of some sail winches which may have a fairly heavy current demand and therefore carry their own separate battery packs. The weight of the equipment in the model may vary from perhaps 7 to 10oz (200–280gm) for an ic engined boat where a servo is linked directly to the engine throttle, to 12–16oz (340–450gm) in an electric model where a speed controller is added, up to 24–32oz (680–900gm) for a racing yacht carrying a winch and additional batteries.

Control is effected by two control sticks on the transmitter, one moving from side to side and spring-biased to return to center for the rudder, and the other moving up and down without springing for the motor speed or sail position. Some equipment uses a spring-biased wheel control for rudder, and this is often easier for a beginner to use, since the wheel is turned without thinking, whichever way the model is required to turn. With a stick, it takes a little practice to know which way to push to get the desired turn when the model is heading across or towards the transmitter, or when it is travelling astern.

The equipment works on an amplitude modulated digital system of a series of pulses and reset pulses forming frames. The Tx sticks alter the timing of the pulses and the Rx decodes the signal and passes it to the appropriate servo. The servo compares the incoming pulses with the position of its control arm and moves the arm to balance out any difference. In most equipment, the servo arm has rotary movement, the link to the control being taken off a radial arm, or a disk, in the form of a pushrod stiff enough to pull or push the control. A typical servo movement is about $\frac{3}{8}$in (9mm) each side of center. Some servos provide linear movement, which can be an advantage when a pushrod has to emerge through a bush in a watertight radio box, as obviously radial movement involves a certain amount of lateral displacement of the pushrod.

Fairly limited frequencies are allowed for model radio use, mostly the 27, 40, and 72mHz bands, depending on the country in which the equipment is used. At present, the only one approaching universal acceptance is 27mHz, but this offers problems in that there are other users, such as doctors' calls in hospitals, walkie-talkies, and communications bleepers in some large industrial complexes such as docks and mines. All of these have comparatively limited range, but can interfere with model control over a radius of several miles.

Quartz crystals, ground to resonate on very precise frequencies, are fitted into the circuits of transmitters and receivers to particularize response and enable several sets to operate without mutual interference within the limits of a confined waveband. For example, the 27mHz band extends from 26.96 to 27.28 megaHertz, a spread of 320 kiloHertz. By using crystals and superheterodyne receiver circuits, a basic separation of 50kHz is possible, and these separated frequencies are given color codes thus:

**Left**

Some people use their thumbs on top of the Tx control sticks, others rest the case against them and use a finger and thumb on each stick. This Tx in waterproof case. *(Courtesy Ripmax Ltd)*

**Bottom left**

For offshore racing, or in rainy conditions, waterproof transmitter covers can be obtained, or, as glimpsed here, the transmitter can be operated through a thin polythene bag.

**Below**

Typical sandwich box radio installation without lid. Rx and Deac wrapped in foam padding. Note box fitted over rudder tube and flexible nylon sleeved rod passing round tank to throttle.

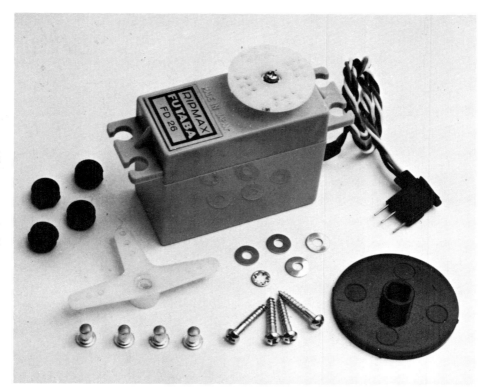

**Left**

A normal servo with mounting grommets and screws etc as supplied. Alternative rotary discs/arms adapt to different installation requirements. *(Courtesy Ripmax Ltd)*

**Below**

An assortment of radio equipment. Transmitters at rear left and front left are two function (two two-stick and one wheel), others are three, four, and six function. Receivers are in front of each. Center foreground is a 'brick'—two servos and Rx in one unit. *(Courtesy Ripmax Ltd)*

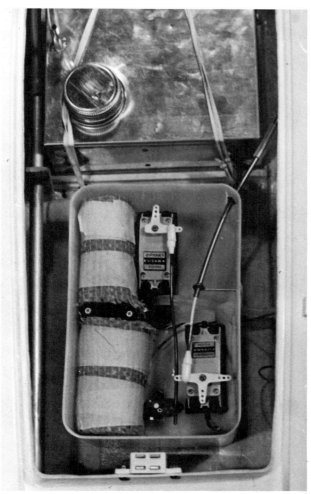

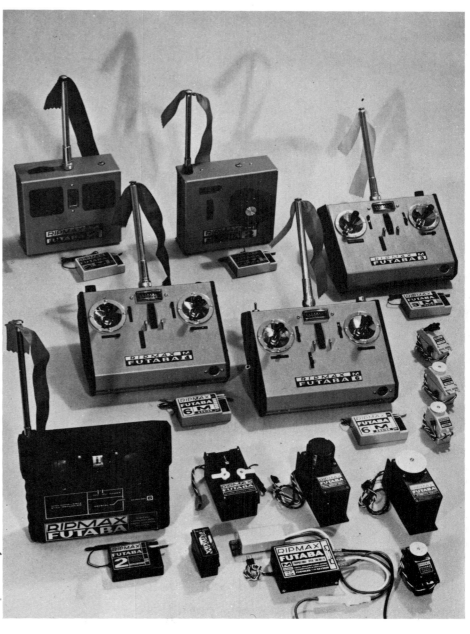

| | |
|---|---|
| 26.995 | Brown |
| 27.045 | Red |
| 27.095 | Orange |
| 27.145 | Yellow |
| 27.195 | Green |
| 27.255 | Blue |

These colors are shown by small flags or ribbons on the Tx aerials, and are the basis of peg-boards used to control operation when a group of modellers - are

159

running together; only the holder of a colored peg or other token can switch on equipment on that specific frequency. Improvement in radio, using closer tolerance components, allows split frequencies (or 'splits') with 25kHz separation to be used; these are identified by the colors on either side, eg, 27.020 is brown/red, 27.70 red/orange, etc, giving the opportunity for 12 models to operate or, with an extra frequency, 27.280 (black) 13 models.

Modern equipment is extremely stable and reliable, and it is really a case of inserting batteries (or charging the batteries supplied), switching on, and it works. No tuning or fiddling is necessary, and this is a far cry from the sets of not so many years ago. Care is reduced to keeping things clean and looking after the batteries, and, in use, keeping it all dry. Waterproof covers allowing transmitter operation in rain can be bought, or it is possible to protect the Tx with a large plastic bag. Today if you are racing, things do not stop for anything but a deluge.

Keeping the gear in the model dry is perhaps less easy, since most models get a little water inside at some time, and if it is salt water it can be a problem. Servos and winches are frequently safe from anything short of total submersion, and receivers, batteries, and all wire junctions or plugs can be stowed in a waterproof box. This is not difficult to achieve except that access is required to change crystals, and it is really better to have the on/off switch and charging sockets inside the box to eliminate any chance of leakage. Alternatively the box can be mounted in the hull under an easily removed but watertight hatch, in which case it need only be proofed against any small amount of water swilling about the bottom of the boat.

High performance power boats offer perhaps more of a problem than other types, especially in windy conditions when a lot of spray may be taken aboard. Many owners seal all the radio into one box either using grommets or rubber bellows to seal control rod exits, or using sleeved flexible control links rather like Bowden cables; the sleeving can be glued to the box. Access for switching etc is through blind rubber plugs

**Left**
Radio yacht racing. The clothes peg on the transmitter aerial is the token representing the frequency color, without which the radio equipment must not be switched on.

**Right**
Experts can squeeze radio into very tiny models. This photo, taken at a club exhibition, shows onlookers intrigued by small ships operating on a shallow 3m square pool.

**Below**
Part of an Italian F7 display team. Not only is the landing craft controlled but it fires rockets and lands the tank which is also under radio control.

such as those sold by car accessory shops. In some cases the radio box is considered as part of the buoyancy aids fitted in the boat. It is possible for the model to sink without water getting to the radio.

Most of the troubles experienced with radio (and they are few nowadays) can be traced to the state of the battery; broken, corroded, or loose connections in the wiring harness or the on/off switch—these items should be thoroughly and regularly checked. It may be possible to isolate the trouble—does the Tx operate someone else's Rx on the same frequency? Or his Tx operate your Rx? If the servos are swapped over, does the same one refuse to work? If the fault is not a simple and obvious one, and you are not an electronics expert, return the equipment to the maker or his service agent. If you use the set often throughout the season, it is well worth having a maintenance check annually, since if regularly serviced it is quite common to get seven or eight years' use at a total cost well below that of a replacement set.

Broken or dislodged wires can arise from unintentional tugs or vibration, so the first rule of any installation is to tuck all wiring neatly out of the way, either tying it with thread or wrapping it with insulation tape to form a tidy cable which can be held in position by tying or taping to the box side. The Rx should be rubber-banded in place on a block of foam rubber, or stuck in place using one or more of the proprietary foam pads supplied with adhesive on both sides. Servos are usually supplied with grommets to fit their mounting lugs, screws or bolts passing through the grommets, or they can be positioned with an adhesive pad. Plastic servo mounts are available and sometimes supplied with the equipment when purchased. Vibration may not be thought to be a problem with a yacht, but the model has to be transported to and from the water, and this is frequently when damage occurs.

Always check for water when returned from a sailing session, and remove dry batteries between outings. A small linen bag of silica gel crystals in the radio box will absorb condensation and small amounts of water, but needs to be removed and dried out periodically. Use care in plugging and especially unplugging connections; the tiny plugs and sockets used in radio often mean that the wires are pulled when disconnecting so do it gently.

The remaining possible source of trouble is the receiver aerial, which is of a definite length to which the equipment is tuned. Any modification to the aerial arrangement should bear the length in mind, and any connections made should be clean and firm. With the comparatively short ranges used for boats, little trouble should be experienced when running a boat on its own, but when several boats are operated simultaneously, aerials should be as efficient as possible to reduce the chances of one set swamping another. A vertical aerial gives the greatest ground range, because ground (or water) absorption weakens the signal, and the higher the aerial above ground level, the further effective control is maintained.

New equipment beginning to appear, in the VHF band of 459mHz and using frequency modulation, offers up to 39 individual frequencies with far fewer interference problems. At the present time it is more expensive than existing conventional equipment, but with the progress made both technically and commercially in the short history of radio control, it seems likely that in a very few years modellers will look on today's sets as curios.

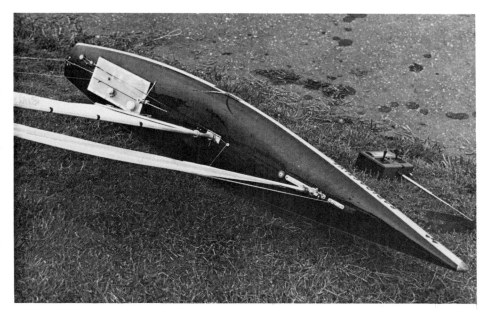

**Above**
Radio 10-rater is fairly typical in that after disconnecting sheeting and tiller, entire radio box can be removed for servicing, storage indoors, or even transfer to another model.

**Far left**
The end of a race. A skipper brings his R10R in, an advantage not shared by non-radio boats, but which enables water with restricted access to be used.

**Left**
Fairly complex installation in an F7 model which fires flares and maroons as part of a noisy but exciting battle in which several landing craft assault a land fort.

# Period Ships

As was explained earlier, the term 'period ships' is applied to scale models of any sailing vessels prior to about 1900, with perhaps special reference to the years between 1400 and 1800. Ships before and after that period tend to be particularized, eg Viking ship, Phoenician bireme, tea clipper, billy-boy, etc. With so long a history and so many different approaches to building and design, the subject is vast, and one can spend a lifetime studying it, learning new facts every day.

In recent years, researchers have made successful if sometimes hazardous voyages (by raft in the Pacific and leather curragh in the Atlantic, to give only two examples) to demonstrate historical probabilities, using the materials and constructional techniques of centuries ago to produce craft identical to the originals. Vessels have been built from information gained from ancient wrecks, to establish what difficulties might have been faced and how they might have been overcome, adding threads to the tapestry of man's development. In these and many other activities, models play an important part, especially for feasibility studies and record work.

The average builder of a period model may be motivated by a variety of reasons. He may simply think that a ship model is a handsome decoration or a certain conversation piece, or, more strongly, that a model brings a touch of romance and beauty. He may find the intricacy of such a model a challenge, or his imagination may have been fired by the work of one or more of the great sea writers; one German company in fact produces several ship kits based on vessels featured in the stories of C S Forester. There are those who wish to model a ship on which an ancestor sailed, and those who find period ships an outlet for their creative urge and craftsmanship. Some build for local museums, to provide a record of a famous ship or type of vessels associated with the locality, and some work with national museums, filling gaps in collections, work for which they may or may not receive payment. There are experts who build for their own pleasure, but are prepared to sell the models when completed, and there are a very few professional builders who will undertake commissions to build specific models.

These different approaches to the subject are catered for in a variety of ways. It is possible to buy kits ranging from small and simple models with little pretence at accuracy of detail, to really superb models which with care can be built to museum standard. Plans can be obtained for decorative 'galleon type' models which bear little resemblance to actual ships, or a wide range of actual shipyard technical drawings can be purchased. Very few plans are available drawn specifically for model building, that is, with constructional parts shown separately, ready for tracing on to timber, so that some knowledge of how to go about building a ship model is required. There are several extremely useful books on the subject, and anyone considering putting in the many hours needed to build a model is again advised to read everything he can lay his hands on.

The simpler kits often provide a central keel member and two blocks of wood bandsawn to plan and profile, which sandwich the central keel and are then carved to shape. Some supply a hull block spindle-molded to shape and provided with a groove into which a central member is fitted. A solid hull of this type can look perfectly satisfactory provided it is finished and painted with care, and since it is relatively quick, it enables the builder to progress to the deck detail and rigging which he may find more interesting. Probably most early vessels, carracks and caravels and the like, are kitted in this form; it enables a relatively inexpensive kit to be marketed, and the purchaser who seeks no more than a decorative model is quite happy.

An advance on this is to make the lower half of the hull from solid block, but then to fit half-frames and plank the sides. Studying pictures of ships will show that many were quite flat-sided above the line of maximum beam, so that planking presents few difficulties except for the bow where the planks may curve in sharply and warming or steaming may be necessary. An alternative is to use a full depth block or blocks, or bread-and-butter construction, and hollow down to the appropriate deck level, then plank the exterior with thin veneer planks. The sides can be carved away internally to leave a very thin shell, but because many sailing vessels had quite a degree of tumblehome, fitting any decks to the interior can be a little tricky.

A fully-planked hull follows normal construction as described in Chapter 3, except that it is customary to include many more frames in a period ship than in a working model. The frames were adzed or sawn from timber grown, by accident or design, into a curve, and pieced together, but are usually fretsawn from sheet timber or, where they will not be seen, ply, for model construction. The number of frames may vary from nine or ten for a small, fully planked model, up to thirty to forty for a moderate size half-planked ship; with half-planking, the frames should not be of ply and will need to be nicely finished. Top-class ship models would have them built up in the various futtock pieces, as in full size, a difficult and time-consuming undertaking for even the expert modellers.

One point of difference in hull planking is the use of thicker planks at intervals to form strong bands called wales, hence gunwale etc. The use of these thicker planks indicates the necessity of keeping the run of planking accurate throughout. Their purpose was to compensate for the number of apertures, gunports etc, in a ship's side. Stealers, or shorter planks which died away before reaching the ends of the hull, were used to

**Left**
Napoleon's State Barge, another good model by E P Heriz-Smith, and one which is quite unusual and interesting. Photographed through its case at an M E Exhibition.

**Below**
The *Adler von Lubeck* makes a colorful model, from a Graupner kit. Treatment of the sails in this model adds to the overall appearance.

the plating lightly on the hull and paint it a streaky coppery green.

Scribing can also be used to indicate planking on a solid block hull, especially if it is to be painted. Planking variations with hand-worked timber are likely to be quite prominent; one has only to look at some of the surviving sailing craft, built in most cases with the aid of mechanical saws, to realize that individual planks would show on earlier craft.

Hull construction to produce an accurate scale effect is quite an involved art, and once again, reading as much as can be found and examining museum models with a critical eye are the two essentials. Quite a lot of museum models are hull only, showing stumps of masts and no rigging, and if a modeller's interest is confined primarily to how a ship's hull was built, this is the approach to study. One advantage is that a very much smaller and more conveniently shaped glass case is required!

Decks and deck details vary enormously and what can be shown depends on the scale and the builder's ability and imagination. It also depends on how the ship

avoid too great a taper and waste of wood on the strakes (planks) which could also mean inadequate width for secure fastening of the ends. At times when many ships were being built and timber was in short supply, top and butt planking was used above the waterline on smaller vessels, permitting the use of timber from smaller trees and adapting to the taper of the tree to produce the strongest possible structure despite the use of comparatively short lengths (Figure 14).

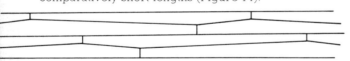

**Figure 14**

Before planking, it is necessary to shape the frames, (bevel them) to form a smooth seating for the planks throughout. At the extreme ends of the hull, the degree of bevel would be excessive if the frames were at right-angles to the keel, and they are therefore angled progressively forward or aft; these are called cant-frames Unless a half-planked model is being built, these areas are rarely visible after planking and are usually therefore built over normal frames, with the considerable bevel giving a bigger area of support for the sharp curves of the planking. Compared with a working model, the planking on a period ship is quite thin, hence the need for more frames and better support.

Early ships used various compounds based on pitch on their bottoms, to reduce worm attack and delay fouling. Sheet lead was tried without a great deal of success, and by the 1600s it was normal for an outer layer of fir planking to be nailed on. Coppering was used from about 1760 onward, but care is needed to reproduce this, since even on full-size ships the thickness of the heaviest sheets used was little more than 1mm or about 3/64ths of an inch. Reduced down to $\frac{1}{8}$in scale gives half a thousand or little more than 1/100mm as the copper thickness, which is thinner than a coat of paint. Probably the best way to represent it is to cut scale plates from cigarette papers, or simply to scribe

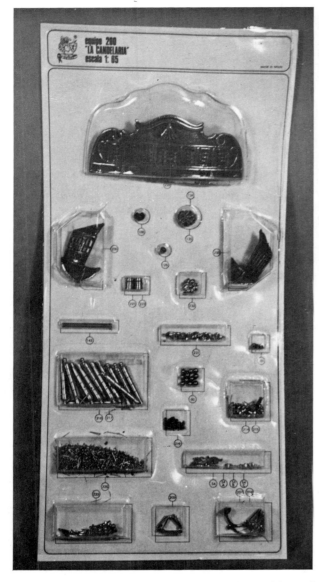

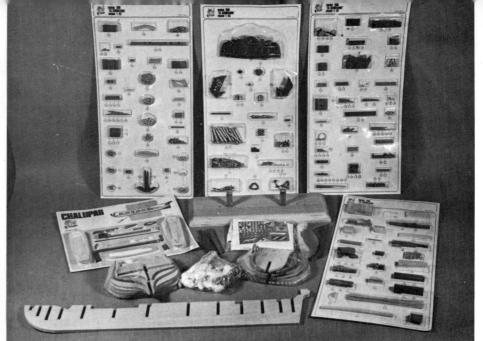

is being shown. A formal full-hull model would need clear decks and only items of permanent equipment, whereas a waterline model shown at anchor or at sea would be cluttered with hen coops, pigs and even cows, sometimes in the ships' boats or in sties or pens, plus hay etc for their feed; there would be spare spars, perhaps barrels and boxes, sails under repair, hammocks in the nettings, and dozens of other details, many varying according to the weather envisaged, the type of ship, even the time of day. Basic fittings are shown on most technical drawings, but other models, or photographs of other models, drawings in books, and accounts of voyages can all yield additional detail. Concentrate on similar sized ships of similar date, as variations can usually be fairly accurately dated.

One of the common faults in period ship models is incorrect gun proportions. The angle of swell at the muzzle, inadvertent stepping between the astragals, the difference between astragals and reinforcement rings, and the taper of carriages are the most frequent areas of criticism. The arrangement of breeching tackles and other ropes should be studied, particularly when the guns are housed (they were not just left standing around on the deck). Ships' boats, too, repay study, since they changed from time to time and their sizes often varied with the size of ship they served. The quality of the boats can make or mar the whole model.

Masts, spars, and rigging create a tangled web to the uninitiated, but there is of course absolute logic in the arrangements. One little realized fact is that masts were more often than not 'made,' that is, constructed from a number of lengths of timber skilfully jointed together and bound with iron hoops. Solid one-piece masts

168

were used only for the aftermast (mizzen in ships and
main in brigs), or for very small vessels. The shortage
of suitable fir trees for large masts was the reason for
made masts, but when trysails were carried on the
mizzen, the iron hoops and rope wooldings used to bind
the masts interfered with raising and lowering these
sails, so single poles available were used for these
masts.

The taper of a mast is subtle. It is at its thickest at the
partners (approximately where it first appears above
deck) and then it tapers in a long curve to about three-
quarters maximum at the bottom of the head, where it
becomes square to receive hound pieces to support
the trestletrees and then tapers more sharply. At the

top is fitted a cap, extending forward to accommodate
the heel of the topmast which passes down to the trestletrees, and has an iron fid passed through it. A top, a
fairly sizeable platform, rested on the trestletrees and
crosstrees, to provide a base for the topmast shrouds,
and was also used as a lookout platform; on a warship it
became a base for a number of sharpshooters and even
swivel guns. A made mast had long vertical cheeks
each side to help support the trestletrees, top, etc.

Topmasts showed only a little taper and were solid,
since they were not much more than half the length of
the respective masts proper. If topgallant masts were
carried, these were lighter again, and had a slightly
more noticeable taper. The bowsprit was almost as
thick as the mast and tapered in a curve on the underside only, down to a little over half its maximum diameter at the outboard end. A light jibboom was often
carried on this, about 30% overlapping the bowsprit
and passing through a cap, outboard of which it would
be lightly tapered.

Yards were tapered, also in a curve, from the center
(the slings) to about 70% diameter three-quarters of the
way out, the last quarter being the yardarm and the
taper reducing rapidly here to half diameter or a little
less. The main and topsail booms would carry iron rings
on top in which slid light studding sail booms to increase sail area off the wind in light conditions. Great
care should be taken with all masts and spars to get the
basic diameters and the tapers correct, as thick and
clumsy spars will ruin a model, no matter how neatly
everything else is made. To avoid subsequent warping,
they should always be shaped from strips split off a pine
plank so that no cross-grain occurs, and they should
first be planed square and to the taper. The corners are
then planed to give an even octagon, the new corners
then planed, and the result finished with glasspaper.
One expert known to the author always used lancewood, but white pine is usually easier to obtain.

Rigging divides into standing and running rigging,
and before about 1875, hemp ropes were used and they
were almost without exception tarred to prevent rot.
After that date, standing rigging should be black, but
running rigging could reasonably be of manila fiber
left a light yellow-brown. Standing rigging supports
the masts, and the ropes (cable-laid up to 1820 or so,

setting up the shrouds. The upper one sat in an eye in the end of the shroud, and the lower one was usually iron-bound, the iron passing through the channel (a horizontal plate on the ship's side) and connecting to three or more long iron links, the lowest of which was secured to the chainplate. Early ships used single-hole heart-shaped eyes for this part of the rigging, but in either case the pair were lashed together with a lanyard. At the upper end the rope was seized into a loop fitting over the mast, the other end passing down to form the next shroud.

A sheerpole, a length of timber, was lashed across the shrouds just above the upper deadeyes, and a similar piece lashed to all but the first and last shrouds below the top; sometimes this latter, the futtock staff, was a rope. The staffs were pulled inward towards each other by ropes called catharpins, which tensioned the shrouds and resisted the pull of the futtock shrouds which extended outwards to the edge of the tops and in turn balanced the pull of the topmast shrouds. Ratlines converted the shrouds into ladders, and were horizontal ropes seized to the fore and after shrouds and clove-hitched to those between, spaced vertically a foot or so (30cm) apart.

The lower masts were also supported by stays leading forward and, in all large ships, doubled. Hearts and a lanyard at the lower end set them up taut, the lower heart forming part of a loop engaged round the bowsprit or similar strong point. The upper masts also had shrouds and forestays, the latter running to the bowsprit or to the tops of the mast ahead; they also had backstays running straight down to deck level. There

hawser-laid after that) were wormed, parcelled, and served, that is, the grooves are filled with yarn, the whole rope wrapped in tarred canvas, and then close-bound with more yarn. Just the serving is adequate for most models, or on small ones, not even that. Just as care is needed to keep the spars delicate, so overthick rigging should be avoided.

Serious modellers often make up a small rope-walk, using three gears arranged radially, driven by a central gear with a hand-crank and hooking the other ends of three strands to a hand-drill. A small wooden pear with three grooves is engaged with the three strands and kept pushed up to the rope being formed. An assistant first winds the three strands into left or right-hand lay (flax thread can be unwound and rewound in the opposite direction as needed) with rather more twist than normal, then the hand-drill is turned to lay the three strands together. Left handed strands laid together right-handed give hawser lay; shroud lay is the same but round a central, fourth strand; and three of either subsequently laid left-handed form cable lay. The laid ropes should be hung with a weight for a day or two to stretch them, then dyed if necessary (shoe dye is excellent) and left to dry. Alternatively, leave dyeing until after rigging, as the cord is slightly easier to use undyed.

Flax (linen) thread seems to be a better basis for ropes than synthetic fibers, and can be obtained in varying thicknesses from upholsterers and harness makers. Once stretched and dyed, it can be pulled over a block of beeswax to lay any fibers and this helps to prevent movement in varying humidity.

Blocks can vary from tiny beads of glue on a miniature to scale-built and sheaved reproductions; some blocks could be as long as 30in (760mm) on large ships. On average, they are shaped from a pre-formed length of boxwood and cut off when as much work as possible has been carried out, leaving a minimum of finishing on the cut side and requiring a groove filed round and a fine wire strap to be added. Holes may be drilled with needles stoned to triangular section before or after cutting off the strip. The higher the blocks in the ship, the smaller they should be.

Deadeyes, usually large blocks of elm, with three holes and a grooved periphery, were used in pairs for

**Left**
Merchant brig of 1853, *Volante*, of New York, at ⅛in scale measures 21in (533mm). Model Shipways supplies plans only if preferred, or wood kits with preshaped parts. *(Courtesy Model Shipways Inc)*

**Right**
Another famous North American vessel was the Grand Banks schooner *Bluenose*, available as a kit from several sources. This one is 24in (610mm) from Scientific. *(Courtesy Scientific Models Inc)*

**Left**
Close-up of part of the Graupner *Mayflower* kit. The ship's boat could be improved by sinking the thwarts but otherwise detail is good for a 23½in (597mm) kit. *(Courtesy Ripmax Ltd)*

were other ropes, pendants, springs, etc.

Yards were secured to the mast by parrels which could be double ropes, ropes with wood balls called trucks, or double ropes fitted with spacing strips of timber (ribs) with trucks on both ropes between the ribs. A footrope hung beneath the yard, supported at intervals by rope stirrups. The weight of the yard was taken by jeers in the center, and to prevent bowing under the weight of men working the sail, by lifts running from the yardarms to the cap above. A lower yard on quite a small warship could have as many as 22 blocks, for lifts, braces, yard tackle, topsail sheet leads, buntlines, clewlines, and leech lines; the last three are for sail control, the others for yard control.

Sails were made up of canvas cloths about two feet in width, reinforced in areas of high stress or high wear, and representing them convincingly is very difficult, especially as they age-darken. There are strong and opposing views on their inclusion on a full-hull model, although a waterline representation might reasonably be expected to show them, even if furled. Probably the best compromise to show their construction is single-line stitching following the pattern of the reinforcing and cloths. Coping with reinforcement bands only a couple of millimetres wide could be a problem, though if the material was clear doped to prevent fraying, the bands sliced off with a razor and stuck rather than sewn to the sail, an acceptable result could be achieved.

Hemp, a strong cream color, or flax, a paler cream were the usual sail materials until perhaps 1825, when cotton, almost pure white, began to be used. The nearest the modeller will get is probably very fine linen, which can be faintly dyed (weak coffee has been used) to a reasonable color. Small models can use paper with the cloths, reef points etc drawn on lightly, but with linen sails the reef points can be knotted fine cotton thread. A bolt rope was sewn right round the

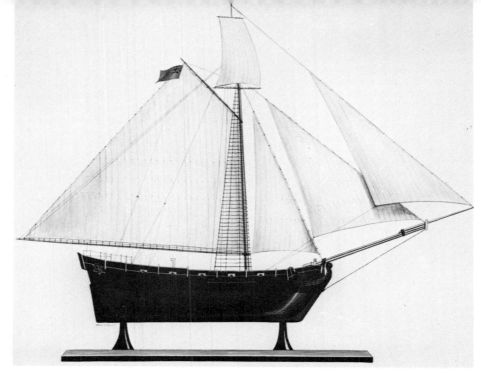

edge of the sail and was quite thick; it is probably best glued on for smaller models. Cringles (small rope loops) numbered as many as ten down each side of the sail and are best represented by cementing scraps of thread between the strands of the bolt rope.

The sails were bent to the yards by pulling sideways and making off earings at the yard tips, then securing the head to the yard by robins (rope bands) passed through eyelets at about one foot (30cm) intervals in the head tabling; the robins were tied round the yard or to a jackstay if fitted, in such a way as to position the sail

**Above**
Another small vessel kitted in the USA is the British sloop *Ferret*, 15½in (394mm) long. Small sloops like this were used for despatches, Revenue work etc. *(Courtesy Sterling Models Inc)*

**Above right**
The American cutter *Hamilton*, though only 14in (355mm) in length, has sufficiently simple rigging to make it an attractive first kit for a beginner. *(Courtesy Sterling Models Inc)*

**Left**
Another Model Shipways kit, the topsail schooner *Eagle* of 1847. Careful research ensures authenticity, and at 3/16in scale (1:64) much detail can be included.

**Right**
Splendid model of the bomb ketch *Granado* by R A Lightley of Capetown, now in the Greenwich museum. Hull separates to show internal fitting out.

head on the foreside of the yard. Furled sails had as much as possible gathered into the center, and bunt gaskets (triangular nets) contained the bulk.

All the lines controlling the yards and sails were led down to deck level and belayed either to bitts sited just ahead or abaft of the mast or to cleats or pin rails secured inside the bulwarks, each rope having its own individual sheave in a bitt, cleat or belaying pin; two lines were rarely belayed on the same point, for obvious reasons. Setting up the running rigging is taxing because of the difficulty of access, but fortunately it does not have to be taut as in the standing rigging.

This chapter has only touched the surface of its subject, but, it is hoped, conveys the fascination and complexity of period-ship modelling. Fortunately there are first-class books available, going into minute detail on construction and rigging, and distilling the essence of many earlier books and manuals. Although a bibliography will be found at the end of this present book, particular reference can perhaps be made to several comparatively recently published works which will be found invaluable:

E W Petrejus, *Modelling the Brig-of-war* Irene
C N Longridge *The Anatomy of Nelson's Ships* and *The Cutty Sark*
H A Underhill, *Plank on Frame Models*, *Masting and Rigging the Clipper Ship and Ocean Carrier*, and other titles
R C Anderson, *Seventeenth Century Rigging*, and others,
and for ideas on research,
D McNarry, *Ship Models in Miniature*.

Apart from good quality timbers and veneers (from specialist suppliers) materials represent an insignificant outlay compared with the hundreds of hours of work, and many cost virtually nothing. Foil from toothpaste tubes and bits of paper doily will provide the basis for ornamental gilt work, old boxwood rulers and cedar cigar boxes provide timber for small parts, beads, lead shot, discarded costume jewellery, stripped electrical cable for fine wire, a model soldier for a figurehead, cocktail sticks, toothpicks—there is no end to the small odds and ends which can contribute. The main ingredients are patience and care.

# Plastic Models

The size of the plastic kit market may be judged by the reluctance of one manufacturer to run off less than 100,000 of any one kit, which, with a score of big manufacturers world-wide averaging a choice of perhaps fifty different models each, suggests an astronomic number of kits sold annually. There were British plastics in the 1930s, mostly aircraft, but modern plastic kits started in the early 1950s in the USA, originally as a few molded parts enclosed with wood kits but very quickly developing into all-molded kits using polystyrene. There were very few ship models at first, but response to one or two tentative offerings encouraged more, till today there is an enormous range, from biremes to nuclear submarines and in sizes from a few inches to three feet or more.

Standards have improved continuously, both in fit of parts and in reproduction of detail. There can be occasional criticisms, such as over-emphasized shell plates or rigging which is much too heavy, but overall, one must have great respect for the skills of the modelmakers and toolmakers. Early kits used to give problems with flash—extraneous plastic attached to a molding where, perhaps, the dies were not fitted together too well—but nowadays kits can virtually be assembled straight out of the box and look good. There are, however, improvements which can be made by a careful builder which add to the pleasure of making the model and produce a better result, or modifications can often be made to convert a kit into a different vessel.

As supplied, most of the parts come still attached to their molding sprues, and they should be left on them while they are identified and, in most cases, while they are painted. The main hull parts are frequently loose, and the second step is normally to assemble the hull and deck. The first step is to study the assembly instructions and establish which part is which and how it fits where! In particular, note the order of assembly, which is important, since incorrect procedure may leave you with items which cannot be fitted at a later stage. If you are modifying, make a note of what parts will need to be cut away or built up.

Where a hull (or other part) is molded in two halves, a little attention to the joint line is usually worthwhile. Although flash is rare, if there is any it should be cut off with a sharp knife and the halves fitted together dry. There will often be a slightly raised ridge along the joint, and this should be scraped away with a sharp blade; scraping produces a much neater result in this type of plastic than filing or sanding. If there are irregularities in the meeting faces, a little scraping or rubbing the surfaces on a piece of fine carborundum paper pinned to a flat board should ensure a good joint. Sometimes the halves are slightly warped and must be held in contact for cementing; this can be done with rubber bands providing that scrap pieces of wood are placed to hold the open top of the hull at the right width.

The deck may need to be inserted between the hull halves when they are joined, so this must be cleaned up and checked for fit. It is also desirable to paint it and the hull sides before assembly as this is the certain way to get a perfect separation line between the colors. Experts frequently immerse all the plastic parts in weak detergent at the outset to remove any trace of grease and leave them ready for cement and paint. There are enamels specially made for use with plastic kits, in a wide variety of colors, and it is recommended that these be used. Use matt enamels only for ship models, except of course where there is no choice—silver, gold, and copper are not normally available in matt finishes. Sable brushes should be used, and with care (see Chapter 12) will last for years. The makers of enamels often supply a solvent for them, but white spirit is normally satisfactory.

**Left**
French plastic kit for the packet boat *Avenir*, 25½in (650mm) long, one of a range by Heller in 1/100, 1/200, and 1/400 scales.

**Right**
*HMS Vanguard*, last British battleship, built from the Frog kit at the somewhat unusual scale of 1/450. At this size (just over 20in or 510mm) much additional detail could be added.

**Below**
A trawler by Heller photographed at a trade fair. Rather thick masts and rigging and an unconvincing steadying-sail mar an otherwise nice-looking model.

As a rule, one thin coat of paint is adequate, but to give density a thin second coat may be applied, especially in the case of light colors used on dark plastic. Avoid flooding with paint, which will collect round rivets and other tiny details and distort them. Leave to dry thoroughly (six hours), then go over the painted pieces and scrape away any paint which has found its way on to joint faces. Cement will not stick well to paint, so that if, for example, a gun turret is to be cemented to a deck, the bottom of the turret and the area of the deck should be scraped with a pointed blade.

Polystyrene cement in tubes needs to be applied very sparingly and any surplus scraped away when dry or almost so. It can have a habit of stringing, where as the nozzle is withdrawn, a hair-like thread of cement is produced. These strings can be plucked away with tweezers, but can be a nuisance. Most experts use a liquid cement (methyl ethyl ketone) applied with a small brush; capillary action draws the cement along the length of the joint. This cement can also provide a filler if a length of waste sprue is shaved and the shavings dissolved into it, though it tends to dry rather quickly. Where gaps exist—hopefully, from modifica-

American clipper *Eagle*, an interesting venture into the plastics field by a Spanish firm. The kit combined cord rigging and cloth sails with plastic hull and fittings.

tion rather than poor assembly—body putty, available in tubes, is best, since it can be applied liberally and does not dry glass-hard so that it can be sanded or scraped to the level required.

While the hull/deck assembly is drying, detail parts can be painted on the sprue. Never break them off the sprue, but cut them and shave away any vestige of the thin connection. Touch in the paint on the shaved area; tiny pieces can be dropped on to a strip of adhesive tape, pinned down sticky side up, which will help hold them for touching in and help to avoid losing them. Inspect them all and decide whether any could be improved by modification. Molding has some limitations, and it may be, for example, that tiny gun barrels would be better cut off, holes drilled with a stoned needle, and, say, short bristles cemented in the holes to give a more delicate and truer scale appearance. Fine wires might be better for whip aerials, or you may care to cut molded chain away and use cheap jewellery chain, or braided thread for tiny models.

There are many such little touches which can be introduced, and one of the most useful materials is the sprue which would normally be thrown away. If a piece of this is rotated above a flame such as a candle, it will soften right through, and when it goes suddenly limp it can be moved from the flame and the ends pulled apart. With a little practice differing diameters can be produced, down to long hair-like strands which are rigid and can be cut and cemented easily, for aerials or stays. Thicker rods can be used for pipes, ladder handrails, and many other extras.

Plastic period ships are often highly detailed and colorful, but if molded plastic rigging is supplied, it is likely to be rather heavy-looking and can overpower the rest of the model. It is better to rig the model with linen thread for standing rigging and fine synthetic thread for running rigging. One method of making up the shrouds is as follows: first trace them on to a piece of stiff card (check that the length is correct, because they form the hypotenuse of a triangle) and nick the card edges. Wind on the shrouds, then wind across them the ratlines, using finer thread. Now paint and/or varnish them, after working a piece of waxed paper underneath so that they do not stick to the card. The paint or varnish will stick the ratlines to the shrouds and stiffen all the threads, so that when dry they can be cut free and gently laid in place and cemented.

Many warships had their appearance altered during refits, and it is possible to modify a kit to show a ship in later or earlier form, provided drawings or several photographs can be found. As an example, the cruiser HMS *London* was built 1926–9 with three funnels, light midships superstructure and an aircraft catapult. She was reconstructed 1940/1 with two funnels, an updated bridge and superstructure, and tripod masts, and virtually all the visible changes occurred between B turret and the mainmast, which would make a simple conversion. Showing both versions side by side would be most interesting, or showing a *London* class ship against a *Kent* class would be attractive; the differences were slight. There are many kitted ships which could be so treated, needing only some scraps of hardwood or plastic card, plus some body putty and odds and ends of sprue, fine wire, etc.

Setting a ship on a sea can be an attractive way to present it, or two or more ships can form a diorama. There are, however, many pitfalls. A choppy sea will not have a white crest on every wave, for example; wave patterns, too, are consistent in open water, so that an incorrect sea will be immediately obvious to any sailor. Reference to color pictures in magazines and books will enable mistakes to be avoided.

Seas are most often made with putty, plaster, polyester resin, plasticine or modelling clay, papier maché, or carved wood, but other materials and methods are sometimes used, including hammered glass and acrylic sheet. The sea state and geographical location portrayed can affect choice of material and treatment, the extremes perhaps being the solid gray of a Channel sea on a murky day and the translucent faint blue of a sheltered tropical bay. For the latter, clear polyester resin, especially cold casting resin, with a hint of pigment, may give what is required (it may need a full-hulled model and a visible anchor cable) but in most cases paint is best. A coat of eggshell varnish will give a suitable wet appearance and a hint of translucence to the surface without killing the model, which the glitter of a very glossy surface might do.

Waterline models of steam and motor vessels lend themselves to construction from scratch in plastic card, stretched sprue, and the usual miscellaneous bits and pieces of fine wire, tiny beads, etc, remembering that hulls are covered with iron or steel plates and that what can be done with sheet (or plate) metal can be reproduced by plastic card. The same general procedures as outlined in 'Plastic Hulls' can be followed and because of the crispness of edges and corners given by this material, and the neatness possible in joints, very fine models can be built. At present only a small number of modellers are exploring this comparatively new field, but the potential is exciting.

**Top**
Unusual subject is Boeing's *Tucumcari* hydrofoil kitted by Aurora Plastics. Relatively small size of plastics enables an interesting collection to be made without taking over the house.

**Above**
Another classic American vessel, the *Robert E Lee*, kitted in plastic at various times by several American and British manufacturers. Careful painting would improve this example.

With all plastic models, the main secrets are good fits and good paintwork, and the latter comes from practice. A neat job cannot be expected if the model is held in one hand and the brush in the other. Stand or prop the model firmly on a block of wood at such a height that, if you are right handed, the left forearm and hand can rest on the bench and the right hand rests on the left with the right elbow on the bench edge. All the brushwork is by wrist and finger movement. Practise on an old kit or even a small cardboard box.

Kits which have heavily molded details will never look right, as can be realized if you study photographs of full-size vessels and pick out the prominent features. Do not be afraid to shave or scrape them away or even sand them with 400 carborundum paper. Some of the techniques for miniature model construction described in the next chapter can be applied equally well to plastics to replace heavy detail. It is estimated that only about one in eight plastic kits ever gets painted, because so many are sold to young modellers who are happy just to stick the bits together; on the other hand, some kits are turned into miniature masterpieces by detailed research and skilled alterations.

# Display Models and Miniatures

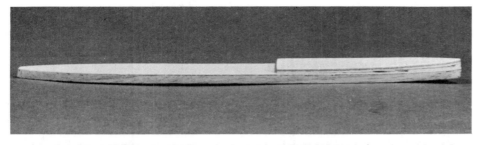

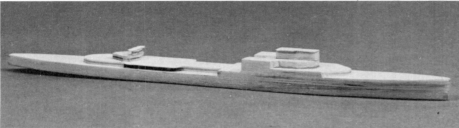

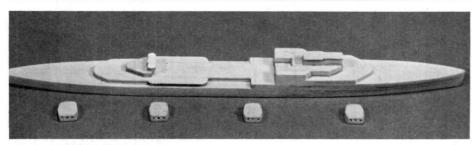

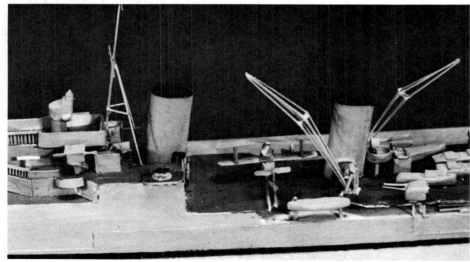

The models discussed in the previous two chapters also qualify for the title 'Display Models' and some are, of course, miniatures too. Lack of a precise title for non-working models of steam or motor vessels has been evident for many years, but possibly, since it is a relatively small part of marine modelling, the absence of any specific description such as 'period ship' has implied a power vessel. The ship's name, in most cases, is an indication, carrying some identification such as SS (steamship), PS (paddle steamer), TSS (twin-screw ship), MV (motor vessel) and so on, though this falls down on naval ships, HMS or USS etc.

Cased models may be full-hull or waterline or, very occasionally, sectioned or cut-away, having part of the hull shell removed to show internal arrangements. The average amateur model, seeking to represent a ship as seen, is likely to be waterline, with the hull carved from either a bread-and-butter assembly or, for a small model, a solid block. Hollowing of the hull is unusual unless internal lighting is installed, or the ship is shown, say, working cargo with one or more hatches off, but if it is hollow, it is more likely to be built up with ply or plastic card sides with perhaps a carved bow and stern. External plating, applied with paper or card, could be expected on any model more than 12in (30cm) long.

The superstructure would normally be built up, a popular choice of material being Bristol board. This is a good quality hard white card sold by artists' suppliers, available in a range of thicknesses, which can be cut cleanly with a sharp blade and has a smooth, grain-free surface which is excellent for painting. Water-soluble adhesive is often used, as surplus can be removed with a dampened paint brush, and water-soluble paints (poster colors or watercolors) are used because of the ease with which color can be varied and natural-looking effects created. Alternatives are plastic card in various thicknesses, with liquid cement, and matt oil enamels or acrylic paints, or close-grained natural veneers such as holly.

For deckhouses or fittings of awkward shape, or too small to make up from card, solid, close-grained timbers are used—lime, apple, cherry, box, holly, sycamore and hornbeam are all excellent. Most would need to be stained to represent darker timbers such as mahogany and teak, though pear darkens quite rapidly when exposed to light. For bent or curved parts, such as a capping rail round the stern, apple is probably best, especially as it can be sawn or sliced into incredibly tiny sections without losing its strength and consistency.

Many of the small fittings on a ship model can tax the ingenuity of the builder, especially where there are several identical items in close proximity. One method is to make a master in metal and press it between two halves of a cuttlefish bone (sold at pet shops). The face of the soft bone has to be sanded flat first, of course. On separating the halves, a filler channel can be cut in the bone, plus one or more vents to allow air to escape, and a number of castings can then be made, using Woods metal, a very low melting point alloy. For larger repetitive items, a mold can be made in a flexible vinyl molding material, available for cold casting, using resin, or in grades capable of accepting low temperature alloys.

Acetate sheet, or thin styrene sheet, can be molded as already described, and provides one simple way of producing cowl vents, always a headache. It is possible to carve a slightly undersize pattern, wax it, and laminate a vent from tissue paper and shellac or thin glue, or to paint on a dozen or more coats of thick cellulose dope. With either method, the resulting 'molding' has to be cut in half vertically to remove it from the pattern, and carefully rejoined ready for painting. Beating copper foil over a steel ball or shaped brass rod, annealing

**Above**

A simple model of HMS *Southampton* demonstrated by expert R Carpenter. At 100ft–1in model is almost exactly 6in long (152mm). First picture shows bare hull with tiny sheer at bow. Second picture shows basic superstructure added, also seen with the addition of the main turrets in the third picture. Funnels and details are added in picture four, while picture five is a close-up. The side armor has been included. To give a better idea of size, the crane jibs are just about ½in (12mm) in length.

ENGLISH SHIP
c. 1600

'ROYAL KATHERINE'
1664-1741
BY D. HUNNISETT          50'=1"

**Above**
Miniatures sealed in cases inside further display cases are hard to photograph, especially when they are only three or four inches (say 100mm) long. This model is a masterpiece.

**Top**
Another of E P Heriz-Smith's models, an English ship on the ways, demonstrating building methods and many other features of the early 17th century. (Also photographed through double glass.)

from time to time, is a way to produce a cowl which can then be soldered to a brass tube.

Lattice or other complex mast structures and cranes etc are best made from brass rod and wire, making up a jig from scrap balsa to hold the basic pieces in place while they are soldered. If the sides or the basic framework are silver soldered or soldered with a high melting point solder, the finer cross-braces etc can be soft-soldered at a later stage without having everything collapse. Delicacy is all-important, and often what looks accurate when assembled in the raw state looks over-scale when painted. Rarely is a model seen in which detail is too light, so, given a choice, err on the side of too thin rather than too thick.

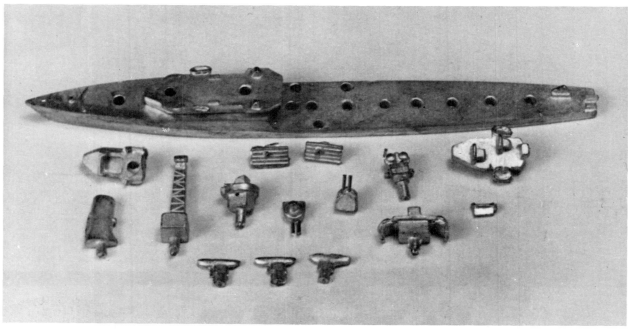

The author's criterion for a good scale model is that, if a photograph of a part of the model is examined, is it difficult to decide whether it is a model or the full-size ship? From this it follows that detail photographs of the prototype, or of ships' gear of similar type, are an invaluable aid to getting proportions and appearance correct. Everything your local library has with illustrations of ships should be studied; it is amazing how much help advertisements in full-size shipping journals can be, for example.

For absolute authenticity, there is nothing to beat a visit to a ship being modelled, or choosing from the outset a subject which can be visited. This is only occasionally possible, especially as basic drawings are needed as well, but a visit to a ship of similar size and type can be helpful, or failing this, a study of models of similar vessels in a museum will provide useful ideas. Certain basic details common to all ships vary very little–door heights, ladders, handrails, hose reels, gooseneck vents, liferafts, navigation lights and scores of others, which, if correct on a model, lend to its overall conviction.

Alignment is a vital matter, and to ensure it, jigs need to be made up. Parallel treads or rungs on a ladder, for example, can only really be ensured by cementing a strip of wood slightly narrower than the tread width to a wider piece, then accurately marking and, with the aid of a template for the angle, sawing slots into which the treads can be slipped. One side is then glued on, the free ends checked for length, and the second side glued. The finished ladder is then slid out and the jig is available for what further ones are needed. If it is a small-scale vertical iron ladder, the sides (wires) are pinned or taped over lines drawn on a strip of wood, thinner wire wound round (again over pencilled lines), tapped true, then all that is needed is a touch of solder paint on each joint and a hot iron. At this stage the com-

pleted ladder is cut free from the surplus wire.

Notice the block arrangement on lifeboat falls, and the griping gear which holds the boat secure. Look at the block arrangements for derricks, the lead of the whistle lanyard, quick-release lifebelt stowage, what happens at the foot of the timberheads (bulwark supports) to allow water to drain along the waterway, and the thousand and one other things which contribute to the successful operation of the ship. It may not be a working model, but if something patently could not work the way you have represented it, it will not be a good model.

Miniatures are a world of their own, and demand even more ingenuity. Hulls are normally carved from seasoned white pine, but it is difficult to get a perfect sheer line. Some builders therefore use a shallow hull base and a thick veneer deck curved to the sheer by inserting a suitable wedge at bow and stern. This naturally leaves gaps which can be filled with body putty, or in some cases it is possible to cover the exterior of the hull with smooth writing paper or the thinnest Bristol board, even incorporating any plated bulwarks in this covering. Alternatively, depending on how the full-size hull was built, plating can be suggested by covering the hull with strips of cigarette paper.

Superstructures are probably easiest built up deck by deck with prepainted Bristol board, with internal board strips to prevent the decks sagging. Prepainting both sides with very thin matt enamel and then sanding most of it off also protects the board against damp. Great precision is needed to keep the strips of board forming the sides at exactly the correct heights, and the corners are accurately cut to a miter, using a new single-edge razor blade.

A method of planking decks is to glue veneer face-to-face to form a block the width of the deck. The edge of

the block is then planed flat with a very sharp plane, then an all-over shaving is carefully planed off. This shaving, composed of tiny strips of veneer, is carefully trimmed and positioned to form the deck. If one side of each piece of veneer is rubbed with a piece of graphite before laminating, there can even be a hint of caulking.

Windows and doors can be cut from a strip of pre-painted cigarette paper (gray or blue/gray for windows, brown for doors) and glued on with the merest trace of glue, remembering that at 1/1200 scale a door will be about 1/16in (1½mm) high but, of course, twice

**Below**
Few small-scale wood kits are available, but this 1900 US East Coast steam tug, *Taurus*, is a nice one. Machined hull and die-cut plank-scored decks are two features. Length is 9in (229mm). *(Courtesy Model Shipways Inc)*

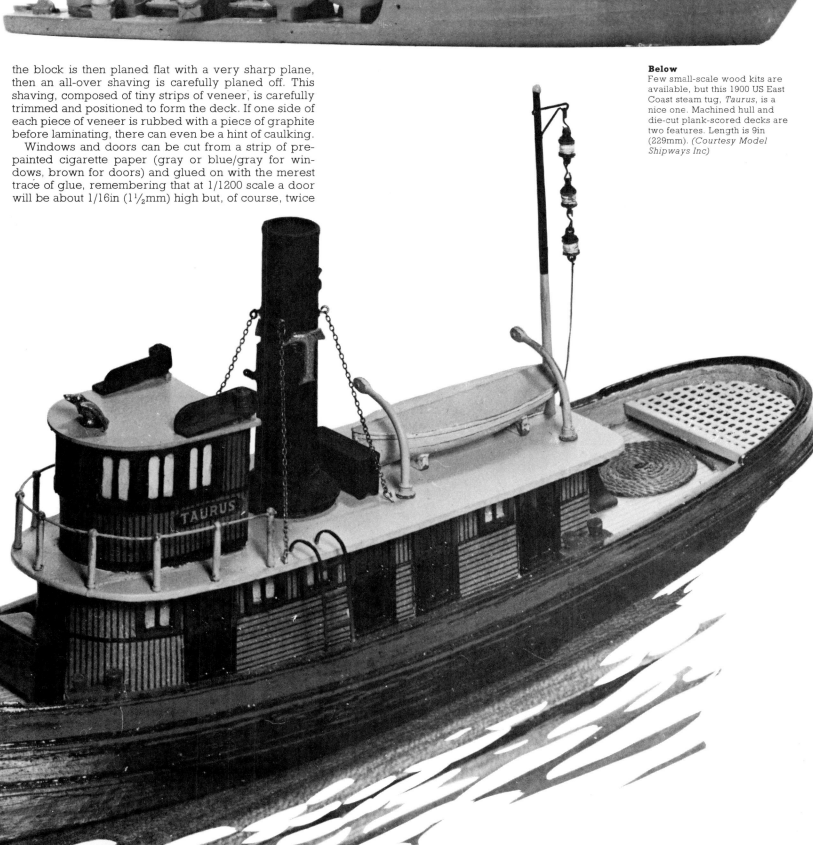

that at 1/600. No painting is likely to produce such neat and consistent rows of windows etc but at 1/600th it is possible to cut the windows and doors out of a paper strip and glue the strip over a prepainted superstructure side.

Deck details are usually shaped from parts of good quality matchsticks or pieces of close-grained veneer, using a new blade and avoiding sanding, which rounds off corners. Cowl vents are made from suitable seeds cut in half, mustard seeds being particularly good. The hemispheres are glued on dowels shaped from matches and faired in either by smoothing the glue with a damp brush or by applying watercolor straight from the tube. Tube color used neat is also useful for filling joints as it has the advantage of a surface reworkable by a damp brush. It can also be used for support brackets, blocks, and other details too tiny to carve.

Rails and tubular ladders are made by stretching fibers unravelled from synthetic thread on a lightly waxed strip of wood and winding or laying thread stanchions or rungs across. Two very thin coats of matt enamel both stiffen and stick the threads together. They are then cut off in the exact lengths needed and glued in place. Throughout, water soluble glue is used, applied with a pin point, and any surplus removed on a very fine damp brush. Rails are not strictly necessary on a 1/1200 model but should be fitted to 1/600, where they would be approximately 1/16in (1.5mm) high. Probably two threads and a top rail are the maximum that most people would care to use.

Rigging and aerials etc are probably best left off the smallest scale, but for 1/600 or larger fine human hair or tungsten wire, which is about average hair thickness (two thousandths of an inch) is usually used. Comparatively recently 'invisible thread,' a fine synthetic monofil in gray or neutral, has appeared, and might be worth trying.

The amount of detail needed on 1/1000 or 1/1200

*The Robt. E. Lee*

models is actually fairly small, comparable with what could be made out in a photograph taken at a distance. The hull, masts, superstructure block, and/or deckhouses, funnel(s), any samson posts, large derricks, or prominent ventilators, and the main hatches on a merchantman, or the cranes and main guns on a warship, are probably all that is needed. Of the smaller detail it would perhaps be worth suggesting the anchor windlass and possibly any breakwater, but unless there is some really prominent feature, it is not necessary to go further.

Someone new to miniatures is advised to try a simple ship without a lot of repetitive detail as a first attempt, and to use one of the larger scales. A tug or trawler at 1/16in or 1/200 scale will be about 6 or 7½in (150 or 190mm) long, big enough to show most fittings. The same model can then be repeated at 1/500 or 1/600, a third the size, an illuminating exercise.

Cases for models are always a problem. Some clear plastic moldings are available, but suffer a little from static and after regular dusting can become a little cloudy because of very fine scratches. Acrylics such as Perspex and Plexiglass can be sawn and polished and are easy to cement with either their own solvent or chloroform, but these too are liable to scratching, although with care scratches can be polished out. Glass is best, but needs framing neatly; it is possible to have the edges ground and cement the panels together, but difficult to make a really neat job as the cement tends to show. Your local glass merchant may advise. Showcase manufacturers (for shops and restaurants) may be a source of something suitable, either as a finished case or for supplies of suitable framing. It may be possible to buy light framing (accepting glass on two planes) from a specialist wood molding supplier. The corner joints are difficult, which is perhaps why most cases have the outer faces of the framing veneered after the case is assembled.

Small cases can have the glass panes cemented together and narrow strips of veneer applied directly to the glass to cover the cement joints. The base should be quite heavy, and the model mounted on a shallow block exactly fitting the glass. A molding of the same depth glued round outside then sandwiches the glass which can be glued in place or left removable. If glued, the final sealing should be carried out on a dry, warm day to avoid the possibility of condensation inside the glass at a later time. *Passé partout* or strips of adhesive film (as sold for covering shelves) can be used instead of veneer, but do not look so elegant; a good model deserves a good case.

**Above**
A miniature drifter, a bare 9in long, made by the late Capt A Thomson. Note the perfection of the clinker-built dinghy, only 1½in (37mm) long, and the delicacy of the rigging.

### Ships in Bottles

An ideal and easily available glass case is a clear bottle, but inserting a ship is a specialist approach. It is difficult enough to make a detailed miniature outside a bottle, and to make the masts fold and the yards pivot, or to assemble and rig a model inside a bottle, is really making complications! For these reasons, ships in bottles are usually simplified to a great extent, and spars etc tend to be rather thicker than scale; serious ship modellers regard them as novelties although they do appreciate the skill and patience needed to produce a good bottled ship.

Choice of bottle is important, as standards vary and a bottle with uneven thickness will cause unacceptable distortion. Some lightly tinted bottles are used, but most people prefer clear glass. The neck diameter is important, since it determines the beam and hull depth

Scope for dioramas is offered by a miniature collection. This elaborate one has a naval dockyard and a commercial harbor side by side and includes over 50 ships.

of the model, not to mention ease of access, and about ³/₄in (18mm) is considered a minimum for a beginner. Inside dimensions need to be checked, particularly height, which is easily done by glueing the center of a thin strip of paper to the end of a wire or stick and pushing it in, trimming the ends until the paper can stand upright. Model size can be determined from this, allowing for sea thickness.

Clean the inside of the bottle and allow it to dry thoroughly. Colored putty or Plasticene is usually used for the sea, inserting in rolled 'sausages' and tamping down with tools made from bent heavy wires. One of the thicker wire clothes hangers used by cleaners is quite a good source of wire, but it needs to be at least 3/32in (2mm) to be stiff enough. Avoid touching the bottle with the putty except where it is to lie, as removing oily marks is difficult. Rolling each sausage lightly in whiting before insertion helps with putty. Form the sea pattern, including the beginnings of the ship's wake, and touch in the odd whitecap with white paint if required. Make a stand if the bottle is rounded.

Although most people think of a sailing vessel as the subject for a bottle model, steam or motor ships can be very attractive and can be scenic, perhaps tied up at a wharf or off-loading cargo into lighters at anchor, with a little background painted on the bottle. The hull is finished outside the bottle and the superstructure and other detail made to fit it but not glued on. Once the hull is inserted and firmly pressed in place on the sea, say bow towards the neck, the details are inserted and glued in their prepared positions, starting in this case from the stern forward, perhaps poop deckhouse, mainmast, main superstructure, funnel and engine-room vents, bridge and foremast, depending on the height. A large ship towed by tugs would probably mean that the tugs could be inserted complete except possibly for masts. Another idea would be a trawler working nets, the crew perhaps being dobs of water-color on a tiny wire armature, plugging into a pre-drilled hole. There is enormous scope: one well-known subject was a sailor inside the bottle, putting a ship into a tiny bottle!

A full-rigged ship is, however, still the subject with the greatest mystique, and for any square-rigged sailing vessel the technique is much the same. A beginner might choose a Stuart yacht or a brig as having fewer masts, or a two-masted topsail schooner. The first step is to produce a drawing to a size which just fits in the bottle, and an easy way is to photograph a chosen drawing and have it printed by a photographer to a specified maximum height. There have been several books on the subject including suitable sized drawings, and two or three are still in print, or you can draw your own since only quite a simple plan is needed.

Almost all models have the hull carved from a block of close-grained wood up to the bulwark tops, and the deck area is then hollowed out, leaving the bulwarks under 1/16in (1½mm) thick, still a little thick for scale. To make it easier to handle, the hull is secured to a strip of wood with two small screws from beneath, the strip being glued and screwed to a shorter block which can be held in a vice. The screws securing the hull must of course be capable of removal. Drill a hole for the bowsprit, then paint the model with acrylics, water-colors or whatever.

The positions of the shrouds and backstays are now marked on the bulwarks by first marking them on a strip of paper laid on the plan, then placing the paper on the hull and transferring the positions by pressing a pin point into the base of the bulwark. Drill a hole through the bulwark at each mark, using a needle stoned to a triangular point, at deck level, and keeping the holes evenly spaced. Some builders pass the lines through the hull and across underneath, others through from inside the bulwarks, but the best appearance comes from passing the first line down outside the bulwark, through its hole, then back out through the second hole and back up to the top.

**Above**
Early State Yacht at 1/100 scale and a ship in a bottle among models displayed at an open air exhibition in Germany. The bow of a galley appears on the left.

Masts and spars can be boxwood strips, although cocktail sticks or toothpicks are usable if thinned and tapered. Some builders drill the center of each yard and the mast and use fusewire to secure the yards so that they swivel, others use thread. Holes drilled across the mast allow lifts to be run from each yardarm through the mast and down to the opposite yardarm; braces run in the same way but downward to holes through the mast behind, or through the bulwark for the mizzen. The yards can thus swing, the thread sliding through the holes.

There are three basic ways to collapse the masts. The trickiest is to have them with short pointed ends located in shallow holes in the deck. An alternative is to glue them to the deck and make a diagonal cut sloping down from the foreside just above the deck, so that the masts can be bent back without breaking right off; a spot of glue is put in the cut as the masts are pulled back up. The third and easiest method is to fit a tiny wire inverted U through the heel of each mast and glue the legs of this hinge into holes in the deck. In this case the masts finish at deck level and are not fitted into holes in the deck.

The model is rigged on its stand, everything being secured at the ends except the forestays which are led through holes in the bowsprit and jib boom. If main and mizzen lower mast forestays are fitted they must pass through the hull and emerge underneath, or through the heel of the mast ahead, lying along the deck at present. All these loose stays must be long enough to

**Above**
Six-masted schooner in a bottle. Towards the end of commercial sail, multi-masted schooners proved more economical, requiring a much smaller crew.

**Left**
Rather larger is this galleon in a flask, made into a table lamp. At least it's dust-free! Another approach is to insert a model in a light bulb, turning it after completion to make it really mystifying.

extend through the bottle neck. Sails are usually bond paper rolled round a pencil, colored with water-color and glued to their yards, avoiding glue coming into contact with any of the holes or sliding threads.

When all is ready, the yards are all swung nearly parallel with the masts and the masts collapsed backwards. A little slow-drying glue is placed on the appropriate area of sea and the model inserted and pressed in place. As it enters the bottle, the forestays can be gently pulled to give room on deck for a thick wire to press the ship down while the cottons are pulled taut and the masts fully erected. The yards are then straightened and set at the required angle and the taut stay ends taped to the bottle neck outside while glue is applied to each where it emerges beneath the bowsprit and, if used, through each mast heel. When dry, the surplus is cut off with a broken piece of razor blade glued in a slot in the end of a piece of dowel and any finishing touches added before sealing the bottle.

Tools are mostly shaped from wire but long tweezers and forceps are helpful. A useful tool to make is a clamp from a piece of brass tube through which passes a length of studding. One jaw soldered to the studding and one to the end of the tube, plus a nut at the outside end of the tube, enables small items to be held firmly, even at the far end of the bottle.

This outline of the technique is necessarily brief, but should provide enough information to enable a model to be tackled. Although not considered serious modelling, ships in bottles have been made almost since bottles were made, and for many years were the closest thing to a ship model seen by many members of the public. A description of so time-honored and traditional an aspect of ship and boat modelling is an excellent way to bring this book to a close.

# Index

# Bibliography

There are vast numbers of books available in major reference libraries, especially in respect to full-size period ships. The following bibliography is composed of books known personally or by repute to the author as being among the most useful to modellers, almost without exception in English, and most not too difficult to find. Many, indeed, are either in print or have been reprinted comparatively recently. Apologies are offered to living authors/publishers for inadvertent omissions.

Anderson, R C *The Rigging of Ships in the Days of the Spritsail Topmast, 1600–1700*, Salem 1927
*The Sailing Ship, 6000 Years of History.*
*Seventeenth Century Rigging*, London 1955
*Oared Fighting Ships*, London 1962
Bathe, B W *Ship Models at the Science Museum*, London 1966
Battson, R K *Period Ship Modelling*, London 1949
*Modelling Tudor Ships*, London 1955
Benson, J, and Rayman, A A *Experimental Flash Steam*, Hemel Hempstead c. 1972
Biddlecomb, G *The Art of Rigging*, London 1848
Bowen, F *From Carrack to Clipper*, London 1948
Bowness, E *Modelling the Cutty Sark*, London c. 1954
*The Four-masted Barque*, London 1955
Boyd, R N *Manual of Naval Construction*, London 1859
Campbell, G F *China Tea Clippers*, London 1954
Carr, F G G *The Story of the Cutty Sark*, London 1969
Chapelle, H I *The Baltimore Clipper*, New York 1930
*The History of American Sailing Ships*, New York 1935
Chapman, F H *Architectura Navalis Mercatoria*, Stockholm 1768
Clowes, G S Laird *Sailing Ships in the Science Museum*, London 1932
Craine, J H *Ship Modelling Hints and Tips*, London 1948
Daniels, W J, and Tucker, H B *Model Sailing Craft*, London 1932
*Build Yourself a Model Yacht*, London 1936
*Model Sailing Yachts*, London 1951
Davis, C G *The Ship Model Builder's Assistant*, Salem 1926
*The Built-up Ship Model*, Salem 1933
Deason, G H *The Model Boat Book*, London 1949
Falconer, Wm *Dictionary of the Marine*, London 1769
Fincham, J A *A Treatise on Masting Ships and Mastmaking*, London 1829
*A History of Naval Architecture*, London 1851
Freeston, E C *Prisoner of War Ship Models, 1775–1825*, Lymington 1973
Greenhill, B *The Merchant Schooners*, Newton Abbott 1968
Griffin, R *Model Racing Yacht Construction*, Hemel Hempstead 1973
Grimwood, V R *American Ship Models and How to Build Them*, New York 1942
Hambleton, F C *Famous Paddle Steamers*, London 1948
Hobbs, E W *How to Make Old-Time Ship Models*, Glasgow 1929
Hubbard, D *Ships in Bottles*, Newton Abbott 1975
Isard, A P *The Model Shipbuilder's Manual of Fittings and Guns*, London 1946
Jeffries, C R *Radio Control Model Yachts*, Hemel Hempstead 1974
Kemp, Dixon *A Manual of Yacht and Boat Sailing*, London 1878
*Yacht Architecture*, London 1897
Landstrom, Björn *The Ship*, London 1961
*Ships of the Pharoahs*, New York 1970
Lauder, J P *Ships in Bottles*, London 1949
Lever, D'Arcy *The Young Sea Officer's Sheet Anchor*, London 1819

Longridge, C N *The Cutty Sark*, London 1949
*The Anatomy of Nelson's Ships*, London 1955
MacGregor, D R *The Tea Clippers*, London 1952
*Fast Sailing Ships*, Lymington 1973
*Square Rigged Sailing Ships*, Hemel Hempstead 1977
March, E *Spritsail Barges of the Thames and Medway*, London c. 1948
*Sailing Drifters*, London c. 1950
*Inshore Craft of Britain*, Newton Abbott 1970
McNarry, D *Shipbuilding in Miniature*, London 1955
*Ship Models in Miniature*, Newton Abbott 1975
Moore, Sir A *Sailing Ships of War 1800–1860*, London 1926
Morris, E P *The Fore and Aft Rig in America*, New Haven 1927
Nares, Sir G *Seamanship*, London 1862
Needham, J *Modelling Ships in Bottles*, London 1972
Paget-Tomlinson, E W, and Smith, R B *Ships (Liverpool Museum)*, Liverpool 1966
Paris, Adml E *Souvenirs de Marine*, Vols 1–4, Paris, 1882–6, 1908
Petrejus, E W *Modelling the Brig of War Irene*, Hengelo 1947
Priest, B H, and Lewis, J A *Model Racing Yachts*, Hemel Hempstead 1965
Purves, A *Flags for Ship Modellers*, London 1950
Rayman, A A *High Speed Marine Steam Engine*, Hemel Hempstead 1965
Rogers, H *Ship Models at the United States Naval Academy*, 1954
Smeed, V E *Boat Modelling*, Hemel Hempstead 1956
*Model Maker Manual*, Hemel Hempstead 1957
*Power Model Boats*, Hemel Hempstead 1959
*Model Maker Annual*, Hemel Hempstead 1963
*Simple Model Yachts*, Hemel Hempstead 1972
*Working Models*, London 1964
*Model Yachting*, Rickmansworth 1977
Smeed, V E, and Connolly, P *Radio Control for Model Boats*, Hemel Hempstead 1970
Smith, A *Building an Open Column Launch Engine*, Hemel Hempstead 1977
Spies, M H *Veteran Steamers*, Humleback 1965
Steel, D *Elements and Practice of Rigging and Seamanship*, London 1794
*The Shipwright's Vade Mecum*, London 1805
*Elements and Practice of Naval Architecture*, London 1812
Thorne, P *Secrets of Ships in Bottles*, Hemel Hempstead 1960
Underhill, H A *Sailing Ship Rigs and Rigging*, Glasgow 1938
*Masting and Rigging the Clipper Ship and Ocean Carrier*, Glasgow 1949
*Deep Water Sail*, Glasgow 1952
*Plank on Frame Models*, Glasgow
*Sail Training and Cadet Ships*, Glasgow
Wilcock, A *Vane Steering Gears*, Hemel Hempstead c. 1968
Wingrove, G *Techniques of Ship Modelling*, Hemel Hempstead 1976
Worcester, G R G *Junks and Sampans of the Yangtse*, Shanghai 1947
*Sail and Sweep in China*, London 1966

**MUSEUMS** known or mentioned to the author as of interest to ship modellers include:

**Britain**
Bristol Museum
Whitehaven Museum, Cumbria
Brixham Maritime Museum, Devon
Exeter Maritime Museum
Glasgow Museum
National Maritime Museum, Greenwich
Liverpool Museum
British Museum, London
Imperial War Museum, London
Science Museum, London
Newcastle Museum
Nelson Museum, Portsmouth
Sunderland Museum, Tyne and Wear
Whitby Museum, Yorks

**USA**
US Naval Academy, Annapolis
Museum of Science and Industry, Chicago
Mystic Seaport, Connecticut
Hart Nautical Museum, Massachusetts Institute of
    Technology
Peabody Museum, Salem, Massachusetts
Mariners Museum, Newport News
Seattle Museum
Smithsonian Institution, Washington

**Others**
National Scheepwartmuseum, Antwerp, Belgium
Musee Maritime, Paris, France
Hamburgische Geschichte, Germany
Staatliche Museum, Berlin, Germany
Nederlandsch Historisch Scheepwart Museum,
    Amsterdam, Holland
Ryksmuseum, Amsterdam, Holland
Prins Hendrik Museum, Rotterdam, Holland
Museo Navale Romano, Albenga, Italy
Museo d'Antichita, Ravenna, Italy
Museo Storico Navale, Venice, Italy
Imperial Museum, Tokyo, Japan
Bygdoy Museum, nr Oslo, Norway
Norske Folkemuseum, Oslo, Norway
Museu de Marinha, Lisbon, Portugal
Maritime Museum, Gothenburg, Sweden
National Maritime Museum, Stockholm, Sweden
Vasa Museum, Stockholm, Sweden
Museum fur Volkerkunde, Basle, Switzerland
Transport Museum, Lucerne, Switzerland

There are many preserved ships which can be visited, eg HMS *Victory* at Portsmouth, HMS *Belfast* and the *Cutty Sark* as well as several small vessels in St Katharine's Dock, in London, the several craft at Exeter, the barquentine *Mercator* at Ostend, Belgium, destroyer HMCS *Haida* at Toronto, USS *Missouri* at Bremerton, and collections of ships at San Francisco, Mystic, St Louis, and so on.

**English Language Periodicals of direct interest to Modellers:**

| | | |
|---|---|---|
| *Model Engineer* | 1898– | Hemel Hempstead |
| *Mariners Mirror* | 1911– | Greenwich |
| *Sea Breezes* | 1919– | Liverpool |
| *Model Maker & Model Boats* | 1950– | Hemel Hempstead |
| *Warship International* | 1966– | New York |
| *Ships Monthly* | 1966– | London |
| *Scale Models* | 1969– | Hemel Hempstead |
| *Model Ships & Boats* | 1976– | New York |

Also
| | | |
|---|---|---|
| *The Model Yachtsman* | 1928–33, | becoming |
| *Marine Models* | 1933–39 | London |
| *Ships & Ship Models* | 1930–39 | London |
| *Model Ships & Power Boats* | 1947–56 | London |